The Grounds of English Literature

The Grounds of English Literature

CHRISTOPHER CANNON

OXFORD
UNIVERSITY PRESS

OXFORD

UNIVERSITY PRESS

Great Clarendon Street, Oxford OX2 6DP

Oxford University Press is a department of the University of Oxford.
It furthers the University's objective of excellence in research, scholarship,
and education by publishing worldwide in

Oxford New York

Auckland Bangkok Buenos Aires Cape Town Chennai
Dar es Salaam Delhi Hong Kong Istanbul Karachi Kolkata
Kuala Lumpur Madrid Melbourne Mexico City Mumbai Nairobi
São Paulo Shanghai Taipei Tokyo Toronto

Oxford is a registered trade mark of Oxford University Press
in the UK and in certain other countries

Published in the United States
by Oxford University Press Inc., New York

© Christopher Cannon 2004

The moral rights of the author have been asserted
Database right Oxford University Press (maker)

First published 2004

First published in paperback 2007

British Library Cataloguing in Publication Data

Data available

Library of Congress Cataloging in Publication Data

Data available

ISBN 978–0–19–927082–8 (Hbk.)   978–0–19–923039–6 (Pbk.)

1 3 5 7 9 10 8 6 4 2
Typeset by Laserwords Private Limited, Chennai, India.
Printed in Great Britain
on acid-free paper by
Biddles Ltd, King's Lynn, Norfolk

Acknowledgements

Much that I value in this book came to me in the form of a sage suggestion or correction and, as I finish it, I am conscious of nothing so much as the intelligence and generosity of my friends. Foremost among these are James Simpson and Derek Pearsall, who read and helped greatly with the earliest versions of this work, Sarah Kay, who gave the Introduction and Chapter 1 critically improving scrutiny (when I needed guidance and support the most), Jill Mann and Paul Strohm, who improved early versions of my manuscript as well as the whole of this book in its penultimate version, and Juliet Fleming, who read these words at nearly every stage of their progress to print, and kept showing me how to write more clearly and think more precisely. To Juliet I also owe the nature and very ambition of this book, since I never would have embarked on anything like it, upstairs in her cottage in Chrishall Grange, had she not been writing *Graffiti and the Writing Arts of Early Modern England* downstairs.

Debts to Larry Benson go back to graduate school, when he first encouraged me to think seriously about early Middle English and showed me how to do so. Elizabeth Scala, Elizabeth Fowler, Simon Gaunt, and Nicolette Zeeman issued key invitations and offered valuable encouragement along the way. Bruce Holsinger was the first to understand what I was up to in Chapter 1 (in a very early version) and also provided an invaluable reading of Chapter 4. Douglas Mao helped me with the concepts of tradition and beauty. Two anonymous readers for Oxford University Press offered extraordinarily judicious and helpful readings and Emily Jolliffe, Tom Perridge, Elizabeth Prochaska, Frances Whistler, and Mary Worthington shepherded the manuscript into print with exemplary kindness and care. Sophie Goldsworthy has been the kind of supportive editor academic authors normally only get to dream about.

Valuable material support was provided by the Arts and Humanities Research Board of the United Kingdom in the form of an extra term of leave in 2000 which allowed me to complete a manuscript. A fellowship from the John Simon Guggenheim Memorial Foundation in 2002–3 allowed me to transform that manuscript into a book. I owe thanks to the Fellows of St Edmund Hall and the Faculty of English in Oxford for allowing me to take up the first award, and to the Fellows of Pembroke College and the Faculty of English in Cambridge for allowing me to take up the second. In Oxford, I also relied greatly on Lucy Newlyn and Adrian Briggs, and, in Cambridge, on Barry Windeatt for much kindness and counsel.

Although their arguments are significantly transformed and augmented here, an earlier version of Chapter 2 appeared in *ELH* (vol. 67 (2000)) and an earlier version of Chapter 3 appeared in the *Forum for Modern Language Studies* (vol. 33 (1997)). Chapter 4 appeared in the *Journal of Medieval and Early Modern Studies* (2004) much as it appears here. I am grateful to the editors of each of these journals for permission to reuse this material.

Contents

    Katherine-**group**   139

    The Place of AB Language   145
    Place Itself   154
    Anchorage   161

6. **The Spirit of Romance:** *King Horn, Havelok the*
    Dane, **and** *Floris and Blancheflour*   172

    Romance Form   176
    The Soul is the Prison of the Body   192
    The Grounding of a Thing in Air   200

    Works Cited   210
    Index   229

List of Illustrations

Abbreviations

EETS os   Early English Text Society, Original Series
EETS es   Early English Text Society, Extra Series
MÆ   *Medium Ævum*
MWME   *A Manual of Writings in Middle English*, ed. J. B. Severs, et al.,
          10 vols. [to date] (New Haven: Connecticut Academy of Arts and
          Sciences, 1967–).
MED   *The Middle English Dictionary*, ed. Hans Kurath et al., (Ann
          Arbor: University of Michigan, 1954–).
OED   *The Oxford English Dictionary*, 2nd edn., 20 vols., ed. J. A.
          Simpson and E. S. C. Weiner (Oxford: Clarendon Press, 1989;
          1st edn. 1888–1933).

A Note on Translations

For the sake of clarity, with the exception of quotations from Chaucer, I have provided Modern English translations for all medieval texts. Where those texts provide examples for a broad intellectual history (rather than for a particular concept or term), I have provided the original, but most usually in a note. In the case of ancient writers, such as Plato and Aristotle, and post-medieval writers, such as Hegel and Marx, I have often provided only an English text since that is the text I have worked from.

Introduction

Matter smiled at man with poetical sensuous brightness.
(Karl Marx)

Suppose Hegel was right and spirit was a phenomenon, thought an informing principle, and thinking an instrument for shaping the things of the world. Suppose, too, that Marx was Hegel's most ardent disciple in this matter, and, despite his later disgust with Hegel's conclusions and champions, what he took from Hegel was a belief in the determinate presence of thought in the form of every made thing. One way in which we would have failed to appreciate the implications of such an earnest and general formalism is in our study of that category of things we call 'literature'. Rather than seeing formal description as a dispensable part of literary analysis—the sprinkling round of observations about 'versification', 'metre', 'image', and 'genre' in the course of more important investigations—we would believe that all accounts of meaning were accounts of form. Rather than projecting formalist rigour onto a single mode of criticism (Marxist, say), we would accept that any act of reading was formalist.[1] We would still look at a poem and see its 'whole body' as the 'dancing of an attitude', as did Kenneth Burke, but we would not have to feel that such a vision necessitated a return to that mode of criticism so latterly 'New' that it was now quite old.[2] We would once again have a method of reading we could call 'practical', not because it could do without immediate reference to other writing, but because

---

[1] See e.g. Fredric Jameson, *Marxism and Form: Twentieth-Century Dialectical Theories of Literature* (Princeton: Princeton University Press, 1971). Although Jameson's project in this volume is also to recapture the Hegelianism latent in Marxist thinking, his conception of 'form' is more precise (often addressed explicitly to 'literary' form rather than form as such) and, therefore, less practical for the broad revaluation I attempt here (for an instance of the salient difference see e.g. the distinction Jameson makes between 'form and content', 327–59).

[2] Kenneth Burke, *The Philosophy of Literary Form: Studies in Symbolic Action* (Baton Rouge, La.: Louisiana State University Press, 1941), 9.

it understood a poem or an essay as an object no different in kind from a table or a pair of shoes.[3]

A book on the literature of what is generally called 'early Middle English' will seem an odd place to rely on such suppositions—or to press them. But they are peculiarly practical here, because the things requiring description are so strange, and produced under such anomalous conditions, that they differ, not only from what came before (what we now call 'Old English'), but from all that came after (what we otherwise call 'English literature'). As Thomas Hahn has recently observed, no period in the history of English literature either before or after gives such an 'extraordinary impression that every act of writing requires a reinvention of vernacular literacy'.[4] Early Middle English writers have Anglo-Norman and Latin models and sources, of course, and each necessarily emerges from a rich culture which ancillary documentation can partly reconstruct. But the startling general condition of all these texts is their profound isolation from immediate vernacular models and examples, from any local precedent for the business of writing English. The result is a set of differences themselves so varied that they are hard to categorize, a set of texts whose only unifying principle is their ability to thwart systematization. The chapters which follow will detail this variety, but some idea of what must be taken in hand can be given in the older languages of formal account: examined in these pages are a legendary history in alliterative long-lines which often break into rhyme (Laȝamon's *Brut*), a collection of biblical homilies in unrhymed septenaries (the *Ormulum*), a beast fable in octosyllabic couplets (*The Owl and the Nightingale*), a rule for anchoritic devotion, three saints' lives, and an allegorical description of the soul in prose (*Ancrene Wisse* and the *Katherine*-group), and a collection of romances in rhyming couplets of varying syllabic count (*King Horn, Havelok the Dane, Floris and Blancheflour*). In addition to these radical differences in genre, prosody, and subject—as if vernacular possibility had been divvied up and only one writer was allowed to pursue each course—these texts can also be differentiated by an equally varied set of intellectual

[3] For my definition of 'practical criticism' see *OED*, s.v. 'practical, a. (n.)', III.6 as well as I. A. Richards, *Practical Criticism: A Study of Literary Judgment* (London: Kegan Paul, Trench, Trubner, 1929).
[4] Thomas Hahn, 'Early Middle English', 61–91 in *The Cambridge History of Medieval English Literature*, ed. David Wallace (Cambridge: Cambridge University Press, 1999), 85.

concerns and affinities, stated or implied aims, and even by the relationships they establish between writing and propositional truth. This is not to say that early Middle English writings have not been loved. Few scholars have resisted the charms of *The Owl and the Nightingale*, and it is hard not to notice how perfectly this poem anticipates Chaucer's—even if it seems impossible for Chaucer to have known it.[5] But even affection and the glimmer of a tradition have not helped literary criticism to know what the *Owl and the Nightingale* is about. The larger consequence of the individuality of the literary object in this period has been literary history's general sense that there is nothing there, since the lack of a continuous tradition has so generally (and subtly) been equated with a lack of literature; even when particular texts have been scrutinized carefully it has often been to explain how they do not repair this lack. It is the general aim of this book to provide a theory of form in which such individual and isolated literary works can finally have unapologetic consequence. For what early Middle English can teach all students of English writing, in any period, is that the capacity to read texts apart from all informing precedent or lineal relation, in isolation not only from similar works, but from familiar categories, lies within our philosophy, if beyond our current competence.

A THEORY OF FORM

The model for the kind of enquiry I undertake in these chapters is Marx's description of the 'commodity' in the first volume of *Capital*.[6] Marx's suggestion that the problem with such objects is that they think too much of themselves (because they are puffed up by their exchange value) is, on its face, no more than typical Marxian wit: an exquisite figure for the general observation that capitalism converts relationships between people into relationships between things. But the figure's principles are also basic to Marx's claim that the commodity is a thing which 'congeals' or 'embeds' not only a certain

---

[5] On the suggestiveness of this relationship see Ian Robinson, *Chaucer and the English Tradition* (Cambridge: Cambridge University Press, 1972), 36–41.

[6] For a more thorough analysis of Marx's understanding of making see the 'Structure of Belief and Its Modulation into Material Making', Chapter 4 of Elaine Scarry, *The Body in Pain: The Making and Unmaking of the World* (Oxford: Oxford University Press, 1985), 181–277 (esp. 243–77).

amount of activity, but the thought which directs that labour, where the weaving which makes the linen or the tailoring which makes the coat do not merely shape matter, but in so shaping it, 'deposit' human attitudes into it *as* its form. As a set of attitudes and practices surplus to that labour, capitalism is not only an ideology, but a method for depositing still further thoughts into the object by the activities of 'exchange', a way of causing twenty yards of linen to 'believe', for example, that its value is equivalent to a single coat:

We see, then, all that our analysis of the value of commodities has already told us, is told by the linen itself, so soon as it comes into communication with another commodity, the coat. Only it betrays its thoughts in that language with which alone it is familiar, the language of commodities. In order to tell us that its own value is created by labour in its abstract character of human labour, it says that the coat, in so far as it is worth as much as the linen, and therefore is value, consists of the same labour as the linen. In order to inform us that its sublime reality as value is not the same as its buckram body, it says that value has the appearance of a coat, and consequently that so far as the linen is value, it and the coat are as like as two peas.[7]

It might seem more sensible to describe such relations as a social formation (as Marx soon does), to say that it is not the haughtiness of the linen but the demands of the capitalist which make the long length of fabric appear to have the same shape as a coat. But it is precisely Marx's insight that attitudes become so internal to things when those things are carried through the world only by means of those attitudes that these things are effectively re*shaped*. Linen in capitalism *is* the coat it can be exchanged for, precisely because the capitalist does not perceive such an exchange to be the function of his or her belief but of the object, as it actually is.

It is therefore also basic to Marx's description of the commodity that we are ideologically blind—our consciousness is false—because we make objects rather than our own minds the bearers of our most important thoughts.[8] The commodity is 'transcendent', 'abounding in metaphysical subtleties and theological niceties', because what is embedded in its form are a set of principles which determine human action without us knowing it ('we are not aware of this, nevertheless

---

[7] Karl Marx, *Capital: A Critique of Political Economy*, vol. 1, trans. Samuel Moore and Edward Aveling, ed. Frederick Engels (London: Lawrence & Wishart, 1954), 58.
[8] For the theory I rely on in this paragraph see the 'The Fetishism of Commodities and the Secret Thereof', Marx, *Capital*, 1: 76–87 (for the phrases I quote see 1: 76–9).

Introduction   5

we do it'). Marx's commodified table 'stands on its head' and 'evolves
out of its wooden brain grotesque ideas' because it is more than the
product of any carpenter's hewing—more, too, than his or her designs
and intents. Its independence and creativity are a function of the
thinking of that whole network of valuers and thinkers who make
capitalism work; we are therefore also in a position to *learn* from the
form of the table the thoughts which it has been made to bear. As
Marx imagines this outcome, an economist opines that 'value . . . is
a property of things, riches . . . of man', but all he is doing when he
speaks in this way is ventriloquizing the voice of the commodity
which itself speaks thus: 'Our use-value may be a thing that interests
men. It is no part of us as objects. What, however, does belong to us as
objects is our value. Our natural intercourse as commodities proves
it. In the eyes of each other we are nothing but exchange values.'[9]
Apart from the critique of capitalism which is its larger point, this
is a view of things as eloquent expressions of a certain knowledge,
repositories of thoughts we may not know we have had.

An analysis of form that takes these views for its governing principles takes neither a thing nor a thought as its analytic object but,
rather, the common ground between them; its founding premise is
that *form is that which thought and things have in common.*[10] In the
case of the table made topsy-turvy by capitalism, for example, form is
both the physical object which might be exchanged and the ideology
which governs the exchanging of such an object. But since, as I have
already suggested, the making of a table involves a greater complex
of thoughts than exchange even in capitalism, the table knows more
than this ideology too. A flat piece of wood with four wooden legs
supporting it is, for example, the solidification of the idea of a 'supporting surface', an initiating thought extended into the flatness of a
table top which invites the placing of objects upon it, and the even-
ness of the legs which hold that top in a steady and inviting position.[11]

[9] Marx, *Capital*, 1: 87.
[10] 'Structure' is the other name which can be given to this common ground, as
Althusser did, when describing the 'object' of *Capital*. See Louis Althusser, 'The Object
of *Capital*', 71–198 in Louis Althusser and Étienne Balibar, *Reading Capital*, trans.
Ben Brewster (London: Verso, 1979), esp. 182–93.
[11] For more nuanced and complex descriptions of the relationship between thought
(or as she calls it, more precisely in the case, 'sentience') and objects see 'The Interior
Structure of the Artifact', Chapter 5 in Scarry, *The Body in Pain*, 278–326. For
example: 'The chair is therefore the materialized structure of a perception; it is
sentient awareness materialized into freestanding design. If one pictures the person in

It is easier to think of such simple elements of design as properties of objects rather than intentions of producers because, as the extended analysis of things in *Capital* also proves, even the most mundane object can embed such a complex set of thoughts that it may exceed the competencies of any individual consciousness to know it. This is also true, as Michael Baxandall has shown, because the 'patterns of intention' discernible in 'historical objects' (his example is the Forth Bridge) might just as well be described as 'causes' ('why at all and why thus') which extend far beyond an individual will to an enormous variety of 'circumstances', those 'cultural facts' which anyone might know but which might also only become visible and clear upon careful scrutiny.[12] The form of the thing may require careful description because the material out of which the table was hewn has soaked up, not only the designing thoughts of the maker, but the thoughts that maker unwittingly absorbed from his or her entire culture (for example, contemporaneous assumptions about table-making, the availability of resources, the structure of other tables, their typicality or eccentricity, all those constelled interests and needs which are taken as the demand which the making of a table will meet).

It is therefore in the nature of this theory that the idea leading to the thing can be reconstructed in terms of thinking (initiating principles, causes, cultural facts) but, also, in cases where such thoughts cannot be easily accessed, that thinking can itself be reconstructed through a sufficiently careful description of the thing itself. In very difficult cases, suspicion in one mode can lead to confirmation in the other—the barely perceptible shape (or idea) can be more easily understood with reference to the precisely defined idea (or shape). Spinoza (1632–77), who embraced a version of this theory, understood this

---

the action of making a chair—standing in one place, moving away, coming back, lifting then letting fall his arm, kneeling then standing, kneeling, half-kneeling, stooping, looking, extending his arm, pulling it back—and if one pictures all these actions as occurring without a tool or block of wood before him, that is, if one pictures only the man and his embodied actions, what one at that moment has before one is *not* the *act of perception* (his seeing of another's discomfort and wishing it gone) but *the structure of the act of perception visibly enacted*. What was originally an invisible aspect of consciousness (compassion) has now been translated into the realm of visible but disappearing action. The interior movement of perceiving has been translated into a willed series of successive actions, as if it were a dance, a dance entitled "body weight begone"' (290, emphases Scarry's).

[12] Michael Baxandall, *Patterns of Intention: On the Historical Explanation of Pictures* (New Haven: Yale University Press, 1985), 25–32 (esp. 30).

as its particular explanatory power. For him it did not matter whether you approached an object as it stretched itself through the world, or by way of the 'causes' that stretched it out; the 'order' in question was the same:

A circle existing in Nature and the idea of the existing circle, which is also in God, are one and the same thing, which is explained through different attributes. Therefore, whether we conceive Nature under the attribute of extension, or under the attribute of thought, or under any other attribute, we shall find one and the same order, or one and the same connection of causes, that is, that the same things follow one another.[13]

The order at issue in subsequent chapters may, in this sense, take shape as a version of that discourse we call 'literary criticism' or 'reading' but it may accomplish similar tasks when it assumes the shape of 'intellectual history'. Such descriptive agility makes this theory of particular value to the study of historically distant objects, since it amounts to the claim that the thing carries a whole culture within it—that formal description is allied to, as well as a form of, cultural criticism.

'Form' is an idea with its own intellectual history, of course, and it is well to be clear that what I undertake here is not a contribution to that history, even though there is no question that form was a concept of great importance to thinkers in this period. The thirteenth century in Britain is, in fact, precisely that period and place to which Marx, on at least one occasion, attributed his own understanding of form ('even Britain's scholastic Duns Scotus [1265–1308] wondered: "Can matter think?"').[14] What Duns Scotus's own broad and subtle

---

[13] Benedict de Spinoza, *Ethics*, ed. and trans. Edwin Curley (Harmondsworth: Penguin, 1996), 35.

[14] Marx, *The Holy Family*, 131–55 in *Selected Writings*, ed. David McLellan (Oxford: Oxford University Press, 1977), 151. Marx is probably mistaken about what Duns Scotus wondered, but only because the key work is no longer ascribed to him. In the *De rerum principio* it is suggested that 'matter' [materia] is 'a kind of understanding' which was both 'a living and thinking substance' ('per se subsistens, est de genere intellectualium, ac per hos substantia vivens et intelligens'), and this text was credited to Duns Scotus until well into this century. For the text see John Duns Scotus, *De rerum principio* 4: 267–717 in *Opera omnia*, 26 vols., ed. Luke Wadding (Farnborough: Gregg International, 1969; first published Paris: Vivés, 1891–5), q. viii, art. 6 (p. 388). See also the chapter on 'Form and Matter' in C. R. S. Harris, *Duns Scotus*, 2 vols. (Oxford: Clarendon Press, 1927), 2: 75–121 (esp. 2: 76–80). It is now recognized that the *De rerum principio* is by Vital du Four. For this ascription see the 'Introduction', 1–23 in Allan B. Wolter, *The Philosophical Theology of John Duns Scotus*, ed. Marilyn McCord Adams (Ithaca, NY: Cornell University Press, 1990), 15.

Introduction

writings on this issue reveal most clearly, however, is the very complexity of thought about form abroad at this time: definitions were inevitably attempts to resolve what Aristotle had said 'in various places' [in diversis locis]; as a result, 'form' [forma] and 'matter' [materia] might be two distinct 'principles' [duo principia], or 'form' could be 'matter' in 'the character of act' [ratio actus]; or form might be the 'quiddity' [quidditas] or very essence of the 'thing-in-itself' [secundum ipsum].[15] Attempts to sort out these complex differences were further complicated as Aristotle's terms and definitions were re-examined in the light of Christian theology, for it was no longer only a question of what form had to do with matter or ideas but whether, say, an angel partook of these principles, or activities, or essences ('Can God bring it about that an angel inform matter?' [Utrum Deus possit facere angelum informare materiam]).[16] Thomas Aquinas (1225–74) understood better than most that, precisely because form described the borderline between thought and things, it was a concept which might itself mark out what was 'thinkable' in one way of understanding, but not in another: 'Plato thought that the forms of natural things existed apart without matter and are therefore thinkable . . . But Aristotle did not think that the forms of natural things existed independently of matter, and forms existing in matter are not actually thinkable.'[17] But this means that, if there is a history of form to be written, it would not be about either thought or things but about how various modes of apprehension have caused such phenomena to be.[18] Although it might document all the different forms that 'form' itself has taken—how it has been thought, thing, property, or immateriality as such—generally speaking, it would be

[15] John Duns Scotus, *God and Creatures: The Quodlibetal Questions*, trans. Felix Alluntis and Allan B. Wolter (Princeton: Princeton University Press, 1975), 2.59 (pp. 48–9); *Questiones quodlibetales*, 25: 1–586 in *Opera omnia*, II.20 (p. 90).

[16] Duns Scotus, *God and Creatures*, 9.1 (p. 218); *Quaestiones quodlibetales*, IX.1 (p. 379).

[17] 'Posuit enim Plato formas rerum naturalium sine materia subsistere, et per consequens eas intelligibiles esse . . . Sed quia Aristoteles non posuit formas rerum naturalium subsistere sine materia, formæ autem in materia existentes non sunt intelligibiles actu', Thomas Aquinas, *Summa theologiae*, vol. 11, ed. and trans. Timothy Suttor (London: Eyre & Spottiswoode, 1970), 1a.79.3 (pp. 154–5). Cited in Brian Davies, *The Thought of Thomas Aquinas* (Oxford: Clarendon Press, 1992), 126, from which I take this translation.

[18] On 'form' [forma] and 'quidity' [quiditas] see also Thomas Aquinas, *On Being and Essence*, trans. Armand Maurer, 2nd rev. edn. (Toronto: Pontifical Institute of Mediaeval Studies, 1968), 31–2; *Sermo seu tractatus de ente et essentia*, ed. Ludwig Baur, Opuscula et Textus, Series Scholastica, I (Münster: Aschendorff, 1933), 16–17.

a history of the tension between idealism and materialism as general views.

In subsequent chapters I look back to older theories of form in order to outline the way such a tension may define the form of a particular thing, but the theory that I employ is finally Hegelian rather than Marxist because it bestrides rather than attempts to resolve this tension; it is dialectical in so far as it engages no particular moment in the history of thought about form but rather the whole of that thought.[19] As I have already done here, I often approach and describe this thought through examples taken from Marx, since unlike Hegel, Marx was particularly concerned with the class of object that also most concerns any history of literature, what I have tended to call throughout these pages a made thing.[20] In every case, however, the form of such things, even as Marx sees them, is an illustration of Hegel's general claim that the 'universe of mind' simply *is* the 'universe of nature', that thinking occurs *by means of* that 'infinite wealth of forms, shapes, appearances' which constitute the material world, that ideas are simply the 'inward pulse' that can be detected 'still beating' in those 'outward appearances' we call things.[21]

In relation to a set of objects sorely neglected for so very long, such a theory has the advantage of assigning value to objects without recourse to their 'beauty' or 'excellence'. It is a necessary consequence of the view that form is the materialization of thought that the object then scrutinized will be valued for what it *knows*, that, as Heidegger put it in his own recourse to this theory, a made thing is a 'mode of knowing', and what is 'fixed in place in the figure' is a knowledge as unique as the object and therefore to be valued above all for its rarity.[22] This also means that this theory is prejudiced

[19] As Hannah Arendt observed, 'the very concept of dialectical *movement*, as Hegel conceived it as a universal law, and as Marx accepted it, makes the terms "idealism" and "materialism" as philosophical systems meaningless', Hannah Arendt, 'Tradition and the Modern Age', 17–40 in *Between Past and Future: Eight Exercises in Political Thought* (New York: Viking, 1961), 39. Emphasis Arendt's.

[20] On Marx's Hegelianism generally see Louis Althusser, 'Marx's Relation to Hegel', 161–86 in *Politics and History: Montesquieu, Rousseau, Hegel and Marx*, trans. Ben Brewster (London: NLB, 1972), esp. 181–5; Jameson, *Marxism and Form*, esp. 327–8; and Charles Taylor, *Hegel* (Cambridge: Cambridge University Press, 1975), 546–58.

[21] G. W. F. Hegel, *Philosophy of Right*, trans. T. M. Knox (Oxford: Clarendon Press, 1952), 10–11.

[22] Martin Heidegger, 'The Origin of the Work of Art', 139–212 in *Basic Writings*, ed. David Farrell Krell, rev. edn. (London: Routledge, 1993; 1st published 1978), 184 ('mode of knowing') and 189 ('fixed in place').

toward the more rare and the more complex thing, since the equation
of material structure with thought necessarily implies that structural
richness is equivalent to both the uniqueness and the thickness of
that thought. It therefore tends to value a painting of a pair of shoes
more than it values the pair of shoes themselves, not because the former is 'art' and the latter is not, but because (generally speaking) the
pair of shoes is similar in structure to any number of other shoes (such
similarity is an important part of the thought they materialize) while
the painting, as Heidegger put it, is at least an attempt to 'brin[g]
forth . . . a being such as never was before and will never come to be
again'. [23] This could be taken as a kind of romanticism—as it doubtless still is in Heidegger—but since this theory also holds that the
thought projected into a thing like a painting of shoes necessarily
exceeds the competence of a designing agent such as Van Gogh,
such prizing is not tantamount to a belief in genius. It is, in fact, also
axiomatic to this view that, because solid objects can know so much
more than persons, they are much more interesting than people, and
because their making can absorb cultural knowledge even their maker
does not know, it is appropriate to refer to the form of the object, not
simply as thought, but as *thinking*. That is, since the unique object
assembles a singular combination of ideas, and form is what things
have in common with thought, such a thing is itself a new thought, its
rarity of combinations itself a contribution to the history of ideas.

THE GROUNDS OF ENGLISH LITERATURE

To the extent that early Middle English writing has yet to be allowed
to exist as a set of consequential things, it helps very much to say that

---

[23] Heidegger, 'The Origin of the Work of Art', 187. Heidegger was criticized by
Meyer Schapiro for failing to say which of the many paintings of pairs of shoes by Van
Gogh he meant when making this point (Van Gogh painted eight such pictures; three
of which match the description Heidegger provides). As Derrida later observed, however, Heidegger never actually evokes a specific picture, and what Schapiro misses
is that 'Heidegger does not intend to speak of the picture', but rather two different
(and not necessarily related) modes of 'being', a 'product' (peasants' shoes) and a
mode of 'exemplarity' ('some particular shoes in some particular picture'), Jacques
Derrida, 'Restitutions of the Truth in Pointing [*pointure*]', 432–49 in *The Art of Art
History: A Critical Anthology*, ed. Donald Preziosi (Oxford: Oxford University Press,
1998), 449. Derrida's comments are extracted from *The Truth in Painting*, trans.
G. Bennington and I. McLeod (Chicago: University of Chicago Press, 1978; 1987),
293–329. See also Meyer Schapiro, 'The Still Life as a Personal Object—A Note on
Heidegger and Van Gogh', 427–31 in *The Art of Art History*.

extant shapes might embed something of consequence within them. The theory of form I advance is therefore not simply applied to early Middle English writing but called out by a set of objects which have seemed, on the whole, to be artifacts rather than contributions to the history of ideas, much more matter than mind. As I shall show in some detail in Chapter 1, such inconsequence has a great deal to do with the way such objects have been made to bear our own time-worn views about 'literature', and, in particular, that view which is easily summarized as '1066'—the belief that a cataclysm destroyed a literature along with a polity, so that for some centuries English literature, for all intents and purposes, ceased to exist. In fact, in order for this gap to open in the record a great deal of extant writing must be made to know the very opposite of what its survival demonstrates: things that exist must be made to say, 'nothing survived'.

It may seem obvious to any reader of this book that such equations are more parochial than the texts they dismiss, but it is also part of my claim that literary history has yet to alter its characteristic modes of apprehension—to recognize that it is the poverty of its categories which are at fault, not the literature which will not fit into them. Turville-Petre's account of the sensibility which governed the decision to use English in the period just after the 'early Middle' helps to measure just how much we may need to adjust: where, after 1290, such use accommodated 'a vision of a single community' and therefore helped in 'consolidating' a 'nation', it is equally clear that, before 1290, the decision to use English was a mode of *differentiation*, a method a particular writer chose should he or she wish to deviate from every general trend and practice.[24] One of the reasons to study early Middle English then is to see all the variety in which 'literature' in English can be made, what a writer can do when freed from the compulsions of a model. In their splendid isolation from vernacular inspiration, early Middle English writers learned to see the creative potential in the rich world of *all* forms, and one of the most important stories to be told by the central chapters of this book (2–5) is what objects such writers then turned to, what thoughts they found embedded there, and how they employed such thought in making something new. Such things include the land of Britain (in Laȝamon's *Brut*), the words of the vulgate Gospels as they appear

---

[24] Thorlac Turville-Petre, *England the Nation: Language, Literature, and National Identity, 1290–1340* (Oxford: Clarendon Press, 1996), 7 ('vision') and 10 ('consolidating').

on a manuscript page (in the *Ormulum*), the birds in an English field
(in the *Owl and the Nightingale*), and the peculiar topography (both
natural and made) of the place usually called the Welsh March (in
Ancrene Wisse and the *Katherine*-group). The word 'grounds' in my
title is designed to highlight this surprising material at the foundations of each of these important early Middle English texts—a
common ground in the most basic sense of that phrase.

Since the beginning of the last century, any talk of 'material' in
relation to writing has tended to focus on the 'material transmis-
sion' of texts (manuscript composition and layout, the methods and
results of book production, etc.) so it is also well to be clear from the
start that what I mean by 'matter' and 'materiality' in what follows is
rarely the material described by bibliography of this kind.[25] Where
the thought of a particular text extends itself out into the procedures
of its inscription, where, for example, that text's spelling is inherent to the conception of writing it wishes to promulgate (as in the
Ormulum) or the shape it takes in any book is itself a version of the
thought it formulates (as in *Ancrene Wisse*), then I consider such matter to be part of the text's form and a crucial part of the object I am
describing.[26] But what I generally mean here by the 'matter' of a given
text is the written shape that unspools on any page in which that text
could be said to appear—the shape it has as a particular instance of
writing (the layout, the sequence, the ordinance) in *all* those versions
that can be taken to be enactments of the thoughts that caused it.

What passes for 'materiality' in current discussions of writing is,
in other words, only one of the many grounds that interest me, and a
much more important part of this project is an attempt to characterize the sheer variety of these grounds that early Middle English
texts drew upon. Although many of these grounds can be reconstructed by describing the form they assumed in texts, it is sometimes
only possible to delineate or make sense of a form with reference to
broader cultural facts. Each of the following chapters therefore also

---

[25] The phrase I quote here is taken from W. W. Greg's characterization of what later
came to be called the 'New Bibliography' in 'What is Bibliography?', *Transactions of
the Bibliographical Society* 12 (1914), 39–53 (quotation from p. 48).

[26] This different sort of bibliography was described by Jameson some time ago: 'It is
worth observing how in the context of MacLuhanism or of Derrida's *De la gram-
matologie* . . . all of those hitherto extrinsic questions of public and of physical book
production now find themselves, as in Eric A. Havelock's remarkable *Preface to Plato*
. . . drawn back inside the work itself and interiorized, being now seen as aspects of
the work's thematics or inner structure', *Marxism and Form*, 394 n. 44.

reconstructs the body of learning that informed a particular text (or set of them). In most cases an Anglo-Norman or Latin source provides my point of departure, but it is usually the case that it is necessary to consult a frame of reference as broad as a whole discipline. Just as each chapter pairs a certain 'ground' with a text, then, it also pairs a particular field of ideas with that ground (jurisprudence in the case of the land, philosophies of language in the case of written letters, natural science and the literature of medieval misogyny in the case of birds, political history and phenomenology in the case of the Welsh March). It is a necessary result of regarding the form of any text as a mode of thoughtfulness that each English writing I examine must also be understood in terms of the contribution it makes to these disciplines. In this sense this book also describes the 'grounds' of English literature in a second sense, discovering the *loci* (or *topoi*) that—as Cicero (and Aristotle) had it—furnish the 'places' or 'topics' or 'regions . . . from which arguments are drawn' ['sedes e quibus argumenta promuntur'], the advances that literary objects made on the material through which they thought.[27]

The individuality of such characterizations means that the body of this book is radial rather than progressive—thickening rather than advancing the general claim that early Middle English writing is richer than we have known—but, in Chapter 6, I also offer an account of how this richness came to an end, as literary variety was replaced by a single idea of literature and, thus, a single, normative form. This idea took slightly longer to take hold than the common purposes of English 'use' Turville-Petre describes, but it was finally of larger consequence, since it amounted to the conviction that literature exceeded the boundaries of materiality itself, that it was, in fact, largely an idea and rarely, if ever, a thing. Such a dramatic change was only possible as English writing came to assume some aggregated shape, as there was finally enough writing in English for all of that writing to constitute a form—in short, for literature in English to have achieved that 'primitive accumulation' sufficient to produce a 'revolution'.[28] This accretion and the radical change that was its result can be seen most clearly in the forms we call 'romance' with the

---

[27] Cicero, *Topica*, pp. 377–459 in *De inventione, De optimo genere oratorum, Topica*, ed. and trans. H. M. Hubbell (London: William Heinemann, 1968), II.7 (p. 387).
[28] See 'The So-Called Primitive Accumulation', Marx, *Capital*, 1: 667–70.

result that romance form bears a surprisingly close resemblance to commodity form—it is both haughty and mysterious, puffed up with ideas which seem to be in 'surplus' to the thought which initially caused it. The similarities of shape which allow all romances to mass as an 'accumulation' also means that the idea which shapes these texts is confined to no single one of them, that romance form somehow has both the physicality of a thing and all the transcendence of an idea. The 'grounds of English literature' in my title therefore refers, thirdly, and most importantly, to the emergence of this extraordinary thought-as-thing in early Middle English, a literary object which counts as the most influential contribution of the period, but which, nonetheless, produces the demise of everything that English literature in this period had otherwise been.

This primitive accumulation in literature roughly coincides with the moment that Marx also fixed for the 'transformation of feudal exploitation into capitalist exploitation', and, although, as I have said, this book is not a Marxist description of literature, I have found it particularly helpful to describe the revolution that romance documents in more explicitly Marxist terms: aside from showing how much like a commodity literature soon became, such a discourse makes it possible to notice how 'wealth' in the literary sphere came to be so selectively distributed that an ostensible increase in literary value—marked in (and as) the geometric increase in the quantity of English texts—actually amounted to a general impoverishment.[29] In fact, as a careful analysis of romance form also shows, the quantitative increase in English writing in the course of the fourteenth century is illusory, since such quantity is achieved, in almost every case, by procedures of mass-production, multiplication that proceeds only by means of an increasing insistence on conformity. In this light, the different and unique method of literary making described in every chapter before Chapter 6 can be understood, retrospectively, as that creative variety that English literature abandoned, a set of grounds which, to the extent that they were constituted *by* difference, *could* have made difference itself a ground for subsequent literary production, a freedom with respect to form whose loss was the paradoxical accomplishment of fourteenth-century English literature. In this sense,

[29] 'Although we come across the first beginnings of capitalist production as early as the 14th and 15th century, sporadically, in certain towns of the Mediterranean, the capitalistic era dates from the 16th century', Marx, *Capital*, 1: 669.

early Middle English is not merely what English literature once was, but what it might have been. What has always been understood as *its* poverty is, in fact, what richness actually looks like where the apprehension of literary form has not been turned topsy-turvy by a wealth that is only (as Marx would have put it) 'so-called'.

The Loss of Literature: 1066

Nu is þeo leore forleten,   and þet folc is forloren.
Nu beoþ oþre leoden   þeo læreþ ure folc,
And feole of þen lorþeines losiæþ   and þet folc forþ mid.

[Now that teaching is forsaken, and the folk are lost; now there
is another people which teaches our folk; and many of our
teachers are damned, and our folk with them.]
(*The First Worcester Fragment*, twelfth century)

'The events of 1066', we now believe, 'were a cataclysm of the first
magnitude', and the severe blow dealt to a whole culture necessarily
diminished opportunities to write.[1] Alongside descriptions of battles
and deaths there are eloquent silences in the record which attest to a
more documentary defeat. Perhaps the rawest cessation of this kind
occurs in the version of the *Anglo-Saxon Chronicle* in British Library,
MS Cotton Tiberius B.i (usually labelled 'C' and called the *Abingdon
Chronicle*). Just as the English army did, this account stumbles in
the course of 1066, breaking off in mid-sentence before it has even
finished with the events at Stamford Bridge ('And there Harold king
of Norway was killed, and earl Tostig, and numberless men with
them both Norwegians and English, and the Norwegians . . .'). A
later hand eventually comes along to complete the interrupted sentence ('. . . fled from the field'), and then the same hand continues
the narrative through Harold's victory ('Harold let the king's son . . .
go home to Norway with all the ships'). But the next disaster is so
complete that it obliterates all further opportunity to write; here, the
effects of the Norman Conquest are so severe that they preclude
their own recording.[2]

---

[1] R. C. Van Caenegem, *The Birth of the English Common Law*, 2nd edn.
(Cambridge: Cambridge University Press, 1973; 2nd edn. 1988), 4.
[2] I take my translation of the *Abingdon Chronicle* from *The Norman Conquest of
England: Sources and Documents*, ed. R. Allen Brown (Woodbridge: Boydell Press,
1984), 70–1. '& þær wæs Harold cyning of Norwegan & Tostig eorl ofslagen &

We know the *Abingdon Chronicle* failed at this point, because there are other stories which remain to fill the gap, to tell us not only that we have missed something, but what we have missed. The English view of the Norman invasion was preserved in two other versions of the *Anglo-Saxon Chronicle*, the manuscripts called 'D' (London, British Library MS Cotton Tiberius B.iv) and 'E' (Oxford, Bodleian MS Laud 636), as well as a chronicle kept at Worcester (the *Chronicon ex chronicis* often attributed to 'Florence').[3] Alongside these may be placed the contemporaneous accounts of the Conquest from the Norman point of view by William of Jumièges (*c.*1070–1) and William of Poitiers (*c.*1073–7), as well as a variety of works from the next generation, such as the *Historia ecclesiastica* (*c.*1109–41) by Orderic Vitalis and the *Gesta regum Anglorum* (*c.*1125) and the *Gesta pontificum* (*c.*1125) by William of Malmesbury.[4] There are so many such stories, in fact, that it has been said that there was actually *more* writing rather than less as a result of the kind of loss the Conquest entailed. As tenants and a landed aristocracy watched privileges, possessions, and territory slip away, they resorted increasingly (and then constantly) to writing as a way of recording and asserting their rights.[5] The divisiveness of the political change itself fuelled what David Douglas has called a 'heated polemical vapour'

ungerim folces mid heom, ægðer ge Normana ge Englisca. & þa Normen *flugon þa Englisca* . . . *& þes cyninges sunu Hetmundus let Harold faran ham to Norweie mid alle þa scipe*', *Two of the Saxon Chronicles Parallel (with supplementary extracts from the others)*, ed. John Earle, rev. Charles Plummer, 2 vols. (Oxford: Oxford University Press, 1892–9), 1: 198. Italics in the original.

Elsewhere, contemporary histories wary of positioning themselves around such a severe political change 'elide, or very nearly elide, the moment of change itself', only allowing themselves to acknowledge the enormity of the event by their attempts to smooth it over or the awkwardness with which they change the subject. On this general phenomenon see Monika Otter, '1066: The Moment of Transition in Two Narratives of the Norman Conquest', *Speculum* 74 (1999), 565–86 (quotation here from p. 568).

[3] On these versions see *Two of the Saxon Chronicles*, ed. Earle, rev. Plummer, 1: x–xiii (for a brief survey of the manuscripts) and 2: xxii–cii (for detailed analysis of textual relations). On the 'Worcester Chronicle' (and 'Florence') see Antonia Gransden, *Historical Writing in England c.550 to c.1307* (London: Routledge & Kegan Paul, 1974), 143–8.

[4] For the earliest of the historians of the Norman Conquest, see Gransden, *Historical Writing in England c.550 to c.1307*, 92–104. For the later generations see this volume, 151–65 (on Orderic Vitalis) and 166–85 (on William of Malmesbury).

[5] See R. W. Southern, 'Aspects of the European Tradition of Historical Writing (4): The Sense of the Past', *Transactions of the Royal Historical Society*, 5th ser., vol. 23 (London: Royal Historical Society, 1973), 241–63 (esp. 246–56).

which has lasted until the present day: as the meaning of 'Hastings' and 'the Conquest' and '1066' have themselves been fought over—made and remade to serve a variety of latter-day ends—the 'cataclysm' has become the engine of a 'productive zeal', an endless making of arguments embedded in the kinds of document we tend to call 'history'.[6]

The name we choose to give writing matters very much in this case because, where we have chosen to call it 'literature', and that literature is in English, sudden silencing is not the exception, but the rule: the generations immediately after Hastings have been called a 'hiatus in our literature', a period in which there is no evidence that the vernacular was in 'widespread literary use'. [7] Nor do matters seem to have improved for some time. Even in the twelfth century most of the survivals in English that we have been willing to call literary are fragments, snippets of poetry which sneak into texts in other languages (for example, a song sung by soldiers under the Duke of Leicester in 1173 recorded in Matthew of Paris's *Historia Anglorum*) or short and fugitive (for example, the ten alliterative lines of the 'Charm Against a Wen', *c.*1150).[8] No work of literature of any length has been identified until the middle of the twelfth century (perhaps the earliest is the 700-line *Proverbs of Alfred* (*c.*1150)), but even such length provides no evidence that a significant vernacular impulse has taken hold.[9] Until the fourteenth century, in fact, English literature has seemed an 'unstable continuum', a shape in which the spaces between texts are more common—and therefore seem more definitive—than writings themselves.[10]

---

[6] David Douglas, *The Norman Conquest and British Historians* (Glasgow: Jackson, Son, 1946), 8. According to Christopher Hill, the view that the Conquest inaugurated intolerable restraints on liberty in England was an important rallying cry for the Levellers, Cobbett, the Chartists, and even the modern Labour movement itself. See 'The Norman Yoke', 46–111 in *Puritanism and Revolution: Studies in Interpretation of the English Revolution of the Seventeenth Century* (London: Martin Secker & Warburg, 1958).

[7] *Early Middle English Verse and Prose*, ed. J. A. W. Bennett and G. V. Smithers, with a glossary by Norman Davis, 2nd edn. (Oxford: Oxford University Press, 1968), p. xii.

[8] For these writings see *MWME* 5: 1390 ['Tags in Matthew of Paris']; 10: 3676 ['A Charm Against a Wen'].

[9] For the text see *An Old English Miscellany*, ed. Richard Morris, EETS os 49 (1872), 102–38.

[10] Geoffrey Shepherd, 'Early Middle English', 81–117 in *The Middle Ages*, ed. W. F. Bolton (London: Sphere, 1970), 81.

As the foregoing should have already begun to suggest, however, such a shape is necessarily the product of a kind of attention. As one scholar of the period has recently pointed out, the project of literature is only unstable in this way when the 'complex, trilingual culture' of England in the period is ignored, when we allow ourselves to think of literature as a mono-linguistic enterprise, in this case isolating English from the rich set of relations its production maintained with writing in Latin and Anglo-Norman.[11] The dearth of English literature is also a product of the classifications customary within the language, since it is only to the extent that we insist upon parcelling up writing into kinds that the abundance of history can fail to fill the gaps in the continuum we call 'literature'.[12] Here the old question, 'what is literature?', has an added component, for it must be posed historically ('what is early Middle English literature?') and it therefore also engages the question, 'what is history?' What once appeared as no more than the examination of writing that has survived from the period 1066–1300 reveals itself as a project which will produce the very kind of writing we are trying to separate literature from, where the instrument of our examination will itself be history, or, perhaps, that mixed mode which is usually called 'literary history'.[13]

The history of literary form that I provide in this book can therefore begin nowhere else than with some account of the form of history. The first section of this chapter offers such a description in relation to those histories (not all of them writings) which carry the idea we now generally summarize as '1066' (for it is only in such history that this year survives), and it shows how the ideas generated by retrospection sometimes substitute themselves for the ideas actually embedded in the relics that survive from this moment. The second section assesses the effects such substitutions can have on the meanings carried in a particular relic, *The First Worcester Fragment*, a written form whose near-destruction has come to seem synonymous

---

[11] Linda Georgianna, 'Coming to Terms with the Norman Conquest: Nationalism and English Literary History', *REAL: Yearbook of Research in English and American Literature* 14 (1998), 33–53 (quotation from p. 44).
[12] See *Two of the Saxon Chronicles*, ed. Earle, rev. Plummer, 1: 214 (for the moment of 'D's ending), 2: xxxi–xxxiii (for the manuscript of 'D'), and 2: xlv–lv (for discussion of the complex ending of 'E' and its manuscript).
[13] For a helpful analysis of the general difficulties which attend this mixed mode see Lee Patterson, 'Literary History', 250–62 in *Critical Terms for Literary Study*, ed. Frank Lentricchia and Thomas McLaughlin (Chicago: University of Chicago Press, 1990).

with 1066 but which pays no attention whatsoever to either this year or its consequences. The concluding section looks at how the process which obliterates the meanings of the *Fragment* are typical, not only of the way early Middle English literary objects have been encountered, but of the way we define English literature as such. The equation of rarity with materiality and formal variety with eccentricity which governs so much that has been said about the English writing in the centuries immediately after 1066 turns out to be nothing more than an instance of our general bias against rich and defining thoughtfulness, a manifestation of what turns out to be our *dislike* of metaphysical subtlety in the things we want to call 'literary'—but which, in a defining blindness, we usually understand as our embrace of that subtlety.

HISTORICAL FORM

Despite all the writing devoted to remembering this long moment we will never know what happened in 1066. The events we might care about were—and remain—so politically charged that, even when we limit ourselves to those accounts which Hegel would have called 'original' (by historians who 'simply transferred what was passing in the world around them to the realm of representative intellect'), the variety of account is self-consuming.[14] Sometimes the difference is only a matter of detail: for example, the *Anglo-Saxon Chronicle* ('D') says that William 'ravaged all the region that he overran until he reached Berkhamstead', but William of Poitiers says that he ravaged the region until he reached 'the town of Wallingford'.[15] But such differences in detail can amount to differences in political reality: for example, the *Anglo-Saxon Chronicle* ('D') says that the English 'submitted out of necessity after most damage had been done', but William of Poitiers says that submission came 'with joyful assent,

[14] Georg W. F. Hegel, *The Philosophy of History*, trans J. Sibree (Amherst, NY: Prometheus Books, 1991), 1.
[15] *Norman Conquest*, ed. Brown, 71; '& hergade ealne þone ende þe he oferferde, oð þ[et] he com to Beorhhamstede', *Two of the Saxon Chronicles*, ed. Earle, rev. Plummer, 1: 200; 'Dux progrediens dein quoquouersum placuit . . . ad oppidum Guarengefort peruenit', *The Gesta Guillelmi of William of Poitiers*, ed. and trans. R. H. C. Davis and Marjorie Chibnall (Oxford: Clarendon Press, 1998), ii.28 (pp. 146–7).

with no hesitation, as if heaven had granted them one mind and one voice'.[16] In fact, conflicting details may seem so suitable to the viewpoints from which they are reported that neither seems likely to be true. The *Anglo-Saxon Chronicle* ('D') finds that 'the king had all the monasteries that were in England plundered', while William of Poitiers says William gave 'treasures' to the 'monasteries of various provinces'.[17] The *Anglo-Saxon Chronicle* ('E') says that, in William's reign, 'the more just laws were talked about, the more unlawful things were done', but William of Poitiers says that 'no one ever sought a just judgment of him in vain' because William 'forbade strife, murder and every kind of plunder'.[18]

The uncertainty is endemic because, as Hegel taught us long ago —and as Hayden White has more recently demonstrated—history is a poetics, an 'image' created by a desiring mind (what Hegel called the 'conceptive faculty').[19] To many this is a disabling fault, and, for Marx in particular, this made history one of the most dangerous of political instruments, a way of shackling the present to 'the spirits of the past', shaping current endeavours so that they would satisfy a trajectory which was a modern invention. History's imaginative power was, for him, a mode of proving what never *was* true ('history exists so that the proof of truths may exist'), a kind of 'theoretical eating'.[20]

[16] *Norman Conquest*, ed. Brown, 72; '& bugon þa for neode, þa mæst wæs to hearme gedon', *Two of the Saxon Chronicles*, ed. Earle, rev. Plummer, 1: 200; 'Protestati sunt hilarem consensum uniuersi minime haesitantes, ac si caelitus una mente data unaque uoce', *Gesta Guillelmi*, ed. and trans. Davis and Chibnall, ii.30 (pp. 150–1).
[17] *Norman Conquest*, ed. Brown, 74; 'Se cyng let hergian ealle þa mynstra þe on Englalande wæron', *Two of the Saxon Chronicles*, ed. Earle, rev. Plummer, 1: 205; 'thesauros . . . monasteriis diuersarum prouinciarum distribuit', *Gesta Guillelmi*, ii.31 (pp. 152–3); 'Iudicium rectum nulla persona ab eo nequicquam postulauit'; 'Seditiones interdixit, caedem et omnem rapinam', *Gesta Guillelmi*, ed. and trans. Davis and Chibnall, ii.33–4 (pp. 158–61).
[18] *Norman Conquest*, ed. Brown, 79; 'Ac swa man swyðor spæc embe rihte lage, swa mann dyde mare unlaga', *Two of the Saxon Chronicles*, ed. Earle, rev. Plummer, 1: 218; 'Iudicium rectum nulla persona ab eo nequicquam postulavit'; 'Seditiones interdixit, caedem et omnem rapinam', *Gesta Guillelmi*, ed. and trans. Davis and Chibnall, ii.33 (pp. 158–9), ii.34 (pp. 160–1).
[19] Hegel, *Philosophy of History*, 1. On Hegel's poetics of history see Hayden White, *Metahistory: The Historical Imagination in Nineteenth-Century Europe* (Baltimore: Johns Hopkins University Press, 1973), 81–131. On the fictionality of history more generally see Hayden White, 'Interpretation in History', 51–80; 'The Historical Text as Literary Artifact', 81–100; 'Historicism, History, and the Figurative Imagination', 101–120; and 'The Fictions of Factual Representation', 121–34 in *Tropics of Discourse: Essays in Cultural Criticism* (Baltimore: Johns Hopkins University Press, 1978).
[20] Marx, *The Holy Family*, 131–55 in *Selected Writings*, ed. David McLellan (Oxford: Oxford University Press, 1977), 139.

As Lévi-Strauss went on to develop this view, such fictions not only secure present arrangements by inventing a past for them, they secure our sense that there *is* coherence in a world we only experience as confusion:

> History seems to restore to us, not separate states, but the passage from one state to another in a continuous form. And as we believe that we apprehend the trend of our personal history as a continuous change, historical knowledge appears to confirm the evidence of inner sense. History seems to do more than describe beings to us from the outside, or at best give us intermittent flashes of insight into internalities, each of which are so on their own account while remaining external to each other: it appears to re-establish our connection, outside ourselves, with the very essence of change.[21]

It is therefore appropriate to call history a 'form', not simply because it takes shape as this or that set of written lines (with this or that rhetorical and argumentative shape), but because it is always constituted by the thought that there is order in happening, a 'spurious intelligibility attaining to a temporary internality', a fantasy of structure that actually yields one, the belief that the past is ordered which therefore *creates* that order (what Lévi-Strauss called history's 'fraudulent outlines').[22] Because we are so comforted by the resulting pattern, the making of history also allows us to forget what our daily experience otherwise teaches us: that time does not unfold in parcels which could be described as 'events' to which we may assign any particular meaning. What history allows us *not* to know, is that we always experience the world as 'a multitude of individual psychic moments' which are, in turn, the projections of varied, irrecoverable, and personal 'cerebral, hormonal or nervous phenomena'.[23]

On the other hand, history's capacity to convince us of what was never true may also be described as the form's extraordinary creative capacity. As Hegel also taught us, to distort or reshape thoughts about the past is necessarily to make something, to produce meaning

---

[21] Claude Lévi-Strauss, *The Savage Mind* (*La Pensée Sauvage*) (London: Weidenfeld & Nicolson, 1966), 256.

[22] Ibid. 255 ('spurious intelligibility') and 261 ('fraudulent outlines'). For a summary of Lévi-Strauss's views, drawn upon here, see also White, 'Interpretation in History', 56–7. On the 'formal coherency' of narrative see Hayden White, 'The Value of Narrativity in the Representation of Reality', 1–25 in *The Content of the Form: Narrative Discourse and Historical Representation* (Baltimore: Johns Hopkins University Press, 1987).

[23] Lévi-Strauss, *Savage Mind*, 257.

in place of 'a previously formless impulse'.[24] If history fakes the past by inventing a non-existent coherence then *coherence* is one of the most characteristic structures of the objects we call history. It is perhaps not surprising that one of the more impressive examples of such structuring is the extraordinary coherence one such form achieved for '1066' (or, really 1064–6, for this is the timespan it covers) that historical form we now tend to call the Bayeux Tapestry. The structure of the Tapestry is complex: on a single horizontal plane it combines a central panel of narrative images, Latin epigraphs above these pictures which narrate the same story, an upper border above these words, and a lower border beneath the central panel, which often consists of decorative images but, at times, elaborates the narrative images of the central panel (often from a different perspective or in a slightly phased time). The Tapestry's creative capacity may simply be measured by its size, for it is one of the most massive historical accounts of 1066 ever made (it is 68.38 m long by 45.7–53.6 cm wide)—it is so large, in fact, that it cannot be taken in in one glance.[25] It might therefore also be said that among the things the Tapestry employs in its remaking of the past is time itself. Its 'outlines' are sufficiently complicated that they cannot be apprehended except by the *use* of time (to look or walk around the room in which the Tapestry is hung), by the substitution of a sequence of present moments for the sequence of past moments it describes'.[26]

Such varied and unusual accomplishments are also of particular interest because they are of the kind which tempt us to say that a given history is *less* 'fraudulent' than others, since, to the extent that it is complex, even disordered in its own form, the Bayeux Tapestry is

---

[24] Hegel, *Philosophy of History*, 61.

[25] Representative articles from the whole history of Tapestry scholarship are reprinted in *The Study of the Bayeux Tapestry*, ed. Richard Gameson (Woodbridge: Boydell Press, 1997). Gameson also summarizes those views in his own contribution to this volume, 'The Origin, Art, and Message of the Bayeux Tapestry' (157–211). For an account of the Tapestry focused on its materials and physical shape see, in this volume, Simone Bertrand, 'A Study of the Bayeux Tapestry', 31–8 (originally published as 'Étude sur la Tapisserie de Bayeux', *Annales de Normandie* 10 (1960), 197–206). For the measurement of the Tapestry I quote here see the 'editor's note' in this article (33).

[26] On the conversion of space into time in the visual arts see Otto Pächt, *The Rise of Pictorial Narrative in Twelfth Century England* (Oxford: Clarendon Press, 1962), 1–4. On the size of room required for the Tapestry's display see Richard Brilliant, 'The Bayeux Tapestry: A Stripped Narrative for their Eyes and Ears', 111–37 in *Study of the Bayeux Tapestry*, ed. Gameson.

more likely to capture the rich variety of uncertainty and confusion native to perception and knowing. It models past experience, not only as it fills the time of modern lives, but as its various sequences interact variously and unpredictably, glossing, undermining, and supplementing unitary meanings in each strand. For example, the imminence of the Norman invasion is signalled to anyone who notices the appearance of half-built ships in the lower border before William has ordered any ships built in the main panel, while, at the same time, the English defeat at William's hand is foreshadowed for anyone who notices a comet in the upper border which accompanies their building (Fig. 1). Further along in the sequence, the serious blow to Anglo-Saxon culture witnessed by the interruption of the *Abingdon Chronicle* is itself anticipated for anyone who notices that the masts of William's fleet are so tall that they not only fill the upper border but, necessarily, interrupt the Latin epigraphy which is actually narrating the story (Fig. 2). Later still, the overwhelming force of the Norman attack is captured from multiple perspectives simultaneously, as the lower border is recruited to the depiction of ranks of archers while the main panel is filled by the main charge on horseback (Fig. 3). Finally, as these scenes of attack give way to scenes of slaughter in the main panel, the extent and the cataclysm in space, as well as its inevitability in time, are measured by the piling up of corpses in the lower border, some already in the process of being despoiled by scavengers (Fig. 4).[27]

Such a history is true, it could be argued, to precisely the extent that it succeeds in capturing a constitutive (never fully resolvable) disorder, and yet it is in precisely this sense that a second crucial attribute of historical form emerges: what might be called its *capacity for disguise*. For at the very moment we are willing to accept rather than query the veracity of a given history—when we think we have learned something about a battle or some of its events from this account precisely because history has helped us to understand it— then, however alert we are to the process, history has begun to substitute itself for the past; it has begun to persuade us that it is not a more recently made form but the past itself. Such disguise is in fact so basic to the relation between history and the past that it is even

---

[27] For good photographic reproductions of the tapestry see Wolfgang Grape, *The Bayeux Tapestry* (Munich: Prestel, 1994). For the images cited in my text see this volume, 124 (Fig. 1), 134–5 (Fig. 2), 161 (Fig. 3), 164–5 (Fig. 4).

FIG. 1 'ISTI MIRANT STELLA(M); HAROLD' [These men marvel at the star; Harold]. Detail from the Bayeux Tapestry (eleventh century).

FIG. 2 '(HIC WILLELM[US] . . . TRANSIVIT) ET VENIT AD PEVENESÆ' [Here Duke William . . . crossed the sea and came to Pevensey]. Detail from the Bayeux Tapestry (eleventh century).

FIG. 3 'HIC EST DUX WILELM(US); HIC FRANCI PUGNA(NT)' [Here is Duke William; here the French fight]. Detail from the Bayeux Tapestry (eleventh century).

FIG. 4 'ET FUGA VERTERU(NT ANGLI)' [And the English turned in flight]. Detail from the Bayeux Tapestry (eleventh century).

internal to the word we use to describe these two phenomena: as Hegel
pointed out, history (or *Geschichte* or *historia*) refers to a latter-day
object which tells us 'what happened', the *historia rerum gestarum*,
but it also refers to the unmediated past, the 'things that have happened' themselves, the *res gestae*.[28] Such a disguise is most subtly
(and therefore most powerfully) in operation when we point to the
Bayeux Tapestry and call it a 'history of 1066', for it is as if the acuity
we employ to notice the status of the object we are apprehending
(the part of our awareness that knows it is history and not the past)
somehow prevents us from knowing at the same time that, if it came
from any past, it most certainly did not come from 1066. In this
sense, what gives history's disguise its greatest power is its capacity
to give *some* of the game away—to have outlines that are sufficiently
coherent for us to detect the fraudulence—*but not the extent of it*. In
looking at the Bayeux Tapestry, for example, we have easily detected
the 'rhetorical power' of its pro-Norman bias, how its carefully
crafted arguments 'ride roughshod over the demands of historical
accuracy', and this alone helps us know that it is history and not the
past.[29] Keeping these latter-day ends in sight is itself a way of remembering that even a Tapestry designed by eyewitnesses to the events it
records had to have been made at a later moment (at the earliest, in
the years 1072–7).[30] Yet almost every encounter with the Tapestry
as history fails to care that substantial parts of its complex shape are
not even medieval: nineteenth-century restorations were of sufficient scope (but so poorly documented) that it is now impossible
to tell where the original embroidery ended and modern production
began. Whatever the Bayeux Tapestry may know about 1066, in

---

[28] 'In our language the term History unites the objective with the subjective side,
and denotes quite as much the *historia rerum gestarum*, as the *res gestae* themselves;
on the other hand it comprehends not less what has happened, than the narration
of what has happened', Hegel, *Philosophy of History*, 60. 'Geschichte vereinigt in
unsrer Sprache die objektive sowohl als subjektive Seite und bedeutet ebensogut die
historiam rerum gestarum als die res gestas selbst; sie ist das Geschehene nicht minder
wie die Geschichtserzählung', Georg Wilhelm Friedrich Hegel, *Vorlesungen über die
Philosophie der Geschichte* (Stuttgart: Philipp Reclam, 1961), 114.

[29] Suzanne Lewis, *The Rhetoric of Power in the Bayeux Tapestry* (Cambridge:
Cambridge University Press, 1999), 3. On the Tapestry's Norman bias see the classic
article by Edward Freeman (first published in 1875), 'The Authority of the Bayeux
Tapestry', 7–18 in *Study of the Bayeux Tapestry*, ed. Gameson.

[30] On the Tapestry's date and discussion of its 'historicity' see Gameson, 'Origin,
Art, and Message of the Bayeux Tapestry', in *Study of the Bayeux Tapestry*, ed.
Gameson, 161 and 199–206.

other words, is necessarily defined by the extent to which we forget that some of it is a product of 1821.[31]

But it is also a defining nature of the disguise which defines every historical form that it is strengthened to precisely the extent that a certain proportion of it is detected, that the fraudulence of a whole form is overlooked to whatever extent some of that fraudulence is carefully noted. In other words, where the Middle Ages prized *historia* for its invention, classing it with poetry among the arts of grammar, we now define history as that which *detects* invention, as if history were in fact a species of scepticism.[32] Our confidence in history's truth is actually secured when we look back even the relatively short distance to E. A. Freeman's six-volume account of the Norman Conquest, and, even as we recognize a 'knowledge of the narrative sources of Anglo-Saxon history which has rarely been equalled', we see very clearly that his real project was to annex the eleventh century to nineteenth-century concerns ('[he] treated eleventh-century struggle almost as a matter of present politics').[33] We dismiss Freeman's pedantic insistence that the Battle of Hastings should really be called the 'Battle of Senlac' because this is the hill on which it was 'actually' fought since he allowed himself to come to this conclusion by modern-day tours of that hill.[34] We reject his knowledge of that Battle because it is so generally impeached by a narrative vivid enough to record what was said as well as the emotions of people even as they died:

[31] On the restorations see the description (1st published 1821) by Charles Stothard, 'Some Observations on the Bayeux Tapestry', 1–6 in *Study of the Bayeux Tapestry*, ed. Gameson. On the difficulty of distinguishing such restorations from the Tapestry's original design see Richard Gameson's introduction to this volume, 'Studying the Bayeux Tapestry', p. x.

[32] For 'historia' as part of 'grammatica' see Isidore of Seville, *Etymologiarum sive originum libri XX*, 2 vols., ed. W. M. Lindsay (Oxford: Clarendon Press, 1911), I.xli–xliv. Aristotle also placed poetry and history in the same category. See *Poetics*, 2: 2316–40 in *The Complete Works of Aristotle*, ed. Jonathan Barnes, 2 vols., rev. edn. (Princeton: Princeton University Press, 1984), 1451b1–7 (2: 2323) and 1459a22–29 (2: 2335). On this subject see also Hannah Arendt, 'The Concept of History', 41–90 in *Between Past and Future: Eight Exercises in Political Thought* (New York: Viking, 1961), 45, and Nancy Partner, *Serious Entertainments: The Writing of History in Twelfth-Century England* (Chicago: University of Chicago Press, 1977), 194–6.

[33] Douglas, *Norman Conquest and British Historians*, 18 ('knowledge') and 21 ('treated').

[34] E. A. Freeman, *The History of the Norman Conquest: Its Causes and Results*, 6 vols. (Oxford: Clarendon Press, 1867–77; 2nd edn. of vols. 1–3, 1870–5), 3: 444–5. For Freeman's description of his visits see 3: 756–7.

The Duke bade his archers shoot up in the air, that their arrows might, as it were, fall straight from heaven. The effect was immediate and fearful. No other device of the wily Duke that day did such frightful execution. Helmets were pierced; eyes were put out; men strove to guard their heads with their shields, and, in so doing, they were of course less able to wield their axes. And now the supreme moment drew near. There was one point of the hill at which the Norman bowmen were bidden specially to aim with their truest skill. As twilight was coming on, a mighty shower of arrows was launched on its deadly errand against the defenders of the Standard. There Harold still fought; his shield bristled with Norman shafts; but he was still unwounded and unwearied. At last another arrow, more charged with destiny than its fellows, went still more truly to its mark. Falling like a bolt from heaven, it pierced the King's right eye; he clutched convulsively at the weapon, he broke off the shaft, his axe dropped from his hand, and he sank in agony at the foot of the Standard.[35]

But as we strip off each element of disguise from Freeman's historical form, some of it necessarily sticks to the very position from which our care comes; for it is just under the scepticism it directs at less 'accurate' forms that modern history smuggles in its own powerful fraudulence. The process is particularly noticeable in this case because Freeman was so generally and severely critiqued by J. H. Round. Round's description of this battle is designed to show that Freeman's was a 'purely imaginary creation', while he himself claims to report only 'what the authorities plainly describe':[36]

Let us, then, keep to what we know. Is it not enough for us to picture the English line stubbornly striving to the last to close its broken ranks, the awful scene of slaughter and confusion, as the Old Guard of Harold, tortured by Norman arrows, found the horsemen among them at last, slashing and piercing right and left. Still, the battle-axe blindly smote; doggedly, grimly still they fought, till the axes dropped from their lifeless grasp. And so they fell.[37]

Of course, our own scepticism allows us to see that Round's history is equally imaginary to the extent that it also makes feelings and movements after the fact. The resulting 'picture' is certainly history as it is generally made, but only to the extent that, by calling his

[35] Freeman, *History of the Norman Conquest*, 3: 496–7.
[36] J. H. Round, 'Mr Freeman and the Battle of Hastings', 258–305 in his *Feudal England* (London: George Allen & Unwin, 1964 (1st published, 1895)), 278 ('purely imaginary') and 299 ('what the authorities').
[37] Round, 'Mr Freeman and the Battle of Hastings', 299.

account 'enough'—that is, by proposing a limit for its descriptive scope and power—Round distances himself from his own fantasies.

History is not the only way we can encounter the past, of course, since 'what happened' also lies latent for us in all those objects which past activities and ideas made and then left behind. Indeed, the alternative Marx envisioned to the conjured spirits of history was careful attention to inherited materialities, those 'circumstances, directly encountered, given, and transmitted from the past'.[38] Far easier to detect and put to use retrospectively than such circumstances are those solid and surviving objects, those *relics* (the old table, the used pair of shoes, the text written on the manuscript page) whose made structure offers a rich record of the thoughts which produced them. Benedetto Croce called such objects 'brute facts' because they were so obviously material, but he also described them as 'transcendent', since the past they contain only becomes part of the present by a *present-day* 'act of thought'—as we recover the thinking in this old form and involve that thinking in a modern-day history.[39] As R. G. Collingwood insisted a little later, such history is necessarily a function of the '*a priori* imagination' because it must recognize the past as that which no longer is ('not an object of possible perception, since it does not now exist').[40]

Whether relic or writing, then, the thought that historical forms always bear so that we do not have to—the idea which makes them recognizable as history but which is itself always misrecognized—is that they actually are the past, brought forward into our present, but not made here. Even if we have now read our Croce and Collingwood (and Hegel and White) well enough to know that history is a species of metaphysics, we ensure that the historical forms we make are defended from this abyssal perception by making them ever more rigorously physical. It is for this reason that our history of

---

[38] Karl Marx, *The Eighteenth Brumaire of Louis Bonaparte*, 300–25 in *Selected Writings*, 300.

[39] Benedetto Croce, *Theory and History of Historiography*, trans. Douglas Ainslie (London: George G. Harrap, 1921), 19 ('act of thought'), 72 ('brute facts') and 80 ('transcendent'). R. G. Collingwood also comments on the imaginative nature of facts: 'A person who understands all this will immediately accept as true what a person who did not understand it would reject as a monstrous falsehood: the doctrine that the historian does not find his evidence but makes it, and makes it inside his own head', *The Principles of History and Other Writings in the Philosophy of History*, ed. W. H. Dray and W. J. van der Dussen (Oxford: Clarendon Press, 1999), 54.

[40] R. G. Collingwood, *The Idea of History* (Oxford: Clarendon Press, 1946), 242.

the Conquest has gravitated toward the enumeration of things, as if the massing of objects by means of numbers, histograms, and pie charts, or piecing out of these objects over territory in maps, secures them more firmly in the past.[41] The firmness numbers seem to give to whatever they count is itself responsible for the oracular import- ance of the number '1066' (that it counts something is itself a way of certifying that what it counts are things). But, most importantly of all, such forms secure representations of the Norman Conquest by tricking them out, not as some event or sequence of them, but as a power gradient along which certain outcomes were the results of something as material as addition:

In all, the estates of Harold, his brothers and his mother were valued at £5,400 and twenty-two nights' farm, or about £7,500 and the king's estates about £3,900 and twenty nights' farm or approximately £5,950. The Godwinesons's, therefore exceeded the total value of the *terra regis* in January of 1066 by £1,550 and slightly exceeded the king's estates in nights' farm.[42]

Of course, this gradient *implies* a narrative, and a form so bolstered by facticity of this kind can even allow itself to tell that, for example, Edward's position 'eroded during the course of his reign' because of his 'inability to stop the growing power and wealth of Earl Godwine and his sons', while the 'clientage' attracted by these 'new men' had itself become so fragile that, after Stamford Bridge, it was imposs- ible to organize the 'effective resistance' necessary at Hastings.[43] Such a form calls the matter which comprises it 'evidence' and what that form therefore also knows (as the very warrant of its being) is that such matter has not changed in its journey from the past to the present (that, for example, these figures would have been the same were they run in 1066).[44] In this case, however, such accuracy is itself a coherence which disguises the journey these figures have made, for nearly every one of them is taken from that survey of

---

[41] The example I allude to here is Robin Fleming, *Kings and Lords in Conquest England* (Cambridge: Cambridge University Press, 1991), 145–82. This volume is thick with tables (59), histograms (72), pie charts (225–8), and maps of landholding (221–4).

[42] Ibid. 70–1.   [43] Ibid. 103.

[44] Fleming uses the term 'evidence' to characterize the basis of all her claims: 'What makes it possible to study [this period] is the survival of sufficient evidence to identify many of the kingdom's chief men and their kinsmen and allies', ibid., p. xvi.

landholding called *Domesday Book*—which was not made until 1086.[45]

History is therefore only useful (perhaps only extant) to the extent that its formal nature is denied; its constituting cause is the need to make any who meet it forget how it was made. When we measure such a compounding of fantasies with the metric of accuracy or even truthfulness, we are not wrong, however, for all we can test with the instrument of our scepticism is the security of the (false) coherence and the (undetected) disguise which is 'truth' in this arena: the perfection of a given form's alignment with the past is something we could never seek (since no line can be drawn between something and nothing), and, thus, history only ever succeeds by means of the alignment of each one of its parts with all the others. A given history is 'accurate', therefore, to precisely the extent that it imparts sufficient coherence to make us forget its belatedness and fictionality. This is not how history fails us, however, but how it has substantial value and consequence. As a mode of knowing, history is truly formidable in its capacity to make what has vanished so vivacious that we feel we have not lost it—to make what has died away from the world live again in the richness of its former substance.

THE LOST LITERATURE OF ENGLAND

But such forms and their power are also capable of making a silence where there is actually an eloquent relic, of actually swallowing up some stolid presence by opening a gap right beneath it. Where such an occlusion occurs by inadvertence—when it is not propaganda of some sort but a mistake, where history is so caught up in a general thought about the past that it cannot absorb the thought recorded in a particular relic to the trajectory it is bent on tracing—we ought to be able to detect the omission by means of that critique of coherence which lets us denigrate any history. That is, where the story does not

---

[45] This document (discussed at more length in Chapter 2, pp. 65–8) measured the change brought about by the Norman Conquest by describing landholding in the 'T. R. E', the *tempus regis Æduardi*, the 'day king Edward was alive and dead' (5 January 1066), and 'now' (*modo*), the period in which the survey was completed (between Christmas 1085 and 1 August 1086). On a chronology for the making of *Domesday Book*, see J. C. Holt, '1086', 41–64 in *Domesday Studies*, ed. J. C. Holt (Woodbridge: Boydell & Brewer, 1987), 44.

fit the relic, we can write the story again. But what if history has been insistent enough in the making of its own forms not only to lose some object, but to lose the whole species of things which might alert us to the need for correction? What if the very profusion of historical forms generated by and around 1066 have actually lost the most fecund and rich of survivals precisely because those things disrupt the idea of 'cataclysm' on which the coherence of that history immediately came to depend?

The First Worcester Fragment suggests itself as a likely example of such a loss since it is that relic which has always been seen to embody the general view of 1066 as 'cataclysm', recording the loss of literature from the perspective of literature itself. As the title customarily given to it implies, the *Fragment* even bears this general loss in its own injured form. Although it is now again secure in a codex (Worcester Cathedral MS F. 174), the poem is called a 'fragment' because the leaves on which it and another longer text were copied had been deemed so unimportant that they were used to stiffen the covers of another book (at some point after 1250); we only have these poems to read at all because this binding was disassembled in the nineteenth century.[46] It may well be that we do not have the whole of the text, but what we do have of it is short enough to quote in full:

Sanctus Beda was iboren   her on Breotene mid us,
And he wisliche   bec iwende
Þet þeo Englise leoden   þurh weren ilerde.
And he þeo cnotten unwreih,   þe questiuns hoteþ,
Þa dern diȝelnesse   þe deorwurþe is.   5
Ælfric abbod,   þe we Alquin hoteþ,
he was bocare,   and þe fif bec wende:
Genesis, Exodus, Leuiticus,   Numerus, Vtronomius.
Þurh þeos weren ilærde   ure leoden on Englisc.
Þet weren þeos biscopes   þe bodeden Cristendom,   10

---

[46] For a description of the manuscript see N. R. Ker, *Catalogue of Manuscripts Containing Anglo-Saxon* (Oxford: Clarendon Press, 1990; 1st published, 1957), 466–7. See also Christine Franzen, *The Tremulous Hand of Worcester: A Study of Old English in the Thirteenth Century* (Oxford: Clarendon Press, 1991), 70–1. On the discovery of the fragment see Douglas Moffat, 'The Recovery of Worcester Cathedral MS F. 174', *Notes and Queries* NS 32 (1985), 300–2. A description of the whole manuscript and a diplomatic edition of its English texts can be found in Jan-Geir Johansen Aase, ' "The Worcester Fragments": (Worcester Cathedral MS 174, ff. 63ʳ–66ᵛ): An Edition, with Diplomatic Transcription, Notes, and Glossary', University of Sheffield, Ph.D. Thesis, 1984.

Wilfrid of Ripum,   Iohan of Beoferlai,
Cuþbert of Dunholme,   Oswald of Wireceastre,
Egwin of Heoueshame,   Ældelm of Malmesburi,
Swiþþun, Æþelwold   Aidan, Biern of Wincæstre,
Paulin of Rofecæstre,   Dunston and Ælfeih of Cantoreburi.   15
Þeos laerden ure leodan on Englisc,   næs deorc heore liht, ac hit fæire glod.
Nu is þeo leore forleten,   and þet folc is forloren.
Nu beoþ oþre leoden   þeo læreþ ure folc,
And feole of þen lorþeines losiæþ   and þet folc forþ mid.
Nu sæiþ ure Drihten þus,   *Sicut aquila prouocat pullos suos*   20
ad volandum.   et super eos uolitat.
This beoþ Godes word   to worlde asende,
Þet we sceolen fæier feþ   festen to Him.

> [Saint Bede was born here in Britain with us,
> And wisely he translated books
> So that the English people were taught by them.
> And he unraveled the problems, called the *Quæstiones*,
> That obscure enigma which is precious.   5
> Abbot Ælfric, whom we call Alcuin,
> Was a writer and translated the five books:
> Genesis, Exodus, Leviticus, Numbers, Deuteronomy.
> With these our people were taught in English.
> There were these bishops who preached the Christian faith: 10
> Wilfrid of Ripon, John of Beverly,
> Cuthbert of Durham, Oswald of Worcester,
> Egwin of Evesham, Aldhelm of Malmesbury,
> Swithun, Ethelwold, Aidan, Birinus of Winchester,
> Paulinus of Rochester, Dunstan and Alphege of Canterbury.   15
> These taught our people in English. Their light was not dim, but
>   shone brightly.
> Now that teaching is forsaken, and the folk are lost.
> Now there is another people which teaches our folk,
> And many of our teachers are damned, and our folk with them.
> Now our Lord speaks thus, 'As an eagle stirs up her young   20
> To fly, and hovers over them.'
> This is the word of God, sent to the world
> That we shall fix a beautiful faith upon him.][47]

The poem has almost always been read as a lament after some
drastic cultural change (in fact it has sometimes been called *St Bede's*

---

[47] I quote this text and its translation from S. K. Brehe, 'Reassembling the *First
Worcester Fragment*', *Speculum* 65 (1990), 521–36 (pp. 530–1).

Lament), and it has also been seen to offer proof of that loss in its own shape.[48] As Derek Pearsall put it, this poem is not only 'witness' to, but 'symptom' of, a 'decline': it demonstrates the very loss of learning it complains of as 'it confuses Ælfric with Alcuin and twice dissolves into prose lists despite its attempt to ape the elevated style of Old English verse'.[49] More recently, such ignorance has seemed less an inadvertence than an elegant way of using the passing of an era as the material for a style. Seth Lerer has described the poem's imperfect deployment of old metrical habits as a mode of 'nostalgia', describing all that Pearsall sees as decline as a 'formal means' for acknowledging belatedness.[50] Thomas Hahn has made the more daring proposal that such a form was wise enough to predict its fate, since to precisely the extent that it has 'surviv[ed] by chance'—that it is 'fragmentary'—it 'bod[ies] forth the contingencies of language and writing that it takes for its overt subject'. In this sense the poem's vision of the culture into which it emerges is so acute (it so fully knows 'the nexus of cultural forces that characteristically mark vernacular writing and culture in the early Middle English period'), that it understands even its own achievement to be perched on the edge of imminent destruction.[51]

The First Worcester Fragment was almost certainly written after 1066 (it has been dated anywhere from 1100 to *c.*1170), but what has never been noticed is that it proceeds as if 1066 had not *yet* happened.[52] The proper names which determine so much of the poem's shape are themselves a clear, temporal grid, a network of time-lines (each equivalent to the knowable length of a famous life) which confine the poem's attention to the pre-Conquest period. The last of these figures to die was 'Alfeih' (or 'Alphege' (line 15)) who was

[48] For this title see e.g. Franzen, *Tremulous Hand of Worcester*, 1.

[49] Derek Pearsall, *Old English and Middle English Poetry* (London: Routledge & Kegan Paul, 1977), 76. For the claim that these 'prose lists' are more metrical than Pearsall allows as well as a rebuttal of the view that its learning is generally mistaken see Brehe, 'Reassembling the First Worcester Fragment', 523–7 and 531–5.

[50] Seth Lerer, 'Old English and its Afterlife', 7–34 in *The Cambridge History of Medieval English Literature*, ed. David Wallace (Cambridge: Cambridge University Press, 1999), 24.

[51] Hahn, 'Early Middle English', 61–91 in *Cambridge History of Medieval English Literature*, ed. Wallace, 75.

[52] For the earliest dating see Pearsall, *Old English and Middle English Poetry*, 76; for the later see *MWME* 5: 1435. Brehe dates the poem to 'the late twelfth century' ('Reassembling the *First Worcester Fragment*', 521). According to Ker the poem was copied in the form that we have it in the first decades of the 13th c. (*Catalogue of Manuscripts Containing Anglo-Saxon*, 466).

martyred at the hands of Danish raiders in 1012.[53] The spectre of this invasion looms in the earliest moment the poem points to as well, for 'Aidan' (line 14) founded Lindisfarne Abbey in 634 and it was in the very first of the Danish raids (in 793) that, as the *Anglo-Saxon Chronicle* ('E') puts it, the 'harrying of the heathen miserably destroyed God's church in Lindisfarne by rapine and slaughter'.[54] The poem's attention does fall heavily on a conquest, in other words, but on those devastating (if intermittent) raids and incursions by Scandinavian (or 'Viking') forces which plagued the English from 793 until 1013 (when one of these invaders, Swein, finally ascended the English throne). If the poem is about any 'cataclysm', it is certainly not the Norman Conquest but what we would surely call the Scandinavian (or Danish) Conquest had this earlier event been permanent enough to generate its own abundant history.[55]

The biblical allusions that weight the *Fragment* at its centre, and with which it ends, insist on an earlier cultural context as well. The first five books of the Old Testament which are listed in line 8 are often taken together in this way (as the 'Pentateuch' or 'books of Moses') because they tell a single story, tracing the early flourishings of a religion, through the captivity and subjugation of its adherents, to their release and a new beginning. The 'beautiful faith' referred to in the poem's last lines (20–1) is a phrase from the end of the last of these books, Deuteronomy 32: 11, when the Israelites, poised to enter the Promised Land, look forward to better times. Such allusions necessarily pick out an identical trajectory for the generations of 'English people' subject to the Viking onslaught. In fact, in complete contradistinction to 1066 (when the English sometimes understood themselves to have been defeated because of their 'sins', and a bishop, Odo of Bayeux, was part of the Conqueror's invading force), the

[53] On this bishop's life see the entry for 'Alphege' in the *Oxford Dictionary of Saints*, ed. David Hugh Farmer, 4th edn. (Oxford: Oxford University Press, 1997; 1st published 1978). His martyrdom is described in the *Peterborough Chronicle* entries for 1011–12 (for these see *Two of the Saxon Chronicles*, ed. Earle, rev. Plummer, 1: 141–3).

[54] *The Anglo-Saxon Chronicle*, trans. G. N. Garmonsway, 2nd edn. (London: J. M. Dent, 1972; 1st published 1953), 57; 'earmlice heðenra manna hergung adiligode Godes cyrican in Lindisfarena ee þurh reaflac & man sleht', *Two of the Saxon Chronicles*, ed. Earle, rev. Plummer, 1: 57.

[55] On the first Scandinavian invasions see H. R. Loyn, *The Vikings in Britain* (London: B. T. Batsford, 1977), 55–67. For a summary of events from the earliest raids to the Danish ascendancy, see F. M. Stenton, *Anglo-Saxon England*, 3rd edn. (Oxford: Clarendon Press, 1971; 1st edn. 1943), 239–76 and 364–432.

Viking attacks were everywhere understood by those who experienced them as an assault by 'heathens' on the faithful.[56] It is true
that many of the Scandinavians were eventually (even sometimes
quickly) converted, but the biblical analogy would have been further
reinforced by the way these raids targeted the institutional centres of
the Church until they were more or less eliminated. After a century of
the kind of attacks experienced at Lindisfarne, in fact, Asser claims
in his biography of Alfred (c.893) that the monastic backbone of the
English Church has been completely destroyed.[57]

Because it has always been seen to describe the linguistic changes
that accompanied the Norman Conquest, the replacement of men
who 'taught our people in English' (line 16) with 'another people'
(line 18) may still seem to point to 1066 and no other time. Because
the poem picks out the 'English people' (line 3) as those who were
taught, and emphasizes the fact that they were taught in English (lines
9 and 19) it seems that the teaching that was 'forsaken' (line 17) was
English itself: what else could this be than a description of the way
the Norman invaders systematically replaced English prelates with
non-English speakers, thereby ensuring that Latin supplanted the
unusual role English as a vernacular had assumed in the Anglo-Saxon
Church?[58] But the *Fragment* never says that the new people no longer
taught in English; nor does it ever say that 'English' is the 'teaching'
that is 'forsaken'. The significant change the poem marks is between
a learning which 'shone brightly' and a learning that is dim, between
'bishops who preached the Christian faith' (line 10) and teachers who
are now so errant that they are not only 'damned' but those they teach
are also 'lost' (line 19). This is exactly the change that resulted from
the sacking of so many monasteries and the killing of so many illustrious and learned men during the most severe periods of the Viking
raids. It was, in fact, the widespread abandonment of orthodoxies

---

[56] See *Anglo-Saxon Chronicle*, trans. Garmonsway, 56 (on the Viking invasions)
and 200 (on the Norman Conquest); *Two of the Saxon Chronicles*, ed. Earle, rev.
Plummer, 1: 56 and 1: 200.

[57] On various conversions of the invaders see Loyn, *Vikings in Britain*, 59
(Guthrum in 878), 85 (Olaf Tryggvasson in 994–5), and 90 (Cnut in 1016). On the
effects of the raids on the monasteries see David Knowles, *The Monastic Order in
England* (Cambridge: Cambridge University Press, 1949; first published 1940), 32–6.
For the relevant portion of Asser's text see Knowles's appendix ('The Evidence for the
Disappearance of Monastic Life in England Before 943'), 695.

[58] On the ecclesiastical policy of the 'Norman plantation' see Knowles, *Monastic
Order*, 103–13.

which resulted from the loss of such 'folk' which required the very reforms and new foundations with which 'Dunstan' (line 15) was often associated (but which themselves eventually fell prey to renewed Viking raids).[59]

Although the *Fragment* has almost always been read as if it were defined by such loss, it is also the case that the poem spends fewer than three lines (17–19) lamenting anything, and, as Michael Lapidge has more recently noted, the poem is really concerned to look back to 'the glory days of the Anglo-Saxon church' and to 'commemorat[e] the saintly churchmen who instructed the people'.[60] The lines which describe the Viking raids so movingly are themselves a way of marking out the two extraordinary periods of Christian flourishing in medieval Britain, the conversion of the Anglo-Saxons which preceded those raids, and that energetic rebirth and reform of the English Church which I have just mentioned.[61] The poem in fact begins with this twinned emphasis: Bede and his translations are often synonymous with the enormous success of the apostolic period (he was 'the only teacher of the first rank whom the West knew between Gregory the Great and the eleventh century'), while Ælfric's writings and the translation of the Pentateuch he oversaw are signal accomplishments of the reform.[62] The poem casts its attention in these twin directions in the list of bishops (lines 11–15) that fills almost a quarter of its length. Although, as S. K. Brehe has noted (see p. 35 n. 47 above), these names are arranged in a 'rough geographical order from the north of England to the south', what they map much more carefully than England are two long and important periods. The century between 630 and 730, marked out by the lives of Aidan (d. 651), Paulinus (d. 644), Birinus (d. 650), Cuthbert (634–87), Wilfrid (633–709), Aldhelm (639–709), Egwin (d. 717) and John (d. 721), was the time in which each of these men played an instrumental role in the conversion of the Anglo-Saxons and the institutionalization of Christianity throughout Britain. The century and a half

---

[59] On this period of reform see Stenton, *Anglo-Saxon England*, 433–69 and Knowles, *Monastic Order*, 31–56.

[60] Michael Lapidge, *The Cult of St Swithun*, Winchester Studies 4.ii (Oxford: Clarendon Press, 2003), 712. I am very grateful to Michael Lapidge for lending me part of the text of this study in manuscript.

[61] On the conversion of the English and the growth of the Church see Stenton, *Anglo-Saxon England*, 96–176.

[62] See Knowles, *Monastic Order*, 24 (on Bede) and 61–2 (on Ælfric and his writings).

from 860 to 1010, marked out by the lives of Swithun (d. 862), Ethelwold (912–84), Dunstan (909–88), Oswald (d. 992), and Alphege (953–1012), was the period of substantial rebirth and reform.[63] When the poem says that 'now there is another people which teaches our folk' [nu beoþ oþre leoden þeo læreþ ure folc] it is against these bishops that this 'other' is necessarily defined; these teachers are completely distinct from this past because they could never equal it.

The *Fragment* only thinks about 1066 then to the extent that we ignore its shape and all that it celebrates in past happening. What this form actually knows is not a 'cataclysm' but an accomplishment, how a people and the things that they did, how the books that they made, *lasted*, despite the enormous disasters they endured. It is for this reason that the language of the *Fragment*, rather than enumerating losses or providing imagery of destruction, unfolds in lists (whole lines devoted to the names of books of the bible, or to important bishops) or insistent repetitions (the phrase 'bec awende' (lines 2 and 7), the many different terms for learning it employs, 'ilerde' (line 4), 'ilærde' (line 9), 'lærden' (line 16), 'leore' (line 17), 'læreþ' (line 18)). In fact, to the extent that this form acknowledges a loss it does so in the manner of *history*: it is a form whose very solidity exists, not to make an absence, but to fill it, to trace a vanished past, not because there was nothing there, but because something extraordinary was.

Why then *have* we ignored almost the whole of this shape and its consequence? In this case, it is not simply that other historical forms have been powerful enough to substitute a different past for the one this history recreates, but that the idea this object has been made to bear is that which its very own survival proves wrong. How, in other words, can an object whose surprising achievement is to have survived seem to prove that everything perished? Our need to tell the same story about 1066 would not seem to be enough for the substitution in this case since the *Fragment* can only be firmly attached to this moment by means of that substitution. In this case the historical form which overwrites the *Fragment* before it can itself be read as a form is

[63] For these bishops (with the exception of Aidan) see the entries for 'Aldhelm', 'Alphege', 'Birinus', 'Cuthbert', 'Dunstan', 'Egwin', 'Ethelwold', 'John of Beverley', 'Oswald', 'Paulinus of York', 'Swithun', and 'Wilfrid' in the *Oxford Dictionary of Saints*, ed. Farmer. For Aidan, see *Bede's Ecclesiastical History of the English People*, ed. Bertram Colgrave and R. A. B. Mynors (Oxford: Clarendon Press, 1969), III.3 and III.5.

the story told about English literature and the kind of loss it always is in the long centuries after 1066. As that story goes, it is not capable of misreading or even overlooking *The First Worcester Fragment* because it simply refuses to know that it is there:

> The development of the old vernacular literature was arrested for nearly a hundred and fifty years after Hastings; and, as the preservation of letters depended on ecclesiastics, professed scholars and monastic chroniclers of foreign extraction, the literature of England for practically a couple of centuries is to be found mainly in Latin.[64]

This is the kind of fraudulent outline we normally call *literary* history, and, as here, it generally ends the 'old vernacular literature' with the 'cataclysm' on Hastings field, not only by declaring literary production to have stopped (to have been 'arrested'), but by imagining literature as that which could never be a 'fragment': what is cut off here is not any particular thing, but a throng of them; what 'literature' is in this vision is not a relic, but a 'development', an advancing host. Such a version of the past annihilates 'literature' where it survives in the isolate or fragmentary text because it assumes that 'literature' has died wherever it cannot be detected in many places; as R. W. Chambers puts the point only a decade later, the 'essential thing' is 'continuation'.[65] The need to trace these particular outlines means that even where there is an enormous quantity of writing ('material to fill some thousands of pages of print'), where that quantity even represents an *increase* rather than a diminishment (this material is 'very much more than [we have] for the whole six centuries of Anglo-Saxon England'), what must be emphasized on the whole are the gaps between these things ('much that was composed in English between the Norman Conquest and the Black Death [1349] is lost'), because what literature *is* is 'a human achievement enacted over centuries'.[66]

The 'lost literature of England' was, in its day, a powerfully elegiac phrase which seemed to make it possible to write the history of an irreducible absence; it was a way of creating a historical form on the

[64] *The Cambridge History of English Literature*, ed. A. W. Ward and A. R. Waller, vol. 1 (Cambridge: Cambridge University Press, 1908), 149.

[65] 'But the essential thing is, that side by side with French verse, we have the continuation of the English homily tradition and the tradition of books written for recluses, especially women, in English prose', R. W. Chambers, *On the Continuity of English Prose from Alfred to More and His School*, EETS os 191a (London: Oxford University Press, 1932), p. xciv.

[66] Shepherd, 'Early Middle English', 81.

very premise that the past can be so lost to us that even history cannot make it live again.[67] Part of this form both attends to, and pieces
itself out of, certain relics—manuscript pages where texts have been
scraped away or torn or obliterated, parts of writings which imply
other writings we cannot find anywhere, for all our searching—and
it does have for its referent those real absences of literary objects
which I began by describing. But such a commitment to disappoint-
ment is itself a way of ensuring that absence is the only substance
such history can have. In assuming that 'the whole history of English
literature, prior to Chaucer and Langland, would appear to us in a
different light . . . if the lost poetry had been preserved', it makes the
loss it claims to find.[68]

THE SHAPE OF THE LITERARY THING

If the early Middle English literary object has been so generally erased
by such literary history, what will it take to find it? What definition will admit to the company of literature those English writings
so isolated by circumstance in the centuries after 1066? Since the
problem is of our own making, it is not surprising that the solution
lies dormant in what we have long known. In fact, the demand for
'development' or 'continuity' is not only a definition of literature, but
a bias both toward and against certain *kinds* of form. So accustomed
has literary history become to the expanse of interrelations which
characterize English literature in the period after the early Middle, in
other words, that it declares anything other than this familiar vista
to be aberrant, even noisome: like a sea voyager grown too used to the
subtle undulations and eddies in a vast but largely grey ocean, literary
history grows neurasthenic, even alarmed, before the parti-coloured
boldness of the shapes that greet it on early Middle English shores
('please', such history always seems to plead, 'take those hideous
things away'). What such literary history fails to know about itself,

[67] R. W. Chambers first used the phrase in a suggestive article, 'The Lost Literature
of Medieval England', *The Library*, 4th ser., 5 (1925), 293–321. It was reused by R. M.
Wilson as the title of a much longer meditation, *The Lost Literature of Medieval
England* (London, Methuen, 1970; 1st published 1952). Neither study focuses exclu-
sively on the gap between 1066 and 1300 (Old English and later Middle English are
also scrutinized), but the resonant phrase sums up an attitude from which early Middle
English has suffered most.
[68] Chambers, 'Lost Literature', 294.

however, is that it embraces the monochrome expanse and rejects the jagged outcropping by means of the very same formalism: in fact, literary history is already sufficiently formalist to attend to the objects it has largely insisted are not there.

It is strange to think that a mode of scrutiny which ignores most forms is formalist, but Chambers makes clear that this is true, as well as what the features of the preferred form are, when he describes the 'continuity' he takes to be equivalent to literature as a *chain*, 'a series of links, sometimes working very thin, but never broken'.[69] Such a chain proves itself worthy of such exclusive attention by its scope alone, for it not only extends in space, but across infinite expanses of time ('from generation to generation'), in this sense transcendent, not *in* any one moment but for all time.[70] It is also an object that is compelling because, despite its scope, it is astonishingly simple: while each writing which is part of this chain is independent of all the others, it is connected to each one of these others in so far as it resembles it in shape—in so far as it devotes a substantial proportion of its matter to the process of 'continuing' the larger whole. On the other hand, because 'continuity' occurs through the whole of the chain by means of such formal resemblance, this simplicity also endows each text in the chain with an extraordinarily vast historical and prophetic knowledge: in so far as it is part of the chain, each link carries within its form, not only an awareness of what every text in the chain has been, but what every future text will be. This also means that each writing is part of this chain merely by virtue of knowing that the chain exists: all any text needs to be in order to be literature according to this definition is the statement, 'I am literature'.

It is a form that is therefore vain and stupid to precisely the extent that it is structurally secure, but Chambers is willing to hope against hope that early Middle English writing will somehow yield such a form in 1932, not least because T. S. Eliot had so influentially persuaded literary history in 1920 that this simply *was* 'the form of European, of English literature', a givenness he insisted upon by calling his own chain-like thing 'tradition':

The existing monuments form an ideal order among themselves, which is modified by the introduction of the new (the really new) work of art among them. The existing order is complete before the new work arrives; for order to persist after the supervention of novelty, the *whole* existing order must be,

---

[69] Chambers, *On the Continuity of English Prose*, p. xc.   [70] Ibid., p. xc.

if ever so slightly, altered; and so the relations, proportions, values of each work of art toward the whole are readjusted; and this is conformity between the old and the new.[71]

For Eliot, the exclusivity, the singularity, of the form is in fact its reason for being; it is only 'conformity' to an existing 'ideal' that can annul the passage of time in which the resulting 'order' unspools (it 'has a simultaneous existence and composes a simultaneous order').[72] It was a view of the relation of present to past that suited Eliot's sense of his own 'individual talent' ('one of the many intellectually acrobatic consequences of Eliot's timeless poetic order is that the present is able to alter the past').[73] The view was also so influential because it was not really new to Eliot. In fact, this conception of 'tradition' can be understood as 'dialectical' in a sense that was already old-fashioned by the beginning of the twentieth century ('the smaller idea of limited sequences which are modified by the addition of a new term'); it has even been suggested that the 'rhetorical seductiveness' of Eliot's tradition 'derives in large measure from the way in which the unnamed dialectical character of the notion is passed off on the reader as a new and more dynamic way of seeing things'.[74] Inasmuch as 'tradition' is itself no more than the 'isolation of a category' (the aggregation of literature as a single, large form) by means of a 'diachronic sequence' (how 'the old and the new' are related to one another in that form) the mode of understanding Eliot urges on his contemporaries is, in fact, old-fashioned enough to be called Hegelian.[75]

To stress this connection is to notice that what Eliot calls 'literature'—and what any demand for 'continuity' will also count in this company—is only 'historical' (as Eliot puts it) to the extent that it is metaphysical. Eliot and Chambers may feel that what they are categorizing are relatively solid objects (links in a chain or an 'existing order'), but these objects are only literary in so far as they trail some portion of their being in the ether, as they transcend the exigencies of temporality (being both 'old' *and* 'new'), as they are therefore

[71] T. S. Eliot, 'Tradition and the Individual Talent', 42–53 in *The Sacred Wood* (London: Methuen, 1920), 44–5. Emphasis Eliot's.

[72] Ibid. 44.

[73] Chris Baldick, *The Social Mission of English Criticism, 1848–1932* (Oxford: Clarendon Press, 1983), 121.

[74] Fredric Jameson, *Marxism and Form: Twentieth-Century Dialectical Theories of Literature* (Princeton: Princeton University Press, 1971), 314.

[75] Ibid. 319.

objects with all the capacities of an abstraction. This is a fact Eliot only registers negatively (he claims to 'halt' his own speculations 'at the frontier of metaphysics or mysticism'), but the moment either Eliot or Chambers begins talking about a group of texts rather than a single one it is clear that the matter they have in hand is already stretching itself toward what Hegel called 'the Infinite'.[76] For this reason alone, Hegel's own description of the form of the 'work of art' is actually plainer and more honest than Eliot's, but, in the end, exactly *as* mystical:

> Art [*die Kunst*] spiritualizes—animates the mere outward and material object of adoration with a form which expresses soul, sentiment, Spirit; so that piety has not a bare sensuous embodiment of the Infinite to contemplate, and does not lavish its devotion on a mere Thing, but on the higher element with which the material object is imbued—that expressive form with which Spirit has invested it.[77]

As such a comparison makes clear, when Eliot uses the word 'ideal' (as in 'ideal order') he means a great deal more than 'best': where time may run backwards around a thing (so that the 'old' in the tradition can somehow exhibit its 'conformity' to the 'new'), where a change can be equivalent to no change at all ('for order to persist after the supervention of novelty'), where an 'order' is equivalent to an 'idea' ('this idea of order'), what Eliot otherwise calls a 'work'—like every work that Chambers calls a 'link'—is also invested with 'Spirit'. In fact, what Hegel's metaphysics actually shows is how much *more* mystical 'tradition' and 'continuity' are as forms, for, unlike Hegel's 'art' these forms exclude the possibility that they were ever actually made: while Hegel's artful thing is expressly the product of an extraordinary thought (some 'sentiment' or 'Spirit') as it is projected into a 'material object' by a method which could certainly be described as labour (the 'adoration' that imbues the 'material object' with a 'higher element'), 'tradition' simply makes itself ('the existing monuments form an ideal order among themselves').

---

[76] Eliot, 'Tradition and the Individual Talent', 53.

[77] Hegel, *Philosophy of History*, 408. 'Die Kunst begeistert, beseelt diese Äußerlichkeit, das bloß Sinnliche mit der Form, welche Seele, Empfindung, Geist ausdrückt, so daß die Andacht nicht bloß ein sinnliches Dieses vor sich hat und nicht gegen ein bloßes Ding fromm ist, sondern gegen das Höhere in ihm, die seelenvolle Form, welche vom Geiste hineingetragen ist', *Vorlesungen über die Philosophie der Geschichte*, 549–50.

Of course, we do not need to go back to Hegel to realize that 'tradition' is a concept with a lot to hide (it is, as Williams has described it, 'the most common of . . . false totalities'),[78] but the nature of the deception I am describing here is more than ideological, for, in this case, it is not simply that a certain presumption is spirited in under the guise of self-evidence, but that a certain inattention is hidden under the guise of concern, that the very procedure which understands itself to count for *all* literary objects only accounts for a part of them, that a mode of idealism which is in fact only interested in one idea (the extent to which each form proclaims itself to be 'literature') actually understands itself as a mode of *materialism*. It is in this sense that Eliot's 'tradition' survived in Leavis and *Scrutiny* as a 'trans-historical quality' which could actually be elaborated in terms of 'identifiable developments that were themselves historical'.[79] It is in this sense too that recent historicisms emphasize the specificity and materiality of literature (its 'implication in institutional structures, its deep functional utility') but still prize a 'transhistorical dimension', or even a 'Literary Spirit'.[80] In fact, as John Guillory has recently suggested, wherever an 'established order of literature' is vividly clear to us we are staring at Eliot's ideal.[81] In this sense, we also have this form before us whenever we evoke the category of 'literature' and believe we are referring to solid objects (works we could reach off the shelf

[78] Williams continues: '[Tradition] is seen not as it is, an active and continuous selection and reselection, which even at its latest point in time is always a set of specific choices, but now more conveniently as an object, a projected reality, with which we have to come to terms on its terms, even though those terms are always and must be the valuations, the selections and omissions, of other men', 'Literature and Sociology', 13–30 in *Problems in Materialism and Culture* (London: Verso, 1980), 16. See also Raymond Williams, *Marxism and Literature* (Oxford: Oxford University Press, 1977), 115–17. See also Robert Weimann, 'The Concept of Tradition Reconsidered', *Yearbook of Comparative and General Literature* 23 (1974), 29–41.

[79] Francis Mulhern, *The Moment of 'Scrutiny'* (London: Verso, 1981; 1st published 1979), 116. For such claims see F. R. Leavis, 'Literature and Society', *Scrutiny* 12 (1943), 2–11 (esp. 3).

[80] Stephen Greenblatt, 'What is the History of Literature?', *Critical Inquiry* 23 (1997), 460–81, esp. 462 ('implication'), 470 ('transhistorical dimension') and 476 ('Literary Spirit'). Greenblatt borrows the term 'Literary Spirit' from a translation of Francis Bacon's *Advancement of Learning* (where it is, in the original, 'Genius . . . Literarius').

[81] John Guillory, *Cultural Capital: The Problem of Literary Canon Formation* (Chicago: University of Chicago Press, 1993), 142. Guillory goes on to quote the statement from 'Tradition and the Individual Talent' I quote above in order to suggest that it 'lies behind every subsequent reflection on tradition in twentieth-century criticism, and even behind our own discourse of canon critique' (pp. 142–3).

in some book) rather than an ideal that comprises all of them. As Williams suggested long ago, 'literature' is an idea defined by its capacity not only to conceal its metaphysics, but somehow to convince us that metaphysics is physics ('there is a virtually immediate and unnoticed transfer of the specific values of particular works and kinds of work to what operates as a concept but is still firmly believed to be actual and practical').[82]

If further proof is needed that Eliot's tradition still configures our understanding of what we are accustomed to calling 'literature', the exclusion of early Middle English writings from this category —either by denigration, misprision, or the general claim that this is a period of literary dearth—ought to count as proof enough. In this sense, everything that can be learned about the particular forms I describe in the following pages is itself evidence of the continued force of this formalism—what we have not been able to know because we have only been content to look for an ideal order. It is also the premise of the following chapters that these objects will appear more clearly, not when literary history has abandoned the formalism it practices so surreptitiously, but when it has *embraced* it much more firmly. Where the defining transcendence and self-knowledge that is achieved by the chain or the tradition requires that literature occur in aggregations—where what literature cannot be is a single form— as the above examples should have made clear, only a truly Hegelian formalism can discern spirituality in each and every 'material object', and certainly in every made 'Thing'.

To precisely the extent that it has ignored the individual objects that comprise early Middle English literature, in other words, literary history has not been Hegelian enough. In fact, Hegel can find all the qualities that Eliot and Chambers look for in poetry and prose in any old thing a person might build with an eye to its permanence, in the very house he or she lives in, for example:

The building of a house is, in the first instance, a subjective aim and design. On the other hand we have, as means, the several substances required for the work—Iron, Wood, Stones. The elements are made use of in working up this material: fire to melt the iron, wind to blow the fire, water to set wheels in motion, in order to cut the wood, etc. The result is, that the wind, which has helped to build the house, is shut out by the house; so also are the violence of rains and floods, and the destructive powers of fire, so far as the house is

---

[82] Williams, *Marxism and Literature*, 45.

made fire-proof. The stones and beams obey the law of gravity—press down-ward—and so high walls are carried up. Thus the elements are made use of in accordance with their nature, and yet to co-operate for a product, by which their operation is limited.[83]

It is important in this account that it is not the peculiar nature of the material, nor the special value of the thought, which makes the house last, but the way 'building' involves the one in the other. As thinking directs labour according to a 'subjective aim and design', it embeds itself in the hard materials it shapes (the 'Iron, Wood, Stones'), thereby using that hardness to solidify and preserve an idea. As the very process of that embedding deploys the properties of that material in the service of a thought (as the pressing 'downward' of gravity becomes the movement 'up' that house-building requires) the material itself gains 'subjective' qualities to the extent that it is redirected by thinking. The resulting combination is 'fireproof', not simply because a potentially destructive fire has been used to forge iron, or a potentially destructive wind has been used to generate power, but because it is the character of 'building' to bend matter to some will—converting those aspects of matter which resist thought into the capacity to preserve thought by means of the form that matter is made to assume. It is inherent in any such fireproofing that it may prove temporary (the house may be blown down or burnt at some point), but, so long as it *is* fireproof, it is a monument to the thinking that caused it—a thing in the unique form of the subjective thought that made it.

Because literary history is so used to seeing transcendence in aggregations and chains, each of the forms described in subsequent chapters can itself be understood as more extensive proof that writing can stretch out ideas 'from generation to generation', making the 'old' effectively 'new', even if it does nothing more than survive as a

---

[83] Hegel, *Philosophy of History*, 27. 'Ein Hausbau ist zunächst ein innerer Zweck und Absicht. Dem gegenüber stehen als Mittel di besondleren Elemente, als Material Eisen, Holz, Steine. Die Elemente werden angewendet, dieses zu bearbeiten: Feuer, um das Eisen zu schmelzen, Luft, um das Feuer anzublasen, Wasser, um die Räder in Bewegung zu setzen, das Holz zu schneiden usf. Das Produkt ist, daß die Luft, die geholfen, durch das Haus abgehalten wird, ebenso die Wasserfluten des Regens und die Verderblichkeit des Feuers, insoweit es feuerfest ist. Die Steine und Balken gehorchen der Schwere, drängen hinunter in die Tiefe, und durch sie sind hohe Wände aufgeführt. So werden die Elemente ihrer Natur gemäß gebraucht und wirken zusam-men zu einem Produkt, wodurch sie beschränkt werden', *Vorlesungen über die Philosophie der Geschichte*, 71.

singular and solitary object. Every 'subjective aim and design', every idea, recovered from the shapes built into these things is itself a measure of just how permanent ideas from the past can become, even in forms that devote no part of their own thought to the idea of lasting (which are solid in their particularity, not as they have tried to hook themselves into some 'continuity' or 'tradition'). As is almost inevitable, of course, one of the ideas that lasts in this way is the idea *of* lasting—the idea of literature that Chambers and Eliot understand as given (the belief that writing is consequential by means of a certain 'conformity', that what a particular writing should know best is that it is part of some larger 'order'). This means that the literary history which is ashamed of its metaphysics, and ignores early Middle English, can also be shown to have overlooked a certain part of the single thing it has been *willing* to see (the beginnings of 'tradition' and 'continuity' in the early Middle English period that I shall describe in 'romance' in Chapter 6). And yet it is hardly surprising that a formalism accustomed to describing only a single form should fail to detect the turn that should most delight it in the placid contours it has learned to prefer. In this sense, the care early Middle English writings demand of our formalism may not only redeem a loss by finding a literature we have not known, it should help us to see the literature we have always known much more clearly.

2

The Law of the Land:
Laȝamon's *Brut*

Dicitur vulgariter, 'ut rex vult, lex vadit':
Veritas vult aliter, nam lex stat, rex cadit.

[It is said commonly, 'As the king wills, so goes the law', but the
truth is otherwise, for the law stands, but the king falls].
                                    ('The Battle of Lewis', *c*.1265)

The real hero of Laȝamon's *Brut* (*c*.1200) is no particular person
or peoples but the island now generally referred to as Britain, a place
Laȝamon characteristically refers to as 'þis lond'.[1] This emphasis is
part of a more general programme which the sixteenth and seventeenth centuries came to call *chorographia*, a passion for the representation of territory so general that it spans the graphic and verbal
arts, a conflation of the activities of cartography and narrative so
thorough that it erases the distinction between history and maps.
Since the generalized practice is only named in the later period, it is
there that Richard Helgerson has noticed and identified its origins,
but it may be here—as, perhaps, always—that the Renaissance efflo-
rescence is only better remembered, and it is the medieval centuries
which were the first to have this thought, and therefore this extraordinary form.[2]

---

[1] This is a point also made in Rosamund Allen, 'The Implied Audience of
Laȝamon's *Brut*', 121–39 in *The Text and Tradition of Laȝamon's 'Brut'*, ed.
Françoise Le Saux (Cambridge: D. S. Brewer, 1994), 126; and Michael Swanton,
English Literature Before Chaucer (London: Longman, 1987), 176.
[2] See Richard Helgerson, 'The Land Speaks' (chapter 3), 107–47 in *Forms of
Nationhood: The Elizabethan Writing of England* (Chicago: University of Chicago
Press, 1992), esp. 131–2. Helgerson identifies 1579 as the moment when 'for the first
time [English people] took effective visual and conceptual possession of the physical
kingdom in which they lived'. He concedes that 'there had, of course, been earlier
maps of Britain' (107), but he cites only earlier Tudor maps (321 n.1). See also *OED*,
s.v. 'chorography1'. The word is recorded here in the 19th c., but all other uses are
confined to the 16th and 17th c.

Descriptions of the land are a point of departure for narrative histories of Britain as far back as the *De excidio Britonum* of Gildas (*c*.516–70), and Bede famously begins his *Historia ecclesiastica* (*c*.731) in this way.[3] The high point of this practice, however, is the post-Conquest period, when what had been an introductory paragraph has swollen to encompass half a book (in, for example, the *Historia Anglorum* of Henry of Huntingdon (*c*.1084–1155)).[4] By Laȝamon's day, Matthew Paris (1200–59) was not only describing the island in his *Chronica majora*, but, for the first time that we know of, he drew maps to accompany his histories (Fig. 5).[5] In such an environment, narrative and cartographic forms are similar enough for drawings to tell stories: Matthew's map of Britain is, in fact, organized as an 'itinerary'—tracing the sequence of a journey rather than the relations of a topography—so Newcastle-upon-Tyne, London and Dover are placed in a straight line (even though Dover lies south-east of London) as they would have unfolded for one person on a journey through each of them.[6] Conversely, the Hereford *mappamundi* (late thirteenth century) describes itself as an 'estoire'.[7] And interest in the land is so general in the thirteenth century that the compiler of Jesus College, Oxford MS 29 (*c*.1250) felt he could include two free-standing pages of prose which describe the island

[3] Gildas, *The Ruin of Britain and Other Works*, ed. and trans. Michael Winterbottom (London: Phillimore, 1978), §3 (pp. 16–17 and 89–90); Bede, *Ecclesiastical History*, ed. and trans. B. Colgrave and R. A. B. Mynors (Oxford: Clarendon Press, 1969), i.1 (pp. 14–17).

[4] Henry, Archdeacon of Huntingdon, *Historia Anglorum* [*The History of the English People*], ed. and trans. Diana Greenway (Oxford: Clarendon Press, 1996), i.1–10 (pp. 10–29).

[5] For Matthew's description of Britain see Mathæi Parisiensis, *Chronica majora*, ed. Henry Richards Luard, 7 vols., Rolls Series 57 (London, 1872–3), 1: 21–2. There are actually four different maps of Britain in various versions or adaptations of the *Chronica*. I print the most elaborate here (Fig. 5). On these maps see Evelyn Edson, *Mapping Time and Space: How Medieval Mapmakers Viewed Their World* (London: The British Library, 1997), 118–24; and Suzanne Lewis, *The Art of Matthew Paris in the Chronica Majora* (Aldershot: Scolar Press, 1987), 364–72. On Matthew and 'cartography' see Richard Vaughn, *Matthew Paris* (Cambridge: Cambridge University Press, 1958), 235–50.

[6] P. D. A. Harvey, 'Local and Regional Cartography in Medieval Europe', 464–501 in *The History of Cartography*, ed. J. B. Harley and David Woodward, vol. 1 (Chicago: University of Chicago Press, 1987), 495–6.

[7] For a description and dating of this map see Edson, *Mapping Time and Space*, 139–44. For the text of the map's self-description see David Woodward, 'Medieval Mappaemundi', 286–370 in *The History of Cartography*, ed. Harley and Woodward, 1: 309.

FIG. 5 One of the earliest maps of Britain, drawn by Matthew Paris (*c.*1245) for his adaptation of the *Chronica majora*, the *Abbreviatio chronicorum* in London, British Library, MS Cotton Claudius D.vi.

from top to bottom ('Englelond is eyhte hundred Myle long . . .'),
secure in the belief that some reader would care.[8]
It is in the nature of chorography to make the object it claims to
find—since the land may be a material (which can be touched) or a
concept (the posited boundaries which produce an interior) and may
therefore also be both (a material so complex in its contours that it
can only be compassed by a mind)—so such forms tend to tell us more
about their makers than about the thing they propose to describe.
Their profusion alone testifies to the *importance* of the land in the
thirteenth century. The sudden eruption of graphic representations
also shows how important setting boundaries had become to giving
this land mass an identity. The merging of map and narrative also
suggests that the land was understood to extend, not only vertically
through space, but through *time*, as if what had happened in and to
the land was itself a crucial part of its shape. It is in La3amon's *Brut*,
in particular, that the land's stability through time comes to be its
most important characteristic, as if its principal use and interest to
people was its capacity to remain unchanged through continuous
waves of human happening:

> Swa is al þis lond iuaren   for uncuðe leoden
> Þeo þis londe hæbbeð biwunnen   and eft beoð idriuen hennene;
> and eft hit bi3etten oðeræ   þe uncuðe weoren.

[So this whole land has suffered because of the foreigners who have conquered this land and then been driven out again; and then other foreigners
have got possession of it.][9]

There is a comparable passage at this point in the first version of
the *Brut* story, Geoffrey of Monmouth's *Historia regum Britanniae*
(*c*.1138), although we only learn there that 'foreign invaders'

---

    [8] This text is printed as 'The Shires and Hundreds of England', 145–6 in *An Old
English Miscellany*, ed. Richard Morris, EETS OS 49 (1872), line 1. Hereafter quota-
tions from this text will be cited by line number in the text; translations are my own.
For the contents of Jesus College MS 29 see Neil Cartlidge, 'The Composition and
Social Context of Oxford, Jesus College, MS 29 (II) and London, British Library,
MS Cotton Caligula A.IX', *MÆ* 66 (1997), 250–69. For an attempt to set this choro-
graphy in a larger intellectual context see Betty Hill, 'The History of Jesus College,
Oxford MS 29', *MÆ* 32 (1955), 203–13.
    [9] La3amon, *Brut, or Hystoria Brutonum*, ed. and trans. W. R. J. Barron and
S. C. Weinberg (Harlow: Longman, 1995), lines 3549–51. Hereafter quotations and
translations (with minor adjustments) will be taken from this edition, cited by line
number in the text, and abbreviated '*L*'.

conquered a 'country' [alienigenae qui patriam sibi submittebant].[10]
In Wace's *Roman de Brut* (*c.*1155), Laȝamon's immediate source
for his story, 'the land' [la terre] has emerged as a permanent object
(which is 'often conquered, lost and seized' [sovent conquise | Sovent
perdue, sovent prise]).[11] But Laȝamon makes this permanence more
consequential by extending it, not only to his own day, but beneath
his own feet (it is here, and throughout his *Brut*, '*þis* lond'), and
simply by repeating the term in the short passage I have just quoted
(as he also does incessantly throughout his story) he makes the land a
counter-weight to time itself, a defining permanence that subtends
all change.

Laȝamon's *Brut* is therefore also interesting as a *chorographia*
because criticism has almost always suggested that stability is precisely what this poem and its story lack. As Derek Pearsall nicely
summarizes the general view, 'Laȝamon is at odds with himself for
half the poem, confused to know where to place his sympathies'.[12]
Such criticism has called attention, in particular, to the way this
poem tells the story of British achievement (and mourns the defeat of
British kings) in a style which implicitly celebrates the achievements
of the very Anglo-Saxons who conquered them (using 'many half-
lines [which] reproduce Old English metrical types perfectly' and
Old English compounds and techniques of compounding), while its
immediate source is a French text which never would have been
written had the Normans not finally defeated the Anglo-Saxons in
1066.[13] Understood in this way, Laȝamon's cultural politics have
been thought to be, at best, 'ambivalent', and, at worst, 'mistaken', but,
as I wish to show here, such a form can also be called chorographic

[10] Geoffrey of Monmouth, *The History of the Kings of Britain*, trans. Lewis Thorpe
(Harmondsworth: Penguin, 1966), 106; *The Historia regum Britanniae of Geoffrey
of Monmouth*, I (Bern, Burgerbibliothek, MS. 568), ed. Neil Wright (Cambridge:
D. S. Brewer, 1984), §53 (p. 34).
[11] *Wace's 'Roman de Brut', A History of the British: Text and Translation*, ed. and
trans. Judith Weiss (Exeter: University of Exeter Press, 1999), lines 3777–8. Hereafter
quotations and translations will be taken from this edition, cited by line number in the
text, and abbreviated 'W'.
[12] Derek Pearsall, *Old English and Middle English Poetry* (London: Routledge &
Kegan Paul, 1977), 110.
[13] For an analysis of Laȝamon's relationship to Old English poetic practices see
Daniel Donoghue, 'Laȝamon's Ambivalence', *Speculum* 65 (1990), 538–41 (quotation from p. 539). For a detailed account of Laȝamon's compounds see J. P. Oakden,
Alliterative Poetry in Middle English, 2 vols. (Manchester: Manchester University
Press, 1930–5), 130–65.

to precisely the extent that it is politically agile—in so far as it incorporates more rather than fewer positions—as a tumultuous history not only demonstrates but proves the land's stability.[14] In this sense, La3amon's 'confusion' is his most original and foundational chorographic idea, a way of pouring even the conquests which follow the *Brut* story back into its every line.

This idea can be at once so fundamental and so easily missed because it depends upon the connections thirteenth-century jurisprudence made between the land and the law. What La3amon thought he knew was that the law was really the *land's* idea, a form of thought which took shape according to the structure of that thing from which it emerged, a set of principles which arose from such a stable and unchanging shape that they were themselves capable of stabilizing all the random and violence which comprised human action. In this large and important sense, La3amon saw the law as immanent, a set of principles which were not so much laid down by kings and peoples as discovered by them. Describing the form of La3amon's *Brut* is, therefore, a question of saying how it describes and relies upon the principles of such a law. As these principles emerge, it will also become clear that they adjust and enlarge the poem's *chorographia* into the even more reassuring shape I will call the *consolatio*. For the constancy of change which so troubles La3amon's British (and English) history is, generally speaking, the problem which Boethius adduces as the basic bar to human happiness in the *Consolatio philosophiae*. And La3amon, like Boethius, suggests that such happiness can be permanently restored by an investigation of the problem so careful that it reveals at last that the hope we feel we lack was always there in the very form of the trouble we thought we were experiencing.

THE LAND AS WARRANT

Although La3amon's *Brut* is almost twice as long as Wace's *roman*, La3amon adds very little to the story, expanding episodes mostly by dint of long speeches whose content is already implied in his

---

[14] For La3amon as 'mistaken' see Émile Legouis and Louis Cazamian, *A History of English Literature*, trans. Helen Douglas Irvine, 2 vols. (London: J. M. Dent, 1926), 1: 53. For his 'ambivalence', see, Donoghue, 'La3amon's Ambivalence', esp. 554–63.

source.[15] Even such expansion was not innovative since Wace had already doubled the length of Geoffrey of Monmouth's *Historia* in his own adaptation by extending episodes while adding very little of significance to the larger story. The *Brut* narrative is therefore extraordinarily stable (in all its versions it begins with Britain's founding by the eponymous 'Brutus' of Troy and traces a similar series of events up through the reign of the last British king, Cadwallader), and since a story is itself a shape, at root, Geoffrey's, Wace's, and Laȝamon's text have more or less the same form. The fundamental unit of that form is the reign of a king, and, since these units are themselves formally identical (a ruler gains then loses the land, either by conquest or death), the sequence might also be described as a cycle, a story which extends itself, in large part, by retelling the *same* story over and over again. But the minor changes Laȝamon makes to phrasing, the emphasis he places on certain words by repetition, as well as some minor revisions at strategic points create subsidiary patterns which are sufficient to reorient the thinking of the whole cycle. Small movements can create such a large effect because Laȝamon discovers the jurisprudence that effects the transformation in the *Brut* story itself, while this is itself true because such a jurisprudence governed perceptions of the land in his time. In formal terms, in other words, it is not so much that the *Brut* changes its shape in Laȝamon's hands as that an extant shape is fully clarified by the careful emphases it is given—as if what the *Brut* always *was* can be more easily seen by the boldness with which its outlines have been traced.

The first of these changes makes the law a subject of the poem by mentioning it much more frequently (of the seventy-six references to the 'law' or 'the laws' in Laȝamon only six are present in Wace).[16]

---

[15] For a recent account of the way Laȝamon translated see Françoise H. M. Le Saux, *Laȝamon's Brut: The Poem and its Sources* (Woodbridge: D. S. Brewer, 1989), 14–58. For an extended comparison of Wace's and Laȝamon's narrative procedure organized by topic ('time-setting', 'place-setting', 'character', etc.) see Frances Gillespy, *Laȝamon's Brut: A Comparative Study in Narrative Art*, University of California Publications in Modern Philology 3 (Berkeley, 1916).

[16] The passages in question in Laȝamon are L 578, 585, 587 (for a parallel see W 653), 1040 (and W 1253–4), 1202, 1390, 1404–5, 2124, 2133–4 (and W 2305–6), 2400, 2403, 2415, 2798, 2825, 2991, 3095, 3117, 3123, 3129, 3144–6 (and W 3342–4), 3149–50, 3506, 3569, 4026, 4796, 5022, 5057 (and W 5221–2), 5094, 6021, 6450, 6637, 6729, 6947, 7041, 7071–2, 7072, 7156, 7163, 7179, 7210, 7267, 7278, 7415, 7420, 7766, 8324, 8345, 8378, 8388, 8461 (and W 7989), 9068, 9418, 9676, 9904, 9916, 9929, 9996, 10079, 10856, 11046, 11087–8, 11406, 11470, 11983–4, 12262, 14083, 14171, 14275–6, 14351–2, 14717, 15441, 15599, 15818, 15957, 15964, 16089.

Some of these additions do not refer to the laws of Britain but to, say, 'Cristes' laws (*L* 5057) or 'Romanisce' law (*L* 11984), and sometimes their reference is broad (at *L* 5022 and 8345, for example, a good translation is 'custom' or 'usage'). But gathering such a variety of concerns together under a single term is itself a method for suggesting that the law matters throughout this story; the larger context of most uses suggests that the law is, above other things, *good*. In its most characteristic formation, in fact, the term is connected to kingship (it is a king who 'has' or 'sets' or 'maintains' the laws), and it is the strength of this connection which determines a given king's success in a particular cycle of rule. Ruhhudibras is a 'fine man' [swiðe god mon, *L* 1398] because he 'established peace' [sahtnesse wrohte, *L* 1403], but he only secures such amity because he 'made strong laws' [sette stronge lawen, *L* 1404]. The insistence of this connection is such that the phrase 'good laws' becomes a formula across the length of La3amon's *Brut*, a rigidity of language which itself insists on the necessity of this particular thought.[17]

The second of these changes reaches much more deeply into the story's latent jurisprudence to explain that good laws are powerful because they outlast kings, and that 'setting' them securely is a way for one king to ensure that the goodness of his actions extend beyond his reign. In this sense, such a law overlays this iterative tale to soften the articulation from king to king, to make clear that a change in personnel is not necessarily a change in regime, as if to open out individual cycles end to end, transforming this story (and its thought) into a single long line. The idea that a king might be good simply because he maintained the laws of old is there in Wace (where Aurilie is praised for restoring the 'laws used there before' [les leis ki ainz soleient estre, *W* 7989], but La3amon emphasizes the point by increasing its use quantitatively (making the point on nine occasions when Wace does not).[18] And, in this case, repetition of such goodness is not simply an increase proportional to the amount of reuse, but a way of noticing how repetition is, in effect, internal to such a thought:

---

[17] For the phrase 'good laws' see *L* 2134, 2400, 2991, 3569, 6450, 9068, 11088, 11983, 14276, For the related use of the phrase 'strong laws' see *L* 1390, 1404, 3123.

[18] La3amon repeats this claim about Aurilie: 'and a3ef heom alle þa la3en þe stoden bi heore ælderne dæ3en' (and [he] revived for them all the laws which had existed in the days of their ancestors, *L* 8461). For the nine instances of this formula in La3amon but not in Wace see *L* 2124 (cf. *W* 2280-2); *L* 2133-4 (cf. *W* 2305-6); *L* 3129 (cf. *W* 3325-6); *L* 3149-50 (cf. *W* 3345-7); *L* 5022 (*W* not running); *L* 8461 (cf. *W* 7989); *L* 11087-8 (cf. *W* 9641-4); *L* 14275-6 (*W* not running); *L* 14351-2 (cf. *W* 13337-8).

since the affirmation of precedent is a mode of stability based on repeating what came before, it necessarily sets its own precedent for further affirmations. It is not simply that Arthur creates a continuity with the rule of his father when he expels the Saxons and restores the 'old order' ('Arður . . . sette alle þa la3en þat stoden bi his ælderne da3en' (*L* 11085–7)), but that this linking creates the opportunity for Arthur's successor to continue his laws according to this method.[19] This is a thought La3amon puts in Arthur's mouth when he begs Constantine to keep the kingdom well by this means:

"Constæntin, þu art wilcume;   þu weore Cadores sone.
Ich þe bitache here   mine kineriche;
and wite mine Bruttes   a to þines lifes,
and hald heom alle þa la3en   þa habbeoð i-stonden a mine da3en,
and alle the la3en gode   þa bi Vðeres da3en stode".

[You are welcome, Constantine, you who were Cador's son. I here entrust my realm to you; and defend my Britons as long as you live, and maintain for them all the laws that have been in force in my day, and all the good laws which existed in Uther's time.]

(*L* 14272–6)

And this is also, La3amon tells us, how Constantine transforms the end of the most illustrious reign in the *Brut* story into proof of its success ('and ful wel heolden þa ilke la3en þat stoden on Arðures da3en' [and the same laws which existed in Arthur's day were very firmly upheld, *L* 14352]).

This jurisprudence is at once latent in the story but easily drawn out because it was a form of rule English kings had perfected before Geoffrey of Monmouth wrote a word, and it was the form English kings were still employing to secure their reigns in La3amon's day. The crucial point is, again, 1066, when, at precisely the moment which threatened the most dramatic change, William the Conqueror sought to moderate his position by claiming the Anglo-Saxon law as his own:

Hoc quoque praecipio et volo, ut omnes habeant et teneant legem Eadwardi regis in terris et in omnibus rebus, adauctis iis quae constitui ad utilitatem populi Anglorum.

---

[19] In Wace, Arthur is similarly concerned with precedent but not so explicitly in terms of the law: 'Quant Artur out sa terre assise | E part tuit out bone justise, | E tuit sun regne out restoré | En l'ancïene digneté . . .' [When Arthur had established his realm, and justice throughout it, and restored the whole kingdom to its former dignity . . . (*W* 9643–4)].

[This also I command and will, that all shall have and hold the law of King Edward in respect of their lands and possessions, with the addition of those decrees I have ordained for the welfare of the English people.][20]

Such a reassurance was both shrewd and persuasive because it was itself the adoption of a precedent, since earlier conquerors of England had secured their own position in just this way. In a charter of 1020 Cnut (1016–35) annexed England to the greater Danish kingdom by confirming the laws of the Anglo-Saxon King Edgar (959–75).[21] And Cnut had chosen Edgar rather than a more immediate Anglo-Saxon predecessor because the goodness of Edgar's laws had also been secured by his embrace of precedent:

& to ælcere byrig & on ælcere scyre hæbbe ic mines cynescypes gerihta swa min fæder hæfde, & mine þegnas hæbben heora scipe on minum timan swa hi hæfdon on mines fæder.

[And that in every borough and in every county I possess my royal prerogatives be kept as my father did and that my thegns keep their rank in my lifetime as they did in my father's.][22]

All this distant history was also pressing in the period in which Geoffrey of Monmouth, Wace, and Laȝamon wrote because the post-Conquest kings of England had used this form to unfold their own sequence of reigns into a single jurisprudential continuity: Henry I (1100–35) swore to uphold the law of William (his father) as well as the laws of Edward;[23] Stephen (1135–54) offered a charter

---

[20] 'Statutes of William the Conqueror', in *Select Charters*, ed. William Stubbs, 9th edn. (Oxford: Clarendon Press, 1913; 1st published 1870), 97–9 (quotation from p. 99). On the 'Statutes' generally and for this translation, see *English Historical Documents*, vol. 2, ed. David C. Douglas and George W. Greenaway, 2nd edn. (London: Eyre Methuen, 1981; 1st edn. 1953), 432.

[21] '& ic wylle þæt eal þeodscype, gehadode & læwede, fæstlice Eadgares lage healde þe ealle men habbað gecoren & to gesworen on Oxenaforda' [And it is my will that the whole nation, ecclesiastics and laymen, shall steadfastly keep the law of Edgar to which all have given their adherence under oath at Oxford], 'Canute's Proclamation of 1020', in *The Laws of the Kings of England from Edmund to Henry I*, ed. and trans. A. J. Robertson (Cambridge: Cambridge University Press, 1925), cap. 13 (pp. 142–3).

[22] 'IV Edgar', in *Laws of the Kings of England*, cap. 2a (pp. 32–3).

[23] 'Lagam regis Edwardi vobis reddo cum illis emendationibus quibus pater meus eam emendavit consilio baronuum suorum' [I restore to you the law of King Edward with all the reforms which my father introduced with the consent of his barons], 'The Coronation Charter of Henry I', in *Laws of the Kings of England*, cap. 13 (pp. 282–3). In a more explicit decree, Henry I demanded that his law be administered as it had been before the Conquest): 'Sciatis quod concedo et praecipio ut amodo comitatus mei et hundreda in illis locis et eisdem terminis sedeant sicut sederunt in tempore regis Eadwardi, et non aliter' [Be it known to you that I grant and enjoin, that henceforth my

guaranteeing all the laws of his uncle (Henry I) as well as the laws
granted by Edward;[24] and Henry II (1154–89) proclaimed in a 'charter of liberties' that he would uphold 'the liberties and free customs'
of his grandfather, Henry I.[25] The culmination of this long line of
charters was in fact Magna Carta (1215) whose paramount significance was, as Maitland put it, that 'the king is and shall be below
the law'.[26] As that view finally showed itself to be proverbial later in
the thirteenth-century poem usually called 'The Battle of Lewes' it
amounted to the belief that laws were always more powerful than

county and hundred courts shall sit at those times and in those places, when and where
they sat at the time of King Edward, and not otherwise], *Laws of the Kings of England*,
286–7.

[24] 'Sciatis me concessisse et praesenti carta mea confirmasse omnibus baronibus et
hominibus meis de Anglia omnes libertates et bonas leges quas Henricus rex Anglorum
avunculus meus eis dedit et concessit, et omnes bonas leges et bonas consuetudines eis
concedo quas habuerunt tempore Regis Edwardi' [Know that I have granted, and by
this present charter confirmed, to all my barons and vassels of England all the liberties
and good laws which Henry, king of the English, my uncle, granted and conceded to
them. I also grant them all the good laws and good customs which they enjoyed in the
time of King Edward], 'The First Charter of Stephen', in *Select Charters*, 142; trans.
here from *English Historical Documents*, 2: 434–5.

[25] 'Sciatis me ad honorem Dei et sanctae ecclesiae et pro communi emendatione
totius regni mei, concessisse et reddidisse et praesenti carta mea confirmasse Deo
et sanctae ecclesiae et omnibus comitibus et baronibus et omnibus hominibus meis
omnes concessiones et donationes et libertates et liberas consuetudines quas rex
Henricus avus meus eis dedit et concessit' [Know that for the honour of God and holy
Church, and for the common restoration of my whole realm, I have granted and
restored, and by this present charter confirmed, to God and to holy Church, and to all
my earls, barons, and vassals all concessions, gifts, liberties, and free customs, which
King Henry, my grandfather, granted and conceded to them], 'Carta Regis Henrici
Secundi', in *Select Charters*, 158; trans. from *English Historical Documents*, 2: 440.
Henry also repeated this claim in a flurry of charters granted to English towns at the
beginning of his reign. In one charter Henry II assures all the 'cives Lincolniae' [citizens
of Lincoln] that they will enjoy 'omnes libertates et consuetudines et leges suas quas
habuerunt tempore Eduardi et Willelmi et Henrici regum Angliae' [all their liberties
and customs and laws which they had in the time of Edward and William and Henry,
kings of England], 'Charter of Henry II to Lincoln', in *Select Charters*, 197; trans. from
English Historical Documents, 2: 1038. In another charter he assures the 'burgenses'
[burgesses] of Nottingham that they will enjoy 'omnes illas liberas consuetudines quas
habuerunt tempore Henrici avi nostri' [all those free customs which they had in the
time of King Henry our grandfather], 'Charter of Henry II to Nottingham' in *Select
Charters*, 198; trans. from *English Historical Documents*, 2: 1041. And in a third he
assures the 'cives de Oxenforda' [citizens of Oxford] that they will enjoy 'libertates et
consuetudines et leges et quietantias suas quas habuerunt tempore regis Henrici avi
mei' [their liberties, customs, laws, and quittances which they had in the time of King
Henry, my grandfather], 'Charter of Henry II to Oxford', in *Select Charters*, 198–9;
trans. from *English Historical Documents*, 2: 1042.

[26] Frederick Pollock and Frederic William Maitland, *The History of English Law*,
2nd edn., 2 vols. (Cambridge: Cambridge University Press, 1968; first published
1898), 1: 173.

kings: 'Dicitur vulgariter, "ut rex vult, lex vadit:" | Veritas vult aliter, nam lex stat, rex cadit' [It is said commonly, 'As the king wills, so goes the law,' but the truth is otherwise, for the law stands, but the king falls].[27] This permanence is also emphasized by a third category of alterations which emphasized the fragility of kings by setting them squarely against the solid and immortal land, not only in principle, but throughout the long sequence of royal change. In fact, the whole of the relevant thought is embedded in the general collocation of 'lond' and 'hond' in Laȝamon's *Brut* which everywhere links territory to kingship by internal rhyme, as if inevitably ('he bitahte al þat lond þat Eneas heore fader hefde on hond', *L* 126). In each instance the pairing measures the king's capacity by the size of what it masters (what kingship *is* in this vision is the capacity to take the whole of the land into the palm of a human hand), but, as the phrasing is repeated, the recurrence itself depreciates human power by demonstrating just how temporary it is (although the 'hond' is almost always different, the 'lond' is always the same). Laȝamon makes this explicit when he introduces this verbal formula to the observation (itself present in Wace) that a defining condition of Britain is that it has always been subject to conquest:

þus is þis eit-lond
igon from honde to hond
þet alle þa burhȝes
þe Brutus iwrohte
and heora noma gode
þa on Brutus dæi stode
beoð swiðe afelled
þurh warf of þon folke.

Par plusurs granz destruiemenz
Que unt fait alienes genz
Ki la terre unt sovent eüe,
Sovent prise, sovent perdue,
Sunt les viles e les contrees
Tutes or altrement nomees
Que li ancessor nes nomerent.
Ki premierement les fonderent.

[Thus has this island passed from hand to hand so that all the cities which Brutus founded have been brought low and their proper names which they bore in the days of Brutus obliterated through changes in the people.]

(*L* 1033–6)

[Through many great acts of destruction wrought by foreigners, who have often possessed the land, often seized it, often lost it, the towns and the regions all now have different names from those their founders gave them, who first established them.]

(*W* 1239–45)

---

[27] 'The Battle of Lewes', 72–121 in *The Political Songs of England*, ed. Thomas Wright, Camden Society Publications 6 (London, 1839), lines 871–2 (p. 116). Cited in Austin Lane Poole, *From Domesday Book to Magna Carta: 1087–1216*, 2nd edn. (Oxford: Clarendon Press, 1955; 1st edn. 1951), 477.

Where Wace describes these changes as fearsome ('great acts of destruction' in which an island is 'seized' or 'lost'), La3amon's language neutralizes the sense that conquest involves change (since one vanishing 'hond' is simply replaced by an identical other); while, to the extent that the collocation renders the 'hand' generic (it is always replaceable), it becomes irrelevant. In fact, La3amon's formula can be applied, not only to succession by inheritance (as when the land is passed from Uther's to Arthur's 'hond' (*L* 12371)), but to the most dramatic moments of conquest in British history (from Brutus's initial colonization ['Nu wes al þis lond iahned a Brutus hond', *L* 967] to Arthur's defeat by Mordred ['and þi wunliche lond isæt an his a3ere hond', *L* 14044] and Aðelstan's final defeat of the British ['and hu he al Anglelond sette on his a3ere hond', *L* 15970]). Since every use of this language elides a particular change, the very quantity of its use will tend to erase political articulations in the *Brut* story and convert the political change it describes into a story of stasis: accordingly, La3amon introduces the formula 192 times where it is not prompted by Wace.[28]

The solidity of the land is also brought into the poem as a subject (rather than a point of reference) by a fourth category of revision. This change amounts to no more than two added passages which themselves take their cue directly from Wace, and yet these small additions completely reverse the priorities of land and event in this story, ensuring that La3amon's *Brut* now concerns a given territory, rather than particular people. The passage on which the first of these additions is based is an example of what La3amon's contemporary,

---

[28] See *L* 126, 531, 822, 967, 983, 1033, 1047, 1242, 1262, 1270, 1281, 1448, 1508, 1624, 1668, 1847, 1887, 1891, 1902, 1966, 2041, 2118, 2161, 2228, 2402, 2471, 2611, 2648, 2737, 2988, 3187, 3405, 3572, 3592, 3595, 3658, 3684, 3865, 3898, 4096, 4110, 4119, 4421, 4435, 4495, 4724, 4767, 4803, 4812, 4974, 4997, 5099, 5149, 5158, 5253, 5315, 5329, 5429, 5457, 5500, 5591, 5596, 5741, 5892, 5909, 5929, 5933, 6066, 6161, 6238, 6247, 6294, 6342, 6343, 6499, 6517, 6521, 6530, 6576, 6666, 6673, 6680, 6873, 7079, 7193, 7353, 7371, 7413, 7425, 7656, 7659, 7682, 7702, 7719, 7796, 7822, 8101, 8407, 8431, 8452, 8505, 8606, 8767, 8799, 8975, 9050, 9102, 9124, 9129, 9224, 9226, 9314, 9371, 9376, 9396, 9397, 9428, 9435, 9442, 9603, 9674, 10010, 10163, 10186, 10205, 10261, 10415, 10501, 10696, 10995, 11030, 11056, 11070, 11071, 11109, 11112, 11155, 11177, 11211, 11246, 11287, 11304, 11309, 11349, 11524, 11670, 11679, 11713, 11777, 11796, 11907, 12024, 12371, 12373, 12383, 12472, 12493, 12505, 12520, 12699, 12798, 13180, 13181, 13632, 13684, 14028, 14044, 14070, 14386, 14494, 14497, 14675, 14682, 14822, 14824, 14839, 14978, 15158, 15165, 15205, 15351, 15524, 15566, 15606, 15621, 15704, 15800, 15821, 15854, 15970, 16056.

Matthew of Vendôme (late twelfth century) called *topographia*, a very localized verbal *chorographia* which can therefore lodge itself within other forms rather than shaping the whole of them. Such a figure maps the land by aestheticizing it, insisting on its importance by finding it full of riches:[29]

Brutus hine biþohte
and þis folc biheold,
biheold he þa muntes,
feire and muchele,
biheold he þa medewan
þat weoren swiþe mære,
biheold he þa wateres
and þa wilde deor,
biheold he þa fisches,
biheold he þa fuȝeles,
biheold he þa leswa
and þene leofliche wode,
biheold he þene wode hu he bleou,
biheold he þat corn hu hit greu;
al he iseih on leoden
þat him leof was on heorten.

[Brutus bethought himself and looked upon this people, beheld the mountains, lofty and fair, beheld the meadows, which were of great extent, beheld the waters and the wild beasts, beheld the fishes, beheld the birds, beheld the pastures and the lovely woods, beheld the forest how it flourished, beheld the corn how it grew; everything he saw in the land pleased him greatly.]

(*L* 1002–9)

Brutus esguarda les montainnes,
Vit les valees, vit les plainnes,
Vit les mores, vit les boscages,
Vit les eues, vit les rivages,
Vit les champs, vit les praeries,
Vit les porz, vit les pescheries,
Vit son pople multepleier,
Vit les terres bien guainier.

[Brutus looked at the mountain; he saw the valleys, the plains, the moors, the woodland, the rivers and the river banks; he saw the fields and the meadows, the harbours and the fisheries; he saw his people multiplying and the lands growing fertile.]

(*W* 1209–16)

But Laȝamon also inserts another *topographia*, based on this one, *before* it, so that where Wace simply has Diana telling Brutus to go and seek 'a fine island' [une ille bone], Laȝamon's Diana details the

---

[29] Matthew of Vendôme, *Ars versificatoria*, 106–93 in *Les Arts poétique du XIIe et du XIIIe siècle*, ed. Edmond Faral (Paris: Champion, 1924), §§ 109–11 (pp. 147–8). On the similar figure he calls 'the pleasance' see Ernst Robert Curtius, *European Literature and the Latin Middle Ages*, trans. Willard R. Trask, Bollingen Series 36 (Princeton: Princeton University Press, 1953), 195–200.

richness of the land for Brutus, before he has even seen it (I provide the parallel passage in Wace here to illustrate the change):

"Þar is fuȝel, þar is fisc,
þer wuniað feire deor;
þar is wode, þar is water,
þar is wilderne muchel.
Þet lond is swiþe wunsom;
weallen þer beoð feire.
Wuniað in þon londe
eotantes swiðe stronge.
Albion hatte þat lond,
ah leode ne beoð þar nane.
Þerto þu scalt teman
and ane neowe Troye þar makian.
Þer scal of þine cunne
kinebearn arisen,
and scal þin mære kun
wælden þas londes".

[There are fowl, there are fish, fine beasts live there; there is wood, there is water, there is much open country. That land is very fair, there are fine springs there. In that land there dwell most powerful giants. That land is called Albion, but there are no people there. You shall go there and build a new Troy. There princes of your blood shall arise, and your noble race shall rule that land.

(*L* 620–7)

". . . Une ille bone e abitable
E a maneir mult delitable.
Bone est la terre a cultiver,
Gaiant i soelant abiter.
Albion ad non, cele avras,
Une Troie nove i feras.
De tei vendra reial ligniede
Ki par le mund iert esalciede".

[. . . a fine island, fit to live in and delectable to dwell in, whose ground is good for cultivation. Giants used to live there. Its name is Albion. This you shall have, and you will make a new Troy there. From you will spring a royal lineage esteemed throughout the world.]

(*W* 683–90)

As ever, any mention of the land in his source is an invitation to Laȝamon to mention it often (even within the local revision he uses the word 'lond' four times to Wace's single mention of 'la terre'), and this earlier *topographia* also ensures that when the land and Brutus are subsequently brought together, Laȝamon has not only shown that the land was already there, but, in the very anticipation, ensured that its primary attribute is its physical constancy. Since the land therefore becomes the predicate of the whole human history this poem knows, such a beginning also creates the opportunity to prove this constancy at that history's end. After all the British have been killed or driven into Wales, Laȝamon says that Aðelstan, the first Anglo-Saxon

king (and the last king whose reign he narrates) possesses a land as
rich as the land Brutus found (it is abundant with 'silver and gold'
[fæi3er lond inoh seoluer and gold], *L* 15927) and he also revises
Wace's description of his power, once again, to place equal emphasis
on 'þis lond':

Þis wes þe formeste Englisce mon þe al Ænglelond biwon. He wes icruned and ieled— þis lond wes al his a3en— and seoðen he wuneden here sixtene 3ere. [He was the first Englishman to gain possession of the whole of England. He was crowned and anointed— this whole land was his—and there- after reigned here for sixteen years.] (*L* 15944–6)	A cel tens ert Adelstan reis; Ço fud li premiers des Engleis Ki ot tute Engleterre en baille Fors sul Guales e Cornuaille. [At that time Athelstan was king; he was the first Englishman to control all England except only Wales and Cornwall.] (*W* 14757–60)

Since Wace says Aðelstan controls 'tute Engleterre' La3amon can
say that he controls 'Ængle*lond*', but he also insists on the land's
autonomy, as he always does, by mentioning it more often, also, inevitably, recurring to the term he has used from the beginning to describe
this thing (it is both ' Ænglelond' and 'þis lond' as it ever was). Where
Wace is content only to mention the new king's 'control', La3amon
also emphasizes the permanence of the land by noting the temporal
limit of even a powerful king's reign (however much he controls,
Aðelstan only rules for sixteen years). To this local limit the whole
of the preceding poem has added an enormously long sequence of
regnal change (however mitigated by La3amon's other changes as
it unfolds), and it is therefore also the point of these lines that the
land stands firm before *all* the political changes which have passed
over it.

A poem which imagines the land in this way also understands
it as the source of that power which kings wield (by means of the
law they control), and it is along the axis of this ideology that the
thinking of La3amon's *Brut* is also reinforced by that other important *chorographia* from the post-Conquest period, *Domesday Book*,
that survey of 'England' and its people commissioned by William
the Conqueror in 1086. This book is not usually understood as a
map, but it actually calls itself a *descriptio* in its final colophon, and

although in form it is really a collection of lists, like the *Brut* these lists coordinate territory (counties, boroughs, farms, waste, castles, houses), legal jurisdiction (sake and soke, shires and hundreds), and resident or 'possessing' people (earls, countesses, bishops, bordars, villeins, sokemen, fishermen).[30] Since these lists value all the land they describe in pounds and pence this survey was long thought to be a 'geld book', an instrument for determining the taxes owed to William from his new territories.[31] But the lists follow the contours of the land so closely (with each booklet of the codex corresponding to a county in England, and the sequence of booklets moving in 'bands' from the east to the west, with each successive band progressing north) that they complicate rather than simplify monetary calculations (a large landholder's holdings would be spread across every booklet); in fact, the valuations are themselves a method for quantifying land so as to distribute it in the form of *rights*, to coordinate the internal relations of a territory with the social relations of the people who live upon it.[32] So thorough is the matching of these relations that the *Book*'s only purpose can be to reassure persons of the security of their possessions as their rights are made to emerge from the very firmness of the land; it is no more than a warrant for the law, a 'great evidentiary certification . . . of enfeoffment'.[33]

In this sense *Domesday Book* is not only a map similar to Laʒamon's *Brut* but it is its political unconscious, not only a different disposition of identical elements but an inversion of their priority so that what is most obvious in the *Brut* is latent in the *Book* and vice versa. *Domesday Book* may not seem like a history, for example, but, in every case, its detailed account of the land is spread across a grid of three distinct moments, 'in the time of King Edward' ('tempore regis Æduardi'), 'when William gave it' ('quando rex Willielmus dedit'), and 'now' or 1086 ('modo'). And, although its very commitment to valuation seems to make its map of the land bloodless, even mercenary,

[30] For the rubric see V. H. Galbraith, *Domesday Book: Its Place in Administrative History* (Oxford: Clarendon Press, 1974), 19. For examples of the kinds of lists provided in the *Book* see *English Historical Documents*, 2: 858–62.

[31] Frederic W. Maitland, *Domesday Book and Beyond* (Cambridge: Cambridge University Press, 1987; 1st published 1897), 3.

[32] For the layout of 'Great Domesday' see Galbraith, *Domesday Book*, 54–5. On the *Book* as a 'foedary' see J. C. Holt, '1086', 41–64 in *Domesday Studies*, ed. J. C. Holt (Woodbridge: Boydell & Brewer, 1987), 48–56.

[33] Ibid. 62. As Holt concludes, 'As such [*Domesday Book*] was not intended to "do" anything. It simply "was"' (p. 64).

as can be seen from the original brief given to the commissions who made the survey, the form of the *Book* is nearly aestheticizing in the manner of the *topographia*, embracing every contour of the land so intensely that it absorbs all its abundance (all its power to 'support' such a variety of people) into its words and numbers:

Hic subscribitur inquisicio terrarum quomodo barones regis inquirunt videlicet per sacramentum vicecomitis scire et omnium baronum et eorum francigenarum, et tocius centuriatus presbiter propositus vi villani uniuscuiusque ville. Deinde quomodo vocatur mansio, quis tenuit eam tempore regis Edwardi, quis modo tenet, quot hide, quot carruce in dominio, quot hominum, quot villani, quot cotarii, quot servi, quot liberi homines, quot sochemanni, quantum silve, quantum prati, quot pascuorum, quot mole, quot piscine, quantum est additum vel ablatum, quantum valebat totum simul, et quantum modo, quantum ibi quisque liber homo uel sochemannus habuit vel habet. Hoc totum tripiliciter, scilicet tempore regis Æduardi, et quando rex Willielmus dedit et quomodo sit modo.

[Here follows the inquiry concerning the lands which the king's barons made according to the oath of the sheriff of the shire and of all the barons and their Frenchmen, and of the whole hundred court—the priest, reeve and six villeins from each village. They inquired what the manor was called; who held it in the time of King Edward; who holds it now; how many hides there are; how many ploughs in demesne and how many belonging to the men; how many villeins; how many cottars; how many slaves; how many freemen; how many sokemen; how much woodland; how much meadow; how much pasture; how many mills; how many fisheries; how much has been added or taken away from the estate; what it used to be worth altogether; what it is worth now; and how much each freeman and sokeman had and has. All this to be recorded thrice: to wit, as it was in the time of King Edward, as it was when King William gave the estate, and as it is now.][34]

What *Domesday Book* in its form makes more obvious than Laȝamon's *Brut* is that any effective history, and any thorough map, in a post-Conquest context is necessarily an insistence on the constancy of the law. In this initiating commission, for example, although every current enfeoffment requires some guarantee because of the drastic political change which has occurred (since 'King William gave' all these rights), current authority is itself interested in (and capable of) securing the rights which applied *before* that change ('in the time of

---

[34] *Inquisitio comitatus Cantabridgiensis*, ed. N. E. S. A. Hamilton (London: Royal Society of Literature Publications, 1876), 97–8. I have silently expanded this edition's abbreviations. Trans. here from *English Historical Documents*, 2: 882.

King Edward'). Although William's legal apparatus has replaced the old regime ('all the barons and their Frenchmen'), Edward's legal apparatus essentially remains ('the sheriff of the shire', 'the whole hundred court') and *both* are here shown to have jurisdiction over landholding both before and after the Conquest. So Laȝamon's *Brut* is effectively a legal document—a broad-brush 'evidentiary certification of enfeoffment'—not only in so far as it is a political history, but in so far as it is a *chorographia*. In fact, in so far as it finds the law everywhere as durable as the land, Laȝamon's *Brut* (like the *Book*) shows that the land is mappable, not only by means of its contours, but in that jurisprudence which is its projection, as the form the land takes when it makes its way out into the activities (and thoughts) of kings and peoples.

IMMANENT LAW

Another way to summarize such a historical vision is to say, as Laȝamon says at one point, that the 'laws are *in* the land' [laȝen beoð an ærde, *L* 9676]. Another way to register both the importance and the particular contours of this view is to see how it has even lodged in the other English chorography I have already mentioned, so much more modest and short than the *Brut*, that description of England in Jesus College MS 29. The key distinction here threads its way through a long description of the thirty-two shires, assigning each one to three different kinds of 'laws' each of which is in turn projected onto a particular part of the land:

Þes xxxij schire syndon to-delede on þreo lawan. On is west-sexene lawe. Oþer Denelawe. Þe þrydde Mercena lawe. To west-sexene lawe bi-lympeþ ix schiren . . . To Dene lawe bilympeþ xv schire . . . To Mercene lawe bilimpeþ viij.

[These thirty-two shires are divided into three laws. One is West Saxon law, the second Danelaw, and the third, Mercian law. Nine shires belong to the West Saxon law . . . fifteen shires belong to the Danelaw . . . and eight shires belong to the Mercian law.]

(lines 37–51)

No such division in the law existed in the thirteenth century, but the arrangement is still knowledgeable about old political boundaries, and it therefore exists here as the assumption that law corresponds to territory (it differs only as the land differs) that, like territory, it will not change materially over time. Because it is untrue, such an assumption is the purest form of antiquarianism (the thinking of those 'who have looked into old-fashioned books and have never looked with any curiosity upon the England of their day'), but the assumption is also here proved by the way the shires in this description are everywhere divided into 'hundreds' and 'hides'.[35] For example,

To Mercene lawe bilimpeþ viij schiren, Gloucestreschire xxxiiij hundred hida, wyricestreschire xij hundred hida, Herefordschire xij hundred hida, warewikschire xij hundred hida, Oxenfordschire xxiiij hundred hida, Sropschire xxiiij hundred hida, Chestreschire xij hundred hida, Staffordschire v hundred hida. Þis is under al xxvi þusend hida and on half hundred.

[Eight shires belong to the Mercian law: to Gloucestershire 34 hundred hides, to Worcestershire 12 hundred hides, to Herefordshire 12 hundred hides, to Warwickshire 12 hundred hides, to Oxfordshire 23 hundred hides, to Shropshire 24 hundred hides, to Cheshire 12 hundred hides, to Staffordshire 5 hundred hides. This is, over all, 26 thousand hides and one half hundred.]

(lines 51–8)

Hides were used in *Domesday Book*, and they were still current in Laȝamon's day, but they had been the fundamental unit of the Anglo-Saxon law: a 'hide' had been 'the holding which supported a ceorl and his household'; hides had been grouped administratively by the 'hundred', and 'in the last century of the Old English kingdom each hundred had a court'.[36] Where a map can also be accurate by means of such ancient legal language even an unjustified antiquarianism gains a certain force, and the law seems so thoroughly a part of the land that any map is a form of historical jurisprudence.

Laȝamon's own practice has often been described as antiquarian, but this has only ever meant his use of language—his use of Old English metre and vocabulary—and it has never been said that his poem is also antiquarian in its understanding of the law.[37] Just as

---

[35] H. G. Richardson and G. O. Sayles, *Law and Legislation from Æthelberht to Magna Carta* (Edinburgh: Edinburgh University Press, 1966), 51. These divisions were still evoked in certain 12th-c. legal writings. See e.g. *Leges Henrici Primi*, ed. and trans. L. J. Downer (Oxford: Clarendon Press, 1972), 96–7.

[36] See Frank Stenton, *Anglo-Saxon England*, 3rd edn. (Oxford: Clarendon Press, 1971; 1st published 1943), 279 ('the holding') and 298–9 ('in the last century').

[37] The classic description of Laȝamon's antiquarianism is E. G. Stanley, 'Laȝamon's Antiquarian Sentiments', *MÆ* 38 (1969), 23–37.

Jesus College MS 29 does, however, La3amon not only thinks about old laws, he also thinks about a kind of law he calls 'Mercian' law, although the way he evokes this element of legal custom has the effect of making *every* body of law in his poem as durable as this law was still reputed to be. In La3amon's case, 'Mercian law' is not the legal provision of a certain place, but of an ancient origin (its name commemorates the brilliant woman, 'Marcie', who devised it); it is a law that applied to the whole of the 'country' ('leode'), not merely a part of it; and it names the whole of that law that the Anglo-Saxons made their own when they conquered the British:

> Þa makede heo [Marcie] ane læ3e,   and læide 3eon þat leode.
> Þa þeos la3e wes al iworhte,
> Brutus nemneden þa la3en   æfter þar lafuedi;
> to soðen, wihuten wene,   þe la3e hehte Marciane.
> Seoððen þeræfter   monie hundred wintre
> com Alfred þe king,   Englelondes deorling,
> and wrat þa la3en on Englis   ase heo wes ær on Bruttisc,
> and whærfde hire nome on his dæ3e   and cleopede heo Mærcene la3e.

[She (Marcie) devised, at that time, a code of law, and imposed it throughout the country. When this law was fully framed, the Britons named the law after the lady; without doubt, to be sure, the law was called Marcian. Then, many hundred years later, came King Alfred, England's darling, and he framed the law in English where it had previously been British, and in his time changed its name and called it the Marcene law.]

$$(L \; 3143-50)$$

The particulars of this legal history are the invention of Geoffrey of Monmouth; it is his witty *etymologia* (like the name 'Brutus' itself) which creates a legendary person to substitute for an otherwise forgotten origin; in the passage I have just quoted La3amon is simply being faithful to this originary fantasy (as it was also faithfully preserved in Wace).[38] But the idea that laws written by a British woman

---

[38]   This is Geoffrey's version of these origins: 'Post illum autem Guithelinus diadema regni suscepit quod omni tempore uite sue benigne et modeste tractauit. Erat ei nobilis mulier Marcia nomine omnibus erudita artibus. Hec inter multa et inaudita que proprio ingenio repererat inuenit legem quam Britones Marcianam appellauerunt. Hanc etiam Aluredus inter cetera transtulit et Saxonica lingua Merchenelage uocauit' [Guithelin received the crown of the kingdom after Gurguit. He ruled it liberally and temperately all his life through. His wife was a noble woman called Marcia, who was skilled in all the arts. Among the many extraordinary things she used her natural talent to invent was a law she devised which was called the *Lex Martiana* by the Britons. King Alfred translated this along with the other laws; in his Saxon tongue he called it the

became laws written by an Anglo-Saxon king is not merely fanciful, for it can also be said to translate the jurisprudence which holds that conquest does not alter the law into narrative; it provides yet another form for the belief that the post-Anglo-Norman law was the Anglo-Saxon law. In other words, as Laȝamon subscribes to this view (as it also governs *Domesday Book*), it is an antiquarianism which, however benighted, understands itself to be rooted very carefully in *fact*: it does not simply have faith in the power of the law to remain unchanged, but it believes that this is possible because the law always *has* been the same, and this can be plainly proved.

As a historical thought such antiquarianism generally travels under the name of 'constitutionalism', although, like the chorography with which it is closely involved, this idea is generally identified with a much later period (in this case the seventeenth-century writings of Edward Coke, John Selden, and William Prynne).[39] The fundamental principle of such history is, however, what Geoffrey, Wace, and Laȝamon also believe: that the ancient law is the modern law because neither successive kings nor foreign conquest have ever altered a timeless custom.[40] A more careful history of jurisprudence makes clear that this belief had its origins in precisely those moments when the *Brut* was created, not only because the law had so recently staked its very claim on continuing old provision across enormous rupture

Mercian Law], Geoffrey of Monmouth, *Historia regum Britanniae*, I, ed. Wright, §47 (p. 31); *History of the Kings of Britain*, trans. Thorpe, 101.
    Wace's version is the same in all essentials: 'Guincelins fu de bone vie, | E sa moiller out num Marcie, | Lettree fu e sage dame, | De buen pris e de bone fame. | Sun enging mist tut e sa cure | A saveir lettre e escriture. | Mult sout e mult estudia, | Une lei escrit e trova, | Marcïene l'apela l'on | Sulunc le language breton. | Li reis Alvret, si cum l'en dit, | Translata la lei e l'escrit. | Quant il l'out en engleis tornee, | Marcenelaga l'ad nomee' [Guincelin led a good life, and his wife was called Marcie, an educated and wise woman, much esteemed and renowned. She devoted all her intelligence and care to learning Scripture and her letters. She knew much and studied much, and invented and wrote down a law, which is called Marcien, in the British language. King Alfred, they say, translated the law and the document. When he had changed it into English, he called it Marcenelaga, W 3335–48].

[39] J. G. A. Pocock, *The Ancient Constitution and the Feudal Law: A Study of English Historical Thought in the Seventeenth Century*, 2nd edn. (Cambridge: Cambridge University Press, 1987; 1st published 1957), esp. 30–55.

[40] Later constitutionalists held, more particularly, that 'the standing and even the structure of Parliament, the limitation of the prerogative in taxation, the protection of the individual by the common law, trial by jury, due process, were all part of an ancient structure which royal power had overlain but only partially impaired', J. C. Holt, 'The Origins of the Constitutional Tradition in England', 1–22 in his *Magna Carta and Medieval Government* (London: Hambledon Press, 1985), 3.

(as in *Domesday Book*), but because the jurisprudence of the twelfth and thirteenth centuries was itself so generally devoted to gathering together the old law in order to demonstrate what Maitland termed its 'perdurance'.[41] The *Consiliatio Cnuti* (*c.*1110–30) and the *Instituta Cnuti* (*c.*1095–1135) gathered together the important laws of Cnut; the *Quadripartitus* (*c.*1108–18) reclaimed much of the *lex Edwardi*; and the *Leges Edwardi Confessoris* (*c.*1115–50), although relying more on fancy than evidence from the past, also claimed to reconstruct the pre-Conquest law.[42] According to J. C. Holt, it is this outpouring of legal history that actually constitutes the 'origins of the constitutional tradition in England'.[43] The very close connection of the *Brut* story to such a project is well demonstrated by a passage added to the *Leges Edwardi Confessoris* when it was gathered together in a compendium with other antiquarian legal texts (usually called the 'London Collection').[44] There, we find that the Anglo-

---

[41] Pollock and Maitland, *History of English Law*, 1: 97.

[42] For these texts see *Die Gesetze der Angelsachsen*, ed. Felix Liebermann, 3 vols. (Halle: Niemeyer, 1903–16), 1: 271–371 (*Consiliatio Cnuti* and *Instituta Cnuti* in parallel), 1: 627–70 (*Leges Edwardi Confessoris*). *Quadripartitus* is printed throughout vol. 1 of *Gesetze der Angelsachsen* parallel to the surviving Anglo-Saxon laws it translates. Other portions are given separately (see 1: 529–46). For the dates of these texts I rely on Liebermann, except for the date of the *Quadripartitus* for which I rely on Richard Sharpe, 'The Prefaces of *Quadripartitus*', in *Law and Government in Medieval England and Normandy: Essays in Honour of Sir James Holt*, ed. George Garnett and John Hudson (Cambridge: Cambridge University Press, 1994), 150–1.

[43] See Holt, 'Origins of the Constitutional Tradition', esp. 13–15.

[44] On the importance of Geoffrey of Monmouth in the 'London Collection' see Walter Ullmann, 'On the Influence of Geoffrey of Monmouth in English History', 257–76 in *Speculum Historiale: Geschichte im Spiegel von Geschichtsschreibung und Geschichtsdeutung*, ed. Clemens Bauer, Laetitia Boehm, Max Müller (Munich: Karl Alber, 1965), esp. 258–60. Liebermann prints 'London Collection' interpolations alongside his editions of the Collection's constituent texts in vol. 1 of *Gesetze der Angelsachsen*. For a description of the collection see Felix Liebermann, *Über die Leges Anglorum saeculo XIII Londoniis collectae* (Halle: Niemeyer, 1894).

Wormald offers this concise summary of the 'Collection's' contents: 'The "Laws of King Edward" for [the London Collector] meant more than the notoriously spurious if intermittently well-informed mid-twelfth-century text of that name . . . the author anticipated modern scholarship in locating the *Leges Edwardi Confessoris* alongside the "Articles of William I", coronation charters from Henry I to Henry II, and *Glanvill*. Part I was devoted to a Latin translation of laws actually issued by Anglo-Saxon kings. The London collector did add a more or less fanciful historical commentary. But the laws themselves came from a very much less disreputable source than the *Leges Edwardi*. This was the collection now known as *Quadripartitus*', Patrick Wormald, ' "*Quadripartitus*" ', 111–47 in *Law and Government in Medieval England and Normandy: Essays in Honour of Sir James Holt*, ed. Garnett and Hudson, 111–12.

Saxon law (which is of course the Anglo-Norman law) was, first and
foremost, King Arthur's law:

Hanc legem inuenit Arturus qui quondam fuit inclitissimus rex Britonum, et
ita consolidauit et confederauit regnum Britannie uniuersum semper in unum;
huius legis auctoritate expulit Arturus predictus Saracenos et inimicos a
regno. Lex enim ista diu sopita fuit et sepulta, donec Edgarus rex Anglorum,
qui fuit auus Edwardi regis, propinqui uestri, illam excitauit et in lucem
erexit, et illam per totum regnum firmiter obseruare fecit et precepit.

[Arthur, who in former days was the most renowned king of Britain, devised
this law, and thus united and joined the whole kingdom of Britain ever into
one; by the authority of this aforesaid law, the aforesaid Arthur drove the
Saracens and enemies from the kingdom. Indeed that law was dormant
and entombed for a long time, until Edgar, king of the English, who was
grandfather of King Edward, your kinsman, roused that law and brought it
into the light, and proclaimed it and had it rigorously observed in the entire
kingdom.][45]

Coke returns to the *Brut* story in the seventeenth century when he
says that the law of his day extends backward through the Anglo-
Saxon laws of Alfred to the 'leges Brutonum' established by Brutus.[46]
In this Coke is only perspicuous about the history of his own tradition, recognizing that, where no records exist—in a time too early
for even a rigorous antiquarianism to discover the provisions of the
law—the *Brut* story is itself the historical thought which recovers
ancient custom.

---

[45] *Gesetze der Angelsachsen*, 1: 655. The translation here is my own. Holt ('Origins
of the Constitutional Tradition', 5–6) cites an even more famous and influential version of this claim in Fortescue's *De laudibus legum Angliae* (*c.*1468–71): 'Regnum
Anglie primo per Britones inhabitatum est, deinde per Romanos regulatum, iterumque
per Britones, ac deinde per Saxones possessum, qui nomen eius ex Britannia in
Angliam mutauerunt. Extunc per Danos idem regnum parumper predominatum est, et
iterum per Saxones, sed finaliter per Normannos quorum propago regnum illud
obtinet in presenti. Et in omnibus nacionum earum et regum eorum temporibus
regnum illud eisdem quibus iam regitur consuetudinibus continue regulatum est' ('The
kingdom of England was first inhabited by Britons; then ruled by Romans, again by
Britons, then possessed by Saxons, who changed its name from Britain to England.
Then for a short time the kingdom was conquered by Danes, and again by Saxons, but
finally by Normans, whose posterity hold the realm at the present time. And throughout the period of these nations and their kings, the realm has been continuously ruled
by the same customs as it is now'), John Fortescue, *De laudibus legum Angliae*, ed. and
trans. S. B. Chrimes (Cambridge: Cambridge University Press, 1942), 38–9.

[46] Edward Coke, *Reports*, ed. John Henry Thomas and John Farquhar Fraser,
6 vols. (London: J. Butterworth & Son, 1826), 2: xiv–xx. (The *Reports* were first
published in French between 1600 and 1615; the first English publication was in 1658.)

Since so much of the law was well and truly lost, what such historicism also consolidated under the guise of all this retrospective
account was a principle that made evidence unnecessary—that the
law was permanent *even if it had changed*. More important to such a
jurisprudence than the validity of the claim that the Laws of Alfred
were written by a British queen, or that William had in fact maintained the law which originated with Brutus, in other words was the
view that new provisions were not drafted but *discovered* in the land
still and stable beneath the drafter's feet, that the thought which constituted that law did not originate with people, but in the structure
of the land itself. This general vision was possible, first, because
'the law of land was . . . the basis of constitutional law', and so most
of that mass of accumulated and well-remembered provision for
which thirteenth-century jurists sought a source actually did derive,
ultimately, from feudal arrangements concerning tenure.[47] But the
land could be so wise, second, because tenurial arrangements understood territory to structure human affairs by the projection of a certain quality resident within it, as if the shape of the relations between
person and person was actually determined by the land they 'held'.
Although the law in La3amon's day used terms such as 'property'
(*proprietas*), 'possession' (*possessio*) was the closest relation a person
could have with any particular piece of ground—this is, for example,
the word that *Bracton* uses to describe the relationship between a
'lord' [dominus] and his 'estate' [fundus]—and, consequently, the
law did 'not recognize any absolute right of ownership but merely
. . . relatively good and relatively bad rights to possession'.[48] This

---

[47] See A. D. Hargreaves, *An Introduction to the Principles of Land Law*, 4th edn.
(London: Sweet & Maxwell, 1963), 9. La3amon uses the phrase as I quote it here at the
very first moment the Saxon invaders threaten British rule, thereby anticipating the
form of the law's survival once the Saxons succeed. Earlier he also praises Dunwallo's
laws by saying they '3et beoð on londe' ['are still in the land', *L* 2133]. At this point
Wace says only that 'Dumwallo's' 'leis' [laws] are still employed by the English [que
encor tienent li Engleus, *W* 2306].

[48] *Bracton: De legibus et consuetudinibus Angliae*, ed. George E. Woodbine, trans.
with revisions and notes, Samuel E. Thorne, 4 vols. (Cambridge, Mass.: Harvard
University Press, 1968–77), 2: 294. See also W. S. Holdsworth, *A History of English
Law*, 17 vols. (London: Methuen, 1922–72), 7: 426. This particular complexity is also
the focus of John Hudson in 'Anglo-Norman Land Law and the Origins of Property',
198–222 in *Law and Government in Medieval England and Normandy*, ed. Garnett
and Hudson. See also Hudson's *Land, Law, and Lordship in Anglo-Norman England*
(Oxford: Clarendon Press, 1994). For consideration of the issue of 'property' in
Continental law see Susan Reynolds, *Fiefs and Vassals: The Medieval Evidence
Reinterpreted* (Oxford: Oxford University Press, 1994), 48–74.

resulted in what A. D. Hargreaves has called a surprising 'material-ism' about principles, as if the right emanating from the land, and not the land itself was the thing one possessed (what Maitland described as a 'legal metaphysics' in which a right was 'a thing quite distinct from the land over which it hovers').[49] 'Seisin' (*seisina*) was the term used in statute and writ to describe this thing ('the person seised of land was . . . the person in obvious occupation, the person "sitting" on the land'), and it was a term which also made clear that even the most secure human attachment to the land did not represent the person's power over that territory, but, in effect, that territory's recognition of the person who was *attempting* to control it.[50]

A land whose power extended into the world in this way was as rich in the things it could provide as that world was full of people to sit upon it, for it was always capable of recognizing yet another form of attachment, and could therefore be 'possessed' almost infinitely:

> An obvious consequence of the tenurial system is that a number of persons have interests of some sort in the same parcel of land. At the bottom of the feudal ladder there will be a tenant who has seisin of the land and is called the tenant in demesne, and at the top there is the King; in between there may be a string of mesne lords, who are lords and tenants at the same time.[51]

A land so rich in 'rights' was therefore also rich in every other way (it was, in fact, 'the major source of wealth' in feudalism) and, in addition to crops, timber, and metals, it could actually produce human labour, since almost all the activities a medieval society required (from the bearing of arms to the care of souls) were secured by the extracting of a particular 'right' from a particular piece of land.[52] What this power proved in its very munificence, however, was that the law was actually no more than the land itself, extended out into the world in the thingly form of 'rights'. The capacity to give so many of these rights at the same time was the land's immutable power to control rather than be controlled by the processes of human habita-tion; its capacity to bestow such rights endlessly (as people inevitably died and the unchanged right passed to another living person) was the active form its perdurable power took.

---

[49] Hargreaves, *Principles of Land Law*, p. 46. Pollock and Maitland, *History of English Law*, 2: 4.

[50] A. W. B. Simpson, *An Introduction to the History of the Land Law* (Oxford: Oxford University Press, 1961), 37.

[51] Ibid. 44.   [52] Ibid. 5.

The law might therefore be understood as no more than the name given to the land in its formal aspect, the idea the land has and is capable of sharing in so far as its structure is actively perceived. La3amon does not simply think about the law then, but in that thinking borrows much of the form of his poem from the land (just as *Domesday Book* does with different emphases, and, as indeed, to a lesser extent, does every instance of the *Brut* story). But La3amon's commitments are unusually extensive, as he clearly acknowledges in a passage which looks back to the origins of the 'hide', that term which itself names the relations in question in so far as it was both territorial limit and juridical structure, still in use in La3amon's day, but also to be found in the oldest laws he could have known. In La3amon's version of the story, the origin of the form lies with the first Saxon ruler in Britain, Hengist, who is granted only the amount of land he can 'overspread' [ouerspræden, *L* 7080] with a 'a bull's hide' [anes bule hude, *L* 7080] for a settlement:

> He hafde ane hude   bi3ete to his neode
> of ane wilde bule   þe wes wunder ane strong.
> He hæfden ænne wisne mon,   þe wel cuðe a craften,
> þe nom þas hude   and a bord leide,
> and whætte his sæxes   alse he schæren wolde;
> Of þere hude he kærf enne þwong   swiðe smal and swiðe long;
> nes þe þwong noht swiðe bræd   buten swulc a twines þræd.
> Þa al islit wes þe þong,   he wes wunder ane long;
> abuten he bilæde   muche del of londe.

[(Hengist) had obtained for his purpose the hide of an extremely strong wild bull. He had with him a knowledgeable man, well skilled in handicraft, who took this hide and laid it on a board and, sharpening his knives ready for cutting, sliced from the hide a strip of leather, very thin and very long; the thong was no thicker than a linen thread. By the time he had cut the whole strip, it was remarkably long; it encompassed a great deal of land.]

(*L* 7090–8)

The legal importance of the story is already there in Geoffrey where Hengist asks for the amount of land he can encircle with a 'thong' cut from a bull's skin [una corrigia], but then chooses a spot 'with the greatest possible cunning' [maxima cautela] and builds a fortress.[53]

---

[53] Geoffrey of Monmouth, *Historia regum Britannie*, I, ed. Wright, §99 (p. 67); *History of the Kings of Britain*, trans. Thorpe, 159.

Wace sees (or brings out more clearly) the historical truth inherent in the terms of the narrative, for he makes the trick more elaborate by having Hengist ask for the amount of land he can 'cover' with a 'hide' (or 'un quir de tor', W 6907), which he then cuts up into a 'thong' [une cureie, W 6914], securing much more land for the Saxon settlement than the British had meant to grant. But it is left to La3amon's English to make the story a proper *etymologia*—to discover the word 'hude' [hide] in the hide Hengist cut up—and therefore to notice that the point of the connection is that a jurisdiction comes into existence *as the contours of the land are mapped*, that *chorographia* is legal making because the shape of the land not only produces the law (as a kind of projection) but it *is* that law (in so far as that shape is the idea, which, in the context of the law, is called, say, the 'hide'). Therefore, to whatever extent British history is a map it is not only interested in the land but constituted by the very law which constitutes the land's meaning.

CONQUEST AS CONSOLATION

Such a thought is immanent in La3amon's *Brut*—as the set of ideas its structure has—but it is also attributed by that structure (as if to help in focusing and introducing these complex principles to any reader) to a figure who is invented to *have* such thoughts in the making of the poem. This is not La3amon (some historical person to whom other devices or records attribute it), but 'La3amon', an author-function we know nothing of outside this *Brut*, who is confected in its very first line ('An preost wes on leoden, La3amon wes ihoten' [There was a priest in the land who was called La3amon', *L* 1]). Although such a figure is a standard feature of the *Brut* story ('Geoffrey of Monmouth' and 'Wace' exist in just this way) and, 'La3amon's' role is only implicit in what follows (we do not hear about him after this prologue), the initiating activities of this man are such that they extend his presence through the whole of what follows. Where 'Geoffrey' and 'Wace' are presented (or present themselves) as translators,[54] 'La3amon' is a

---

[54] 'Codicem illum in Latinum sermonem transferre curaui' [I have taken the trouble to translate the book into Latin . . .], Geoffrey of Monmouth, *Historia regum Britannie*, I, ed. Wright, §2 (p. 1); Geoffrey of Monmouth, *The History of the Kings of Britain*, trans. Thorpe, 51.
   'Ki vult oïr e vult saveir | De rei en rei e d'eir en eir | Ki cil furent e dunt il vindrent | Ki Engleterre primes tindrent, | Quels reis i ad en ordre eü, | E qui anceis e ki puis fu, |

thinker ('hit com him on mode, and on his mern þonke' [it came into his mind, an excellent thought of his, *L* 6]), and, in precise anticipation of the formal result, 'La3amon's' thinking takes the form of a journey through the land:

> La3amon gon liðen   wide 3ond þas leode,
> and biwon þa æðela boc   þa he to bisne nom.

(La3amon travelled far and wide throughout this land, and obtained the excellent books which he took as a model.)

(*L* 14–15)

What 'La3amon' seeks with such thinking is, moreover, the truth ('þa soþere word' [the truthful words, *L* 27]). It is therefore hardly surprising that the power of this figure has also been greater than comparable textual effects: it is true that we also believe 'Geoffrey of Monmouth' and 'Wace' existed, but criticism of this *Brut* has represented itself, with surprising frequency, as an attempt to understand not the poem, but its poet. And what has seemed most provoking about 'La3amon' is that his very existence implies that all the conflicting positions and attitudes the English *Brut* adopts can be compassed from a single perspective (accommodated in the single purpose of one intelligence), and, as a result, his 'character' has absorbed all the faults of his poem (in so far as it is confused), and it is this man, not this *Brut*, which has traditionally required 'vindication'.[55]

Despite such fervent attention to this figure, however, it has never seemed relevant that the name 'La3amon' means something, and that what it means is 'man of law'—that a poem which mentions the law so often (if nothing else about its jurisprudential structure were noticed) mentions it first as the property of a person.[56] Tatlock noticed the word's meaning long ago, but he treated it as a fossilized

---

Maistre Wace l'ad translaté | Ki en conte la verité' [Whoever wishes to hear and to know about the successive kings and their heirs who once upon a time were the rulers of England—who they were, whence they came, what was their sequence, who came earlier and who later—Master Wace has translated it and tells it truthfully, *W* 1–8].

[55] See G. J. Visser, *La3amon: An Attempt at Vindication* (Assen: Van Gorcum, 1935), esp. 92–4.

[56] On such anagrammatic self-naming in *Piers Plowman* see Anne Middleton, 'William Langland's "Kynde Name": Authorial Signature and Social Identity in Late Fourteenth-Century England', 15–82 in *Literary Practice and Social Change in Britain, 1380–1530*, ed. Lee Patterson (Berkeley: University of California Press, 1990), esp. 42–54 and 81–2.

professional cognomen, even though he also knew that there were
still 'lawmen' active in some parts of thirteenth-century England (a
'survey of hundreds' by Edward I refers to twelve men of Lincolnshire
as 'lagemanni' in 1275).[57] Even if the word was as old-fashioned
as Tatlock believed, moreover, such an antiquarianism is precisely
'Laȝamon's' style, for the poem's language is full of compounds
which had not been recorded in centuries, as well as new words
created by Old English methods of compounding.[58] The poem itself
may seem to bar 'Laȝamon' from any legal profession, since it gives
him a different job when it calls him a 'priest'; and yet, just like the
law he carefully describes, this priest resides '*in* the land' [on leoden,
L 1], and most men of law in the thirteenth century were priests.[59]
'Laȝamon' is therefore not only a thoughtful presence, but a presence whose very form is determined by the same thoughts as 'his'
poem; 'he' is, in this sense, yet another method for re-enforcing and
emphasizing the larger form's most important contours. It is in this
sense too that 'Laȝamon' associates the larger form with yet another
one, that personal search through the world for truth which Boethius
called the *consolatio*.

Though the form of Boethius's *Consolation of Philosophy* (c.522–4)
may seem to have little in common with the form of Laȝamon's *Brut*,
it also begins with an embedded author-function, and 'Boethius'
is also represented as searching for 'the resplendent light of truth'

[57] See *Rotuli Hundredorum*, ed. W. Illingworth and J. Caley, 2 vols. (London:
Record Commission, 1812–18), 1: 352. For other 'lagemanni' mentioned in this survey see 1: 354 and 1: 356. For still more evidence see J. S. P. Tatlock, *The Legendary
History of Britain* (Berkeley: University of California Press, 1950), 513–14 and
nn. 124–34.
[58] The language of Laȝamon's *Brut* is unusual as it employs, on the one hand,
nominal compounds that had become rare in Middle English (that is, antiquated
compounds characteristic of Old English poetry) and, on the other hand, compounds
unattested in other Middle English texts (that is, nonce compounds coined in imitation
of Old English poetic practice). Oakden notes that, of the 411 nominal compounds
Laȝamon uses, 183 are found in Old English and 228 are not. He suggests that, in
the latter case, Laȝamon made up most of the words (*Alliterative Poetry in Middle
English*, 2: 130–3).
[59] See R. H. Hilton, *A Medieval Society: The West Midlands at the End of the
Thirteenth Century* (New York: Wiley, 1966), 65. It is also significant here that in
Domesday Book, above the names of three of the twelve 'lageman' described in the city
of Lincoln, the scribe writes 'presbyter'. See *Domesday Book*, ed. John Morris, vol. 31,
part 1 (Lincolnshire), ed. Philip Morgan and Caroline Thorn (Chichester: Phillimore,
1986), C2 and S5.

[splendor verae lucis].⁶⁰ What the older text makes clearer than the *Brut*, however, is that 'gentle remedies' [fomenta lena, I.pr6.12–13/52] only come in such a search to the extent that it fully and passionately documents—and therefore inhabits—a problem: it is only because 'Boethius' is so thoroughly defeated by the 'severity of Fortune's attack' [fortunae saevientis asperitas, I.pr4.2–3/41] that he finally succeeds in discovering 'the supreme good and perfect happiness' [summum bonum plenamque beatitudinem, III.pr12.27–8/112]; it is only because Philosophy uses 'Fortune's own arguments' [Fortunae ipsius verbis, II.pr2.5–6/56] that her solutions so fully answer to the demands which prompted them ('with one internal proof grafted upon another so that each drew its credibility from that which preceded' [ex altero altero fidem trahente insitis domesticisque probationibus, III.pr12.7–8/113]). More clear in the Latin *consolatio* is that such solutions come, first, by means of a better apprehension of form, by understanding that a wheel whose turns always disrupt the world is nonetheless ordering that world by the inevitability of its disruptions ('in the very act of changing she has preserved her own particular kind of constancy towards you' [servavit circa te propriam potius in ipsa sui mutabilitate constantiam, II.pr1.18–20/55]). But, second, this acuity is itself a product of perceiving the exact correspondence between what had seemed to be two different forms—of understanding that Fortune's implacable and troublesome 'wheel' [rota, II.pr1.19/56], because crafted by (indeed shaped after the model of) God, is also a 'circle of divine simplicity' [divinae simplicitatis orbis, III.pr12.24/112]. As Elaine Scarry has shown, such a formal reciprocity is not only part of the propositional wisdom purveyed by the Latin *consolatio*, it is also its own 'final shape': the 'wheel' of disorder is seen to be equivalent to the divine 'circle' at the very centre of the circle traced by this text (the end of book 3), for, at that point, books 4 and 5 turn back to problems, and the text finally concludes with queries that would lead us right back to the beginning of the text—if we let them.⁶¹

⁶⁰ Boethius, *Philosophiae consolationis liber quinque*, ed. Karl Büchner (Heidelberg: Carl Winter, 1977), I.pr6.14; Boethius, *The Consolation of Philosophy*, trans. V. E. Watts (Harmondsworth: Penguin, 1969), 52. Hereafter citations to this edition and translation will be given in the text in the following form: book, metre or prose, line in Büchner edition/page number of Watts translation.

⁶¹ Elaine Scarry, 'The Well-Rounded Sphere: Cognition and Metaphysical Structure in Boethius's *Consolation of Philosophy*', 143–80 in *Resisting Representation* (Oxford: Oxford University Press, 1994), esp. 176.

The *chorographia* of the *Brut* is also a *consolatio* in so far as it discovers comfort in the land, but it only discovers that comfort to the extent that the land limits depredation and disaster, that its constitutive stabilities are defined by (are, in effect, brought into *being* by) the continuous onslaught of conquest. For one could also say of the resulting shape in Laȝamon's *Brut*—whether we call it 'þis lond' or 'the law'—that it is only stable because almost everything else changes around it. It is the resulting disproportion between problem and solution which such illustration requires—the former invested in the style of every single line of the poem, the latter resident in long arcs of repetition and subtle patterns of emphasis—which explains why so many readers have seen this *Brut* as nothing but a problem. But such a poem is also a *consolatio* because it is in the nature of this form to be misread in just this way. It is 'Fortune's wheel rather than the well-rounded sphere [which is] the image most often associated with the *Consolation*', according to Scarry, because we 'neglect . . . the work's structure'.[62] And it is for this same reason that we see Laȝamon's *Brut* as 'about' a disorder which reigns over and among people rather than the order such persons borrow from the structure which enriches them in every other way. It is not, then, that the poem says something entirely different than we have known, but that it knows more about what it says than we have ever allowed ourselves to recognize. Its powerful account of human changefulness is searching and, in its own way, deeply despairing, but in the map which comes from such a search, this form finds the thought which mitigates despair, the idea that constitutionalists have since taught us to regard as proverbial, 'the law of the land'.

[62] Ibid. 176.

3
Right Writing: The *Ormulum*

> What we say about words, in the empirical realm, will bear a
> notable likeness to what is said about God, in theology.
>
> (Kenneth Burke)

When the man who calls himself 'Orm' wants to write he looks down
like Laȝamon, but he looks less far; before his eyes reach the land
beneath his feet, they light on the manuscript pages in front of him,
and he uses this more proximate, and equally solid, surface as the
foundation for the text he calls the *Ormulum* (*c*.1180).[1] The book he
is looking at, the results make clear, contains the Gospels, and the
parchment and letter shapes he works up into the materials of his
own practice are the more firm *and* the more abstract because such
words are also 'The Word', embodiments as well as representations
of God. It has generally been recognized that Orm derives his authority and self-importance from such letters, but it is usually claimed
that he uses them (with the assistance of a few other texts such as
the *Glossa ordinaria*) to piece out no more than a set of homilies, or
a sermon, or, at most, the first 'life of Christ' in English.[2] What I wish
to suggest in this chapter, however, is that, embedded in these very
words, Orm finds an injunction to make writing the form of a life, as

---

[1] For the *Ormulum*'s date and provenance see M. B. Parkes, 'On the Presumed
Date and Possible Origin of the Manuscript of the "Ormulum": Oxford, Bodleian
Library, MS Junius 1', 115–27 in *Five Hundred Years of Words and Sounds:
A Festschrift for Eric Dobson*, ed. E. G. Stanley and Douglas Gray (Cambridge:
D. S. Brewer, 1983).

[2] For a full history of such lives in English and the *Ormulum*'s place in it, see
Elizabeth Salter, 'Nicholas Love's "Myrrour of the Blessed Lyf of Jesu Christ"',
Analecta Cartusiana 10 (1974), esp. 78–81. The classic account of Orm's sources is
Heinrich C. Matthes, *Die Einheitlichkeit des Orrmulum: Studien zur Textkritik, zu
den Quellen und zur sprachlichen Form von Orrmins Evangelienbuch* (Heidelberg:
Carl Winter, 1933). But see also two articles by Stephen Morrison, 'Sources for the
Ormulum: A Re-examination', *Neuphilologische Mitteilungen* 84 (1983), 419–36
and 'New Sources for the *Ormulum*', *Neophilologus* 68 (1984), 444–50.

if the making of letters were itself a mode of devotion perfectible to the extent that writing could fill the activity of living.[3]

Such seriousness of purpose has been difficult to detect, because, at first blush, the *Ormulum* looks like the product of someone who could get nothing right. His poem survives in only a single manuscript (Oxford, MS Bodleian Library, Junius 1) which is a hodgepodge of scraped out letters, belated additions, and cancelled passages, a 'workshop draft' in which Orm and an assistant working under his close direction first copied out a portion of a text, and then made repeated passes through it, trying to iron out exceptions, irregularities, and mistakes—but always discovering and making more errors in the process.[4] As a result, although Orm assembled 242 Gospel texts, he managed to translate and write homilies for only thirty-two of them.[5] Orm's obsessions are also responsible for a manuscript page that is almost impossible to read, and even what can be made out is full of 'tedious repetitions, cumbersome conjunctions and otiose adverbs'.[6] The whole performance is so beleaguered, in fact, that, as Geoffrey Shepherd put it, Orm seems most like 'a diligent and

---

[3] Although her interests are more specifically in the form and function of 'literary signature' at the end of the 14th c., Anne Middleton understands *Piers Plowman* as just this sort of practice, a 'life-work', or 'the usable form of a life remembered'. See 'William Langland's "Kynde Name": Authorial Signature and Social Identity in Late Fourteenth-Century England', 15–82 in *Literary Practice and Social Change in Britain, 1380–1530*, ed. Lee Patterson (Berkeley: University of California Press, 1990), esp. 24–37 (quotations from 37).

[4] On the state of the manuscript and its revisions see J. E. Turville-Petre, 'Studies on the *Ormulum* MS', *Journal of English and Germanic Philology* 46 (1947), 1–27; and R. W. Burchfield, 'The Language and Orthography of the *Ormulum* MS', *Transactions of the Philological Society* (1956), 56–87. Burchfield uses the phrase 'workshop draft' (57).

[5] The Gospel texts are listed (on unnumbered pages) after the 'Dedication' at the beginning of *The Ormulum*, ed. Robert Holt, notes and glossary by R. M. White, 2 vols. (Oxford: Clarendon Press, 1878). For a table of the homilies Orm completed see this edition, pp. lxxxii–lxxxvii. Hereafter references will be to this edition and cited by line number in the text. Lines marked '*D*' are taken from the separately lineated 'Dedication', and lines marked *P* from the separately lineated 'Preface', both of which precede the main text. Burchfield believes that 'it is relatively certain' that the *Ormulum* was once a 'complete work' and that 'if the lost portions were carried out on the same scale as the part that survives, [it] ran once to some 160,000 lines of verse' ('Language and Orthography', 58). As evidence of this he notes extracts from portions of the text that are now wanting which were copied by the 16th-c. owner of the manuscript, Jan van Vliet (d. 1666). For these extracts see N. R. Ker, 'Unpublished Parts of the *Ormulum* printed from MS. Lambeth 783', *MÆ* 9 (1940), 1–22.

[6] *Early Middle English Verse and Prose*, ed. J. A. W. Bennett and G. V. Smithers, with a glossary by Norman Davis, 2nd edn. (Oxford: Oxford University Press, 1968), 174.

ingenious missionary in foreign parts struggling to put Scripture for the first time into a barbarous tongue'.[7]

Even such a criticism registers Orm's most obvious competence, however: he could not have so struggled with English had he not already been learned enough to know Latin. As has been more recently suggested, Orm is not entirely without English learning either, since the style of his poem seems to betray some familiarity with the 'conventional homiletic phraseology' of the Old English tradition.[8] And any attempt to dismiss the *Ormulum* must reckon with the fact that Orm himself regarded it as exemplary, writing which was not only 'right', but whose excellence was self-evident:

> Loke he well þatt het write swa,
>   Forr he ne maȝȝ nohht elless
> Onn Ennglissh writtenn rihht te word,
>   Þatt wite he wel to soþe.

[He should look well that he writes (this poem) in this way for he may not write the word right in another way in English, and that he should well know to be true.]

(D 107–10)

As even these few lines themselves make clear, moreover, Orm's writing was the result of an eccentric and elaborate system. Consonants are doubled following short vowels when that consonant is the last one in the word or followed by another consonant (so 'onn' where most contemporaneous writers would write 'on'; 'Ennglissh' instead of 'English'). Word shapes are also regularized across the whole length of the poem ('onn' is always 'onn' and 'Ennglissh' always 'Ennglissh', whenever these words recur). Finally, lines of verse are precisely syllabic (either fifteen syllables per line, if the poem is printed as long lines, or eight followed by seven syllables per half-line as in the standard edition and my quotations here), and they therefore eschew rhyme, any accentual pattern, and alliteration.[9] In a

---

[7] Geoffrey Shepherd, 'Early Middle English', 81–117 in *The Middle Ages*, ed. W. F. Bolton (London: Sphere, 1970), 115.

[8] Stephen Morrison, 'Orm's English Sources', *Archiv für das Studium der Neueren Sprachen (und Literaturen)* 221 (1984), 55.

[9] On some possible Latin models for Orm's practice see Elizabeth Solopova, 'The Metre of the *Ormulum*', 423–39 in *Studies in English Language and Literature: 'Doubt Wisely', Papers in Honour of E. G. Stanley*, ed. M. J. Toswell and E. M. Tyler (London: Routledge, 1996), esp. 428–31.

period in which writing in English has been described as 'lawless', Orm is a man committed to complex laws—but according to no known jurisprudence.[10]

The principles of Orm's method are not set out as a rationale or explained in any conventional sense, but embedded in practices and outcomes, even in the 'infinite tedium' which his writing produces.[11] This is in part because the 'intransigence' of a style—the extent to which it is 'obscure and cumbersome, indigestible'—is necessarily a demand on thought, a mode of resistance to our wish to pass through a set of words to the meaning located behind them, a formal insistence on the 'materiality of language' itself, which annexes to any meaning both the limits and governing conditions of the shapes which are conveying it.[12] In the case of the *Ormulum* such limits and conditions include the difficulty of recognizing words rendered in such redoubled orthography, the otiose verbiage produced by a versification predicated on filler, and that enormous (and endless) failure of rigour which often makes it hard to know exactly what Orm's rules are. To the extent that such writing insists that it be read, but then proves so resistible that readers will prefer to read as little of it as they can (as Pearsall put it, 'the first line will speak for all'), this is a poem which suggests, above all, that its meanings can only be gleaned at some cost.[13] To the extent that such writing understands itself to be perfect, and yet seems to err so much, it also suggests that the price we will pay for understanding it is the recognition that much that *we* have believed to be 'right' is wrong.

This chapter attempts to explain how the writing of the *Ormulum* can be so impertinent, so brave, and, finally, so insightful. My explanation falls into two halves, the first elaborating the ideas which have caused Orm to shape the *Ormulum*'s words and lines in this unique way, the second showing how such ideas unfold in the strange and elaborate shape that is this remarkable poem. It is inevitable, I think, that, given the extent to which such explanations find sense in what

---

[10] On the 'lawless' English of this time see *Havelok the Dane*, ed. Kenneth Sisam, 2nd edn. (Oxford: Clarendon Press, 1915), p. xxxvii. Cited in James Milroy, 'Middle English Dialectology', 156–206 in *The Cambridge History of the English Language*, vol. 2, ed. Norman Blake (Cambridge: Cambridge University Press, 1994), 193.

[11] Derek Pearsall, *Old English and Middle English Poetry* (London: Routledge & Kegan Paul, 1977), 102.

[12] Fredric Jameson, *Marxism and Form: Twentieth-Century Dialectical Theories of Literature* (Princeton: Princeton University Press, 1971), p. xiii.

[13] Pearsall, *Old English and Middle English Poetry*, 102.

has been so generally derided, my account will seem to credit Orm with far too much. But another of the *Ormulum*'s claims to fame may be that it proves better than almost any other text that a form can be smarter than its maker. If Kenneth Burke is right that talking about writing is like talking about God, then Orm is simply benefiting from the converse: his passionate attempts to write about God produce an extraordinary account of the nature of *writing*.[14]

SPELLING PRACTICE

Of course the word Orm gives to what he is doing is not 'writing' but 'spelling', although this verb had a much broader meaning for him than it retains for us. In the thirteenth century the verb *spellen* still preserved the sense of its Old English root (*spellian* or *spillian*) and meant 'to talk or speak', 'to tell a story', and, as emerging from this last meaning, 'to preach'.[15] It is this last and more specific sense which is the fundamental meaning of the term for Orm, as, for example, when he translates the rebuke Jesus delivers to Nicodemus, the Pharisee: 'To fulle soþ I segge þe, | We spellenn þatt we cunnenn, | & tatt we sæȝhenn opennliȝ' [I tell you truly that we preach what we know and what we see openly, 16684–6].[16] It was not until late in the fourteenth century that *spellen* generally acquired the modern meaning 'to set out by letters', and this seems to have occurred not simply by a semantic shift, but by a convergent derivation of the same form (*spellen*) from Old French *espelir* (or Anglo-Norman *espeleir*).[17] Ambiguity was clearly possible for some time, however, since the

[14] Kenneth Burke, *The Rhetoric of Religion: Studies in Logology* (Berkeley: University of California Press, 1970), 13–14.

[15] See *MED*, s.v. 'spellen v1'.

[16] The passage in question is John 3: 11: 'Truly, truly, I say to you, we speak of what we know, and bear witness to what we know, and bear witness to what we have seen; but you do not receive our testimony' ('Amen, Amen dico tibi, quia quod scimus loquimur, et quod vidimus testamur, et testimonium nostrum non accipitis').

[17] See *MED*, s.v. 'spellen v2'. In its earlier uses this word meant 'to read and write laboriously' or 'to mean'. The *MED* combines 'to read or write by spelling out letters' and 'to read or write laboriously' under the same sub-heading ('c'). The earliest example given of the term with this modern sense is in the English gloss (*c*.1333) to *Le Traité de Walter de Bibbesworth* (where 'espau naturement ki les lettres ensemble prent' is glossed as 'spelieth'). The first recorded use of 'spellen' in an English sentence is John of Trevisa's translation of Ranulph Higden's *Polychronicon* (*c*.1387): 'Lanfranc was war þat þe man couþe wel nygh riȝt nouȝt, and took hym a þing wiþ letter for to spel.'

use of *spellen* to refer to 'preaching' does not wholly vanish from the record until the sixteenth century.[18] This linguistic history has itself hidden the exceptional nature of Orm's 'spelling' however, because Orm equates 'preaching' with the setting out of letters. This is not itself news about the *Ormulum*; the unusual orthography of the poem has always been thought to be a kind of phonetic script designed to help other preachers read it out in later times; its letters offer a 'key to pronunciation' for those who may have been 'more used to Latin than English'.[19] But such explanations have never been able to account for the phonological ambiguities of Orm's system (since neither long vowels nor short vowels in open syllables are marked, it has not been clear to philologists how Orm pronounced most words), nor does phoneticism explain the extraordinary effort taken to regularize these new and unfamiliar forms (since even Orm's regular orthography had many letters which expressed the same sound, 'ð' and 'þ' for example, irregularity would still allow for perfect phoneticism).[20] In fact, the connection between writing and devotion lies at a much deeper level; indeed, it is only discoverable to the extent that we abandon any search for ostensive purposes and look for what Bourdieu has called a *habitus*, that set of 'principles which generate and organize practices and representations' without any 'conscious aiming at ends' or even 'a mastery of the operations necessary in order to attain [those ends]'.[21] Orm may mean only 'preaching' when he uses the word *spellen*, in other words, but to the extent that he means making a poem like the *Ormulum* when he means 'preaching', all the procedures of his writing are attached to this larger devotional purpose. If Orm is not everywhere clear about the larger attachment, its most important constituent parts can be discovered by recessing ever more deeply back through

[18] See *OED*, s.v. 'spell vi.' (marked as 'Obs' and adduced no later than 1530).
[19] Pearsall, *Old English and Middle English Poetry*, 102.
[20] Short vowels in open syllables are therefore sometimes marked with a superscript '˘' (e.g. 'hĕre sinne' [their sins], D 86), although this practice is inconsistent. For an excellent summary of the nature of Orm's system as well as an argument that doubled letters indicate 'syllable final sounds' see Robert D. Stevick, 'Plus Juncture and the Spelling of the *Ormulum*', *Journal of English and Germanic Philology* 64 (1965), 84–9. For a summary of the debate over this question and the argument that Orm's doublings indicate 'syllable boundaries' see Robert D. Fulk, 'Consonant Doubling and Open Syllable Lengthening in the *Ormulum*', *Anglia* 114 (1996), 481–513.
[21] Pierre Bourdieu, *The Logic of Practice*, trans. Richard Nice (Cambridge: Polity Press, 1990), 53.

the results of his practice to discover, not so much what Orm thought, but the thinking that impelled what he did.

The most obvious way in which Orm signalled his deep concern for orthography was to invent a term to refer to 'spelling' when he *only* meant 'to set out by letters'. For the first time in English (and for the last time for some centuries) Orm uses a derivation of *espelir* (in the variant form *espeldre*) to coin the word *spelldrenn* when he wants to describe the shape of a particular word: 'Adamess name Adam iss all | Wiþþ fowwre stafess spelldredd' [Adam's name 'Adam' is spelled out with four letters, 16346–7].[22] The specificity and regularity of Orm's orthography is itself a crucial pendant to this invention, since it not only allowed Orm to keep this form of letters distinct from *spellen*, once he had it, but it marked out a conceptual space in which he could embrace orthography as a word-making activity allied with, but separate from, the other word-making activities subsumed under the verb *spellen* (story-telling, preaching, meaning), and from which he could absorb orthography to the practices he thought of as 'preaching'. For, as Orm discovered, once it was 'spelled out' the composite structure of a word such as 'Adam' provided a tool for explaining Adam's significance in scriptural terms (in this case, as the four letters of his name correspond to the four parts of the earth from which he sprang):

> Þe firrste staff iss nemmnedd A
>   Onn ure Latin spæche;
> Þatt oþerr staff iss nemmnedd DE;
>   Þe þridde iss A ȝehatenn;
> Þe ferþe staff iss nemmnedd EMM
>   Onn ure Latin spæche.
> & ȝiff þatt tu cannst spelldrenn hemm,
>   Adam þu findesst spelldredd,
> Þe name off þallre firrste mann
>   Þatt shapenn wass off erþe,
> Þatt name þatt himm ȝifenn wass
>   Þurrh Drihhtin, forr to tacnenn,
> Þatt all hiss offspring shollde ben
>   Todrifenn & toskeȝȝredd
> Inn all þiss middellærd tatt iss
>   O fowwre daless dæledd.

[22] This use is not related to 'spellen v2' in the *MED* because these lines of the *Ormulum* are cited separately (s.v. 'speldren v.') and associated only with two 15th-c. texts that also use a 'd' in their forms.

[The first letter is named 'A' in our Latin language; the next letter is named 'D'; the third is called 'A'; the fourth letter is named 'M' in our Latin language. And if you can spell them, you find 'Adam' spelled [thus], the name of the first man who was shaped from earth, the name that was given to him by God in order to signify that all his offspring would be driven off and scattered through this middle earth which is divided into four parts.]

(16434–49)

Such a technique could be seen to exploit orthography opportunistically, but the interest in, and knowledge of, word shapes is also a legitimate method for investigating the sense of words (i.e. it combines those branches of philology we call morphology and etymology), and it was through just such a precocious interest in word parts and their significance that Orm found a demand for word-making in the verb *spellen* itself. This important point emerges the first time Orm explains why he has made 'this book':

> Icc hafe sammnedd o þiss boc
>> Þa Goddspelles neh alle,
> Þatt sinndenn o þe messeboc
>> Inn all þe ȝer att messe.
> & aȝȝ affterr þe Goddspell stannt
>> Þatt tatt te Goddspell meneþþ
> Þatt mann birrþ spellenn to þe follc
>> Off þeȝȝre sawle nede.

[I have gathered together in this book nearly all of the Gospels as they are in the mass-book [and said] throughout the year in the Mass. And they are faithful to the Gospels, according to their meaning, as one ought to preach (spell) to people for the good of their souls.]

(D 28–36)

Here, preaching is not only defined as writing (or 'gathering together in a book') because the truths which it promulgates originated in a book (the 'messeboc'), but because the name of that book also demands more words: such insistence originates, not only in the view that the book is edifying or 'good' (that it is a '*Godd*spel', worth copying again), but that it is itself already a collection of words, a 'Godd*spel*'. Orm is faithful to the book before him ('aȝȝ affterr þe Goddspell stannt') not only because he repeats its meanings, then, but because, by preaching it, he 'spells' a 'spel' ('mann birrþ spellenn to þe follc'). What such a practice knows best of all, in other words, is that the word *spellen* was derived from the word *spell*.[23]

---

[23] For this etymology of 'gospel' see *OED*, s.v. 'gospel n.'. For the derivation of 'spellen' from the noun 'spell' see *OED*, s.v. 'spell v1'.

Even such an important gleaning from a particular word shape was only a particular instance of an entire verbal epistemology in which such shapes were always held to be knowledgeable, since words were the principal instruments of knowing. For any Christian thinker, such a stance is only one important implication of the claim, at the beginning of the Gospel of John, that God was 'the Word' ('In principio erat Verbum et Verbum erat apud Deum et Deus erat Verbum' ['In the beginning was the Word, and the Word was with God, and the Word was God'] (John 1: 1)) As Marcia Colish has shown, the writings of Augustine had taught the Middle Ages that, on this basis, knowledge was 'fundamentally verbal' and 'all cognitive intermediaries between God and man' were 'modes of verbal expression'.[24] Of course, in a theology where words were such significant tools, care for words could easily usurp the place of the knowledge those words were supposed to communicate. As Augustine also noted the very care with which human words were made—our rules of grammar and habits of orthography—sometimes took the place of a comparable precision about divine precepts:

Look, Lord God, look with patience as you always do. See the exact care with which the sons of men observe the conventions of letters and syllables received from those who so talked before them. Yet they neglect the eternal contracts of lasting salvation received from you.[25]

On the other hand, as Augustine also made clear, words offered an opportunity to register the constraints of earthliness and therefore to make our knowledge more alert to human limitations. In this way, the opening lines of the Gospel of John could be taken to insist that orthography was a good way to recognize the role of temporality in

---

[24] Marcia L. Colish, *The Mirror of Language: A Study in the Medieval Theory of Knowledge*. rev. edn. (Lincoln: University of Nebraska Press, 1983), 44.

[25] 'Vide, domine deus meus, et patienter, ut vides, vide, quomodo diligenter observent filii hominum pacta litterarum et syllabarum accepta a prioribus locutoribus, et a te accepta aeterna pacta perpetuae salutis neglegant', Augustine, *Confessions*, trans. William Watts, 2 vols. (Cambridge, Mass.: Harvard University Press, 1912; repr. 1995), I. xviii. I take my translation from Augustine, *Confessions* trans. Henry Chadwick (Oxford: Oxford University Press, 1991) I. xviii (p. 21).
Augustine continues here: 'This has gone to such lengths that if someone, who is educated in or is a teacher of the old conventional sounds, pronounces the word "human" contrary to the school teaching, without pronouncing the initial aspirate, he is socially censured more than if, contrary to your precepts, he were to hate a human being, his fellow-man' [ut qui illa sonorum vetera placita teneat aut doceat, si contra disciplinam grammaticam sine adspiratione primae syllabae hominem dixerit, magis displiceat hominibus, quam si contra tua praecepta hominem oderit, cum sit homo].

human knowing, that the very spelling of a word letter by letter ('the second after the first, the third after the second, and so on in order' [secunda post primam, tertia post secundam atque inde ex ordine]) is an instance of how human knowledge only exists in some sequence.[26] Such attention to the physical limitations of word-making also provided some basis for imagining God's perfection as a better sort of spelling:

You call us, therefore, to understand the Word, God who is with you God (John 1: 1). That word is spoken eternally, and by it all things are uttered eternally. It is not the case that what was being said comes to an end, and something else is then said, so that everything is uttered in a succession with a conclusion, but everything is said in the simultaneity of eternity.[27]

In this sense, words were epistemologically valuable not only for what they could help us to know, but what, in their very form, they could help us to understand about human knowing.

Orm's embrace of this epistemology is thoroughly Augustinian, but the particular inflection he gives to its procedures is indicated by the text he takes for his homily on the subject, not the first verse of the Gospel of John, but the fourteenth, in which the verbal nature of God is expanded to include Christ and the incarnation ('Et Verbum caro factum est, et habitavit in nobis' [And the Word was made flesh, and dwelt among us, John 1: 14]). For Orm, such relations make all knowledge verbal, but, since Christ in such an account is not only God made flesh but an *utterance*—not only God's 'Son' but a speech act—precisely as he is the Word, he is the product of a divine act of *spelling*:[28]

> All þatt depe & dærne witt
> Þatt iss i Godess herrte
> Iss Godess Sune, & Godess Word,
> & Godess dærne spæche.

---

[26] Augustine, *Confessions*, XI.vi. and trans. Chadwick, XI.vi (p. 225).

[27] 'Vocas itaque nos ad intellegendum verbum, deum apud te deum, quod sempiterne dicitur et eo sempiterne dicuntur omnia. Neque enim finitur, quod dicebatur, et dicitur aliud, ut possint dici omnia, sed simul ac sempiterne omnia', Augustine, *Confessions*, XI.vii. and trans. Chadwick, XI.vii (p. 226).

[28] For the extant part of Orm's homily on this text (the beginning is wanting) see lines 18492–9550. On this analogy see Burke, *Rhetoric of Religion*, 11–16. In addition to the Biblical texts I cite here Burke mentions Revelation 19: 12–13 ('And he had a name written, that no man knew, but he himself. . . . And his name is called the Word of God') and the First Epistle of John 5: 7 ('For there are three that bear record in heaven, the Father, the Word, and the Holy Ghost: and these three are one').

[All the deep and subtle thought that is in God's heart is God's son and God's
Word, and God's subtle speech.]

(18493–6)

As Orm pressed upon this analogy, moreover, Christ's meaning was
discovered to be 'subtle' [dærne] because such a divine 'Word' does
not unfold letter by letter as human words do, but in the shape of the
'deeds' that constitute the whole of a (not incidentally 'right') 'life':

> He wrohhte miccle tacness,
> & talde spell amang þe follc
>   Off þeʒʒre sawle nede,
> & off þatt miccle sellþe & sel,
>   Þatt enngleþed inn heffne
> Wiþþ Godd, all þurrh þe ʒife off Godd,
>   A butenn ende brukenn
> & all hiss lare & all hiss lif
>   & all hiss hallʒhe dede
> Droh till þatt an, to turrnenn follc
>   Inntill þe rihhte weʒʒe,
> Till fulluhht, & till Crisstenndom,
>   & till þe rihhte læfe.

[(Christ) worked many miracles and told many stories among the people for
the good of their souls, and the great blessing and wealth that the angels enjoy
in heaven with God, all through the gift of God, without end. And all his
teaching, and all his life, and all his holy deeds were to that end, to turn people
to the right way, to baptism, and to Christendom, and to the right belief.]

(17893–905)

'Spelling' is the 'right' form of Christian teaching, not only because it
produces knowledge of a verbal God in verbal form, but because it
converts 'the Word' into a 'way' ('weʒʒe'), because it makes the act of
understanding or knowing an act of 'spelling'. It is important in this
sense that Christ was himself a 'speller' ('talde spell amang þe follc'),
that the rightness of his own living converted the knowledge embedded in his actions into the activity (and form of knowing) which is the
making of words. This meant that 'spelling' (in *all* of its senses) was
the most accurate form in which to know God's Word (in all *its*
senses) because 'spelling' was the form of doing which constituted
that knowledge.

As Wittgenstein would later put the larger point, since 'words can
be wrung from us,—like a cry', since, in fact, 'words can be *hard*

to say', 'words are also deeds'.[29] Expanding on this insight Orm developed what could be called the labour theory of spelling, which is why he usually refers to his own production, not as a 'spel' or a 'boc', but as a 'deed' ('Icc hafe don þiss dede', D 112). It is on these grounds too that Orm's preaching is everywhere marked as an activity of word-making, that is effortful, not only 'right' because it is 'spelling' or because it is a form of doing, but, because in the nature of the orthography employed, it is *double* the effort that simply telling the words of God would otherwise be:

> & whase wilenn shall þiss boc
>   Efft oþerr siþe writenn,
> Himm bidde icc þatt het write rihht,
>   Swa summ þiss boc himm tæcheþþ,
> All þwerrt ut affterr þatt itt iss
>   Uppo þiss firrste bisne,
> Wiþþ all swillc rime alls her iss sett,
>   Wiþþ all se fele wordess;
> & tatt he loke wel þatt he
>   An bocstaff write twiȝȝess,
> Eȝȝwhær þær itt uppo þiss boc
>   Iss writenn o þatt wise.

[And whoever wants to write this book again, another time, I ask him to write it correctly, as this book so teaches, all throughout just as it is in this first example, with all such rhyme as is used here, and with all its many words, and that he look carefully to write every letter twice, everywhere that it is so written in this book.]

(D 95–106)

In so far as such a theory of practice also holds that the more you work the righter you are—that to use 'many words' [fele wordess] or to 'write every letter twice' [an bocstaff write twiȝȝess] is to be righter than to use few words or to write letters once—such a writing is also 'right' to the extent that it involves more doing. This is why, apropos of nothing (and, in vain, as it happens), Orm imagines that his own long and difficult book will naturally find someone who wants to write it again ('wilenn shall þiss boc | Efft oþerr siþe writenn'). It is for this reason, too, that Orm imagines that, just as his own spelling perfectly reflects the actions described in the Gospels, his own actions

---

[29] Ludwig Wittgenstein, *Philosophical Investigations*, trans. G. E. M. Anscombe (Oxford: Oxford University Press, 1963), §546. Emphasis Wittgenstein's.

will lead to still more (and identical) deeds in the people who 'hear it
with their ears':

> & tærfore hafe icc turrnedd itt
> Inntill Ennglisshe spæche,
> Forr þatt I wollde bliþeliȝ
> Þatt all Ennglisshe lede
> Wiþþ ære shollde lisstenn itt,
> Wiþþ herrte shollde itt trowwenn,
> Wiþþ tunge shollde spellenn itt,
> Wiþþ dede shollde itt follȝhen.

[And therefore I have translated [the Gospels] into English speech because I
will be glad that all English people should hear it with their ears, believe it
with their hearts, preach it with their tongues, follow it in their deeds.]

(*D* 305–12)

As Orm understands the injunction to which he so ardently
responds, in other words, 'spelling' leads to more spelling and, therefore, never ends. As it converts the whole of the world into words,
such logic is deeply Augustinian, but, inasmuch as it finally absorbs
epistemology to technology (making knowing a *tekhnē* or craft), as it
understands knowledge to be a mode of doing rather than the possession of particular truths, it suspends certain inevitable consequences
by refusing to seek them. Augustine's theology of the Word was predicated on an equivalence of God and the Word that entailed acknowledgement of the lesser equivalence of human speaking and writing:

And what was the manner of his coming, if not this: 'The word was made
flesh and lived among us'? When we speak, the word which we hold in our
mind becomes a sound in order that what we have in our mind may pass
through our ears of flesh into the listener's mind: this is called speech. Our
thought, however, is not converted into the same sound, but remains intact
in its own home, suffering no diminution from its change as it takes on the
form of a word in order to make its way into the ears. In the same way the
word of God suffered no change although it became flesh in order to live
in us.[30]

---

[30] 'Quomodo venit nisi quod verbum caro factum est et habitavit in nobis? Sicuti
cum loquimur, ut id quod animo gerimus in audientis animum per aures carneas illa-
batur, fit sonus verbum quod corde gestamus, et locutio vocatur, nec tamen in eundem
sonum cogitatio nostra convertitur, sed apud se manens integra formam vocis qua se
insinuet auribus sine aliqua labe suae mutationis assumit, ita verbum dei non com-
mutatum caro tamen factum est ut habitaret in nobis', Augustine, *De doctrina
Christiana*, ed. and trans. R. P. H. Green (Oxford: Clarendon Press, 1995), I.xiii.26.

Augustine knew, as Derrida has more recently insisted, that to posit
the 'absolute proximity' of saying and knowing ('of voice and being,
of voice and the meaning of being, of voice and the ideality of meaning') is always to reveal a determinate difference.[31] It is for this reason
that 'the sign and divinity have the same place and time of birth', for
any chance that the sign will be relegated to 'secondariness' has always
required the positing of a 'truth, anterior, exterior, or superior to the
sign'.[32] Thus, for Augustine, 'knowledge itself ought to mean more
to us than the signs by means of which we know'.[33] For Orm, on the
other hand, proximities remain absolute and there is always a simple
and rectilinear path to be traced between a divine 'truth' and its signs,
from God's 'thought' to his 'Son' to his 'word' to his 'speech' ('dærne
witt | Þatt iss i Godess herrte | Iss Godess Sune, & Godess Word, &
Godess dærne spæche', 18493–6), to human thoughts, to human
words, to human deeds. As Orm insists on these particular trinities
again and again, in order to 'believe [God] aright' [rihht himm cwem-
mann, 5597] God's words must be heeded in all these forms, 'in
thought, in word, in deed' [i þohht, i word, i dede, 5601].[34] But 'truth'
of this interrelated and enchained kind can exist in no other form
than its continuous statement, in the constant movement from equivalence to equivalence which prevents any single term from gaining
priority over any other. Aimlessness is therefore exactly the price, in
the coin of spelling, that Orm feels 'right' knowing must pay.

Since Orm's spelling is so embedded in a mode of doing or unfolding it is therefore basic to its success that Orm should never step
outside its labour to explain what he was up to. And yet, Orm does
come close to such an explanation in the very first lines of his poem,
when he describes his writing, not as 'spelling', but as 'filling'. In
Orm's lexicon *fillen* is a verb which may mean little more than 'filling
something up', and this is all that Orm has ever seemed to mean when

---

[31] Jacques Derrida, *Of Grammatology*, trans. Gayatri Chakravorty Spivak
(Baltimore: Johns Hopkins University Press, 1976), 12.

[32] Ibid. 14.

[33] 'Confectum est . . . cognitionem ipsam signis, quibus cognoscimus cariorem
nobis esse oportere', Augustine, 'The Teacher', 113–186 in Augustine, *The Greatness
of the Soul; The Teacher*, trans. Joseph M. Colleran (London: Longmans, Green,
1950), X.31 (p. 170); Augustine, 'De magistro', ed. K.-D. Daur, 155–203 in *Contra
academicos; De beata vita; De ordine; De magistro; De libero arbitrio*, Corpus
Christianorum, Series Latina 29 (Turnholt: Brepols, 1970), X.31 (p. 189).

[34] For other examples of this phrasing (or close variations) see *D* 22, *D* 94, *P* 72,
P 106, 1491, 1594–5, 2703, 2780, 2955, 4141, 4181–2, 5419, 5445, 5601, 7865–6,
8317, 10043–4, 11949–50, 13015, 13437, 13989, 13993, 17883–4, 19652.

he says that he has added 'many' words to the Gospels simply for the
sake of his verse form:

> Icc hafe sett her o þiss boc
> Amang Goddspelless wordess,
> All þurrh me sellfenn, maniȝ word
> Þe rime swa to fillenn.

[I have placed here in this book among the words of the Gospels, entirely by
my own means, many words, in order to fill the rhyme.]

(D 41-4)

It is with this explicit carelessness, moreover, that Orm has seemed
to license all critical neglect of his poem: why should anyone care
about words that even describe themselves as 'filler'? And yet, for
Orm, the primary meaning of the verb *fillen* is actually 'fulfil' (as words
might realize the Word, for example, or as human action might realize
scriptural command), and when Orm says his words 'fill the rhyme' it
cannot shake this other common meaning, very neatly illustrated by
Orm's description of the third prayer of the Pater Noster:

> Þe þridde bede þatt mann bitt
> Uppo þe Paterr Nossterr
> Þatt iss, þatt Godess wille beo
> All filledd her onn eorþe,
> All all swa summ itt filledd iss
> Inn heoffne i Godess enngless;
> Forr whase maȝȝ wiþþ word & weorrc
> Her fillenn Godess wille,
> He winneþþ her þatt he shall ben
> Þurrh Godess wille borrȝhenn.

[The third prayer that one makes in the Pater Noster is that God's will be
entirely fulfilled here on earth, as it is fulfilled in heaven among God's angels;
For whoever may here fulfil God's will with words and work, he labours here
that he shall be saved through God's will.]

(5420-9)

In fact, the connection between the two meanings is crucial to this
later example because, 'God's will' is done 'on earth' as it is 'in heaven'
only to the extent that (again) the heavenly notion takes residence in
some earthly activity, as the divine thought becomes not merely 'words'
but 'work'. 'Filling up the rhyme' with 'many words' [maniȝ word] is
to fulfil God's will because it means that writing is *no more* than
doing, because it unfolds the 'words of the Gospels' [Goddspelless
wordess, D 42] as someone 'labours' [winneþþ, 5428]. This is why

the verb *fillen* is also equivalent to the verb *spellen*: in all the activities to which these words refer, divine words demand word-making; they insist that knowing can never be anything *other* than a practice.[35]

DECONSTRUCTION

A poet so heedless of outcomes might still seem to fail when his poem satisfies neither him nor his readers. For even if all Orm ever wanted was to labour, his habit of returning continually to rewrite what he had written is evidence of a certain frustration, and the very fact that almost no one else ever wanted to copy his text must be taken as evidence that it wholly failed to find an audience in its day (as, indeed, it still does). It is perhaps in these ways alone that the *Ormulum* is unsurprising, for, as Jonathan Goldberg has observed, 'spelling reform in English . . . has never succeeded'.[36] But it is also the case that the *Ormulum* is extraordinary by virtue of its capacity to parlay even this disaster into some kind of success, to absorb what seems like failure to the patterns of its form, and, thus, to its larger project of meaning. In fact, where initiating principles are as stern and unusual as those Orm detected in the Gospels, the resulting shape is necessarily as much a product of resistances and counter-pressures as of rules, of unplanned interactions and deflections as of particular causes. Such a form will necessarily unfold as a kind of self-reflection, a mode of thoughtfulness about the very demands that brought it into being.

It might even be said that the *Ormulum* was constructed by the processes we normally call 'deconstruction', that it is a text built up by 'the careful teasing out of warring forces of signification'.[37] It is not for nothing, in other words, that Orm's founding principles are well defined by a Derridean lens. This may be another way in which the *Ormulum* is less strange than we have thought. As Goldberg also observes, 'spelling reform in English . . . has always been based on the

---

[35] It is both helpful and prescient that the glossary of Holt's edition of the *Ormulum* defines *fillen* as 'practice' (s.v. 'fillenn'). For the meanings of this verb in more general use see also *MED*, s.v. 'fillen v.', 7.

[36] Jonathan Goldberg, *Writing Matter: From the Hands of the English Renaissance* (Stanford, Calif.: Stanford University Press, 1990), 191.

[37] 'The de-construction of a text does not proceed by random doubt or arbitrary subversion, but by the careful teasing out of warring forces of signification within the text itself', Barbara Johnson, *The Critical Difference: Essays in the Contemporary Rhetoric of Reading* (Baltimore: Johns Hopkins University Press, 1980), 5.

dream of reducing writing to a transparency' so that, in any particular case, 'the orthographic dilemma ramifies to the larger question of writing' which is 'the Derridean problematic of writing'.[38] But these ramifications also mean that, to the extent that we have allowed the *Ormulum*'s failures to become the sign of its insignificance, we have ourselves failed to see what this poem achieves. For, if it is in the nature of orthographic dreams to uncover unwittingly the grounds that make such dreams necessary, then what have seemed the most obstructive aspects of the *Ormulum*'s form—what has most seemed to thwart our interest or even the text's clarity—are its most powerful insights, ways in which the poem actually understands that it is impossible to make writing 'right'. In so far as the *Ormulum* is meant to have the form of writing as such (but to be more 'right' than any other kind), all those aspects of its form which remain imperfect are, in fact, equivalent to knowledge of the bars to perfection embedded in all writing practices.

The most obvious and important of these aspects is that systematic *repetition* of words, phrases, and whole lines which commentators have almost always complained about. Orm is of course committed to some repetition by the simple decision to teach by translation ('and therefore I have turned [the Gospels] into English' [& tærfore hafe icc turrnedd itt | Inntill Ennglisshe spæche, *D* 305–6]), for 'turning' not only requires that the Latin scripture ('Fuit in diebus Herodis Regis Judee sacerdos') be followed by the same text in English ('An preost wass onn Herodess daȝȝ | Amang Judisskenn þeode', 109–10), but that the sense of the passage be frequently repeated in order to make its meanings clear:

> Þiss gode mann, þiss gode prest,
> Þatt we nu mælenn offe,
> Wass, alls I seȝȝde nu littlær,
> Ȝehatenn Zacaryas;
> & he wass, alls icc hafe seȝȝd,
> God prest, & Godd full cweme.

[This good man, this good priest, who we now speak about, was, as I said a little before, called Zacharias, and was, as I have said, God's priest and very pleasing to God.]

(461–6)

---

[38] Goldberg, *Writing Matter*, 29 and 191. The 'orthographic dilemma' Goldberg refers to is Richard Mulcaster's *The First Part of the Elementarie* (1582).

Repetition in the *Ormulum* may therefore be said to emerge, as it always does, from the use value of words themselves—on the simple presumption that they are cognitive helps, that they signify something by a process of reference—and, therefore, if a particular set of words is helpful, then more of the same will be more helpful. And yet as Orm's asides in this quotation make clear ('as I said a littler earlier . . . as I said before') to precisely the extent that it is aware of itself, repetition is also the doubt that a set of words may not have worked as they ought to have done, the retracing of a signifying groove that necessarily casts doubt over whether that groove was adequately traced in the first place. As the *Ormulum* unfolds by means of such repetition, as it spins itself out in concentric loops of identical words and sentences, each of them closing ever more tightly in upon itself, as one repetition leads directly to another, as, in short, the poem *becomes* repetition, the resulting pattern recognizes that the impulse to repeat in any form (that there ever are repeated words in a text or between them) actually undermines signification. In fact, it suggests that, if repetition is ever of any use, then what *repetition* knows is that words may not work at all.

Of course Orm writes by means of a logic in which such nullity is significant, where words can do work irrespective of any meaning they may convey. For the act of 'filling' (as 'fulfilling') is so generally important to what Orm's writing knows that an identical set of words must often be repeated in order to show the identity between, say, a divine thought and an earthly deed, or God's word and human works. Such repetitions represent a sub-set, and therefore a sub-pattern, within the larger flood of repetitions which comprise the poem, and they are often recognizable as such by their unusual length; in fact, they often seem like retranscriptions of a previous passage (as if, by eye-skip, one set of words was mistakenly copied again). In order to be efficacious in such nullity however—in order to illustrate a given fulfilment—such reiterations must also be marked out as *different*, the first, for example, labelled as what 'God . . . said',

> Forr Godess Gast itt haffde seȝȝd
> Þurrh hiss profetess tunge,
> Full mikell fresst biforenn þatt
> Þatt Crist comm her to manne,
> Þatt Godess follc, Judisskenn follc,
> Þatt Godess laȝhess heldenn,

      Aȝȝ sholldenn habbenn allderrmenn
       & kingess off hemm sellfenn,
      Aȝȝ—till þatt Godess Sune Crist
       Himm shollde onn eorþe shæwen.

[For God's Spirit said it by the tongue of his prophet, a very long time before Christ came here as a man: that God's people, the Jewish people, who held God's laws, and should always have rulers and kings from among themselves—until God's Son, Christ, should show himself on earth.]

                           (259–68)

the second as what subsequently happened:

      & swa wass filledd opennliȝ
      Þatt word tatt ær wass cwiddedd,
      Þatt Godess follc, Judisskenn follc,
      Þatt Godess laȝhess heldenn,
      Aȝȝ sholldenn habbenn allderrmenn
       & kingess off hemm sellfenn,
      Aȝȝ—till þatt Godess Sune Crist
       Himm shollde onn eorþe shæwenn.

[And so the word that was declared earlier was fulfilled openly, that God's people, the Jewish people, who held God's laws, and should always have rulers and kings from among themselves—until God's Son, Christ, should show himself on earth.]

                           (281–8)

In this way repetition registers another anxiety, not about the efficacy of words, but about the nature of repetition, since, in these cases, the same words only produce a meaning to the extent that repetition has *not* occurred—to precisely the extent that a difference between the first and second set of words has been marked. In fact, in the example I have just given there is only repetition in so far as identical words *fail* to convey why they are a 'fulfilment' (in the first instance, these words are not actually God's words but Orm's version of them; in the second instance, they are certainly not earthly events, nor even a narrative of them, but a sketchy summary). In this sense, what repetition in the *Ormulum* knows about itself is that it is a structure that is meaningful only when *it* does not work.

So, as if to contain these deeply troubling thoughts, a surprising proportion of repetition throughout the poem is *un*marked—words and phrases, whole lines and couplets, small and large sections, are written and then written again, without any acknowledgement that what has been said was said 'earlier', and with iterations often at such a distance from one another that intervening words themselves tend to act as a screen between a first and second use. Unmarked repetition reproduces the worry that words do not work, but it also proves it, since the absence of any clear reason for a recurrence makes it nothing other than evidence that the prior use of the same words failed. Some sense of the power and nature of this effect can be given by a passage from the *Ormulum*'s first homily in which the first and fifth couplets, as well as the third and seventh, are, for no obvious or stated reason, completely identical:

> & Sannt Johan Bapptisste comm
>   Biforenn Cristess come,
> Þa Crist wass her all gilltelæs
>   Wiþþ woȝhe demmd to dæþe;
> & Helyas shall cumenn efft
>   Biforenn Cristess come,
> Þa Crist shall demenn all mannkinn
>   All rihht, & nohht wiþþ woȝhe.
> & Sannt Johan Bapptisste comm
>   Biforenn Cristess come,
> Þa Crist comm hiderr dun, hiss follc
>   To lesenn ut off helle;
> & Helyas shall cumenn efft
>   Biforenn Cristess come,
> Þa Crist shall cumenn efft, hiss follc
>   To ledenn inntill heoffne.

[And Saint John the Baptist came before Christ came, when Christ, entirely guiltless, was condemned to death with wickedness; and Elijah will come again before Christ comes, when Christ shall judge all mankind justly and not with wickedness; and Saint John the Baptist came before Christ came, when Christ came down hither, to release his people from hell; and Elijah shall come again before Christ comes, when Christ shall come again to lead his people into heaven.]

(870–84)

In such cases, moreover, it is not repetition but the words which intervene between the duplication that create the strange sense of weightlessness: as they embed identical words in a slightly different context, drawing a slightly different meaning from those words in each case, these different words amount to a *lack* of awareness that any repetition has occurred. One might even say that what such words seem most to know is that the words which have already occurred have never occurred, as if what repetition accomplished was finally just the opposite of its intent, not the redoubling, but the cancelling of meaning. What the larger pattern of such unmarked repetition may therefore be said to recognize in the *Ormulum* is what any reader who tries to find traction in its seamless circling also knows: using words can actually exhaust their capacity to mean, since it is possible to use them to such an extent that they can actually cause us to know *less*.

If the *Ormulum* were only such knowledge it would only contain one word repeated endlessly, and the very material of repetition is provided by a second pattern whose point is not to emphasize and clarify by means of the same, but to insist on the sameness that underlies difference. Such a structure is also essential to Orm's conception of 'spelling' in so far as it holds that certain crucial differences are, in fact, equivalents ('words', say, are 'deeds'). Since an endless chain of such equivalents constitutes knowledge in the *Ormulum*, any particular equation can acquire more terms endlessly (so, 'words' which are 'deeds' are 'thoughts', which are 'God's' or those of 'English people', etc.) As a result, just as any statement of equivalence may be extended infinitely by means of repetition, it may also be extended by *recursion*, the constant addition of more terms (so A = B becomes A = B = C), which produces such distance between equivalents that they sometimes require restatement within the given statement (so that A = B = C = D = E = F does not forestall another instance of A = B), with the inevitable consequence that, at some point, the whole statement will become internal to itself (at precisely the point in the chain A = B = C = D = E = F that we are also told that F = A). One of the more dense examples of such circularity can be found at the ideational centre of the *Ormulum*, where the homilies have arrived at those lines of John which describe how God is the Word ('In principio erat Verbum' (John 1: 1)), and where the point of the meditation must be to state how such an equivalence governs both a theology and a conception of knowledge:

> Forr Godess word iss Godess witt
>   & Godess aȝhenn kinde,
> & Godess kinde & Godess witt
>   Iss soþ Godd unntodæledd.
> Forr Godd himm sellf, & Godess witt,
>   & Godess aȝhenn kinde
> Sinndenn all an, all an soþ Godd
>   Þatt alle shaffte wrohte.

Forr Godd iss Godd, & Godess witt
Iss ec soþ Godd, & baþe
Þeʒʒ sinndenn an Allmahhtiʒ Godd
Þatt alle shaffte wrohhte
Forþ wiþþ þatt an Allmahhtiʒ Gast,
Þatt cumeþþ off hemm baþe.
& forrþi seʒʒde Sannt Johan
O þiss Goddspelless lare,
Þatt Godess word wass a soþ Godd
To don uss tunnderrstanndenn,
Þatt all þatt strenedd iss off Godd,
Off Godess aʒhenn kinde,
All iss itt all þatt illke whatt
Þatt Godd iss inn himm sellfenn.

[For God's word is God's understanding and God's own nature, and God's nature and God's understanding is true God undivided. For God himself, and God's understanding and God's nature are all one, all one true God, who made all creatures. For God is God, & God's understanding is also true God, and they are both an Almighty God who made all creatures along with an Almighty Spirit that comes from them both, and therefore Saint John said in this Gospel's teaching that God's word was a true God, to make us understand that all that is created by God from God's nature, it is all that same thing that God is himself.]

(18533–54)

Any statement of identity recognizes a difference between two terms (otherwise why bother to insist on their sameness?), but recursion of the kind that occurs here is a way of recognizing that no amount of insistence actually makes terms that are different truly identical. What looks like a form of forgetting (we learn that 'God's wit' is the 'true God', and then we learn it again) could also be construed as a heightened awareness, the recognition that, even after they are pressed together as if one, the two terms are *still* different ('God's wit' never will *be* the 'true God', unless it is somehow no longer 'God's wit'). This passage is particularly knowledgeable in this regard because its statements are not only so generally recursive, but, at its very centre *sameness* is finally internal to itself, as the chain winds itself up into a self-consuming spiral, and we learn that 'God is God' ('Forr Godd iss Godd'). Just as such nonsense is a particularly condensed form of the general pattern, it is also a concise form of what that whole pattern knows: the only equivalence which is truly secure is the equivalence that it is unnecessary to state (A = A). As this pattern extends itself through this poem it becomes the correlative doubt that any of the equivalences the *Ormulum* exists to state (and by means of which it understands itself to exist) *do* in fact hold.

Since this poem understands words not only to mean but to do— and writing not only to be a procedure for signifying and knowing but for living—its form also extends outward into all those behaviours that made it, particularly as those behaviours themselves traced patterns and, in that way, were forms of knowing. Since writing the *Ormulum* was 'right' to the extent that that writing was at once effortful and endless, perhaps the most important (because the most wise) part of this *poem*'s form are therefore those habits of *correction* and *revision* that often threaten to overwhelm the writing to which we normally restrict the name 'Ormulum'. These alterations were themselves patterns of repetition, first, because they all involve a 'common principle' (and therefore each change was, in aim, identical to the others) and, second, because that principle was the 'elimination of variants' (so their aim was to make the writing of each word in the *Ormulum* the same as its writing elsewhere).[39] In the course of his first homily, for example, Orm recognized that he was using multiple forms for the word 'she' (*ȝho* and *ho*) when he reached line 452; he only ever used one of these forms subsequently (*ȝho*), but also went back through the text he had already written, adding a *ȝ* to every earlier instance of *ho*.[40] By recognizing the variant and conceiving the need to correct it *in* the very process of writing, however, such a correction is the recognition that writing always produces the need for correction (that, in effect, the more that is written the more correction there is to do). Other corrections in the manuscript extend this pattern by proving it. New variants became recognizable along the whole long course of this poem's writing (at line 10196, for example, Orm reduced the variants *kaserr/ keȝȝse* to *kaserr* and went back and eliminated *keȝȝse* from all preceding lines), but so many variants finally emerged that there was, eventually, only opportunity to register and correct them in subsequent use (*nahht/nihht* becomes *nahht* after line 6494; 'þ/ð' is reduced to *þ* from line 17566), and no opportunity to go back and correct earlier variants (earlier uses of *nahht* and *ð* remain unchanged). And, as it therefore must, the wisdom

---

[39] Burchfield, 'Language and Orthography', 69.

[40] I take this example as well as those in the rest of this paragraph from Burchfield's helpful table charting the 'elimination of variants in the *Ormulum*', 'Language and Orthography', 74–9 (for these particular examples see this table, 74–6).

of this pattern, and the form in which it is lodged, even involves
the margins of the manuscript page in its knowledge, since it is finally
the dimensions of the parchment available which become the absolute limit to further correction. Indeed, as changes fill the margins
of leaves, and then the foot of every page (with changes linked in by
reference marks), as still more leaves are added to this book to provide a surface for even more revisions (there are twenty-nine such
leaves in the manuscript), the endlessly extending surface on which
the *Ormulum* must be written itself becomes the most solid form in
which this poem recognizes that the production of words is the production of error.[41]

This is why the elimination of variants on a horizontal plane—
extending so far across the surface of the text as to reach its limits
—finally becomes vertical, and in the making of the *Ormulum*, correction was also so 'successive' that it can be described as recursive, as
corrections were themselves corrected (and so the activity was also,
finally internal to itself).[42] This pattern is well traced by means of the
most extensive change made in the course of the poem's writing, the
reduction of the digraph *eo* to *e*. The two forms were not understood
to be variants until line 13864, and, as in similar cases, *e* alone is used
in place of *eo* in the writing of the rest of the text, but earlier lines are
also corrected (with the offending *o*'s in the digraph scraped out).
The very extent of this correction shows that many corrections had
been made before this general programme was undertaken (there is
cancelled text before line 13853 in which the *o* has not been scraped
out of *eo*'s), and therefore that rewriting was everywhere coincident
with writing this text. Since *e* text also occurs alongside uncorrected
but cancelled *eo* text on some occasions, it is also clear that other
forms of correction interrupted the general attempt to reduce *eo* to
e.[43] What this recursion knows, therefore, is not only that writing
produces the need for correction but, for that very reason, the need
to correct will always be in excess of the activity of correction itself.
Thus, even though the 'Dedication' describes itself as the last part
of the *Ormulum* to have been written ('Þiss werrc . . . iss brohht till
ende', D 24–8), still more forms in need of correction were discovered when it was written (where the 'Dedication' has only *wifman*,
the variant *wimmann* was used, and then cancelled, in the rest of the

[41] Turville-Petre, 'Studies in the *Ormulum* MS', 1–6. For a collation of MS Junius 1
see the preface to *The Ormulum*, ed. Holt, p. lxxxviii.
[42] Turville-Petre, 'Studies in the *Ormulum* MS', 1.   [43] Ibid. 6–7 and 15–20.

poem), but, in some cases, there was no opportunity to correct all the
variants in the rest of the poem (for example, we find only *hafenn* in
the 'Dedication' but *habbenn/hafenn* elsewhere, only *redenn* in the
'Dedication' but *rædenn/redenn* elsewhere).[44] And the poem, even in
its endlessly corrected state, is itself replete with variant forms which
Orm never even noticed (the following are only representative):

a/aȝȝ/æfre, 'ever'; *abufenn/bibuffenn*, 'above'; *amang/mang*, 'among';
ba/baþe/beȝȝenn, 'both'; *biforr/biforenn*, 'before'; *fe/fehh*, 'money'; *fon,*
(unnderr-/onn-), fanngenn (unnderr-, onn-) 'receive'; *gan (unnderr-/þurrh-),*
ganngenn (unnderr-/oferr-), 'go'; *hannd /hande,* 'hand'; *hemm/þeȝȝm,* 'them';
here/ þeȝȝre, 'their'; *noþ/noe,* 'Noah'; *operr/oþþr/orr,* 'or'; *stanedd/istanedd,*
'stoned'; *till/to,* 'to'; *wel/well,* 'well'; *wiþþ/midd',* 'with'.[45]

It could be said that all these uncorrected forms actually recognize
that even Orm's writing can never be 'right' since, even where rightness is measured by effort, there is finally a physical limit to the capacity to labour. What we take to be the last corrections and revisions
in the poem occur in a 'cramped and trembling' hand, which seems to
be Orm's autograph 'in old age', an indication that the final bar to the
perfection of the *Ormulum* was the end of the life into which it had
extended itself.[46] But here the *Ormulum*'s form even extends itself
out into lives much later than Orm's, showing not only that the text
is always reproducible (that the effort of making it has not in fact
ended), not least because it has so far been impossible to *reproduce*
this poem without error. When just a few passages of the poem were
copied in the seventeenth century by the manuscript's owner, Jan van
Vliet (d. 1666), he introduced a number of irregularities which were
not in the original text.[47] Modern technologies of printing (and edit-
ing) have made no appreciable difference either. It has been observed
that the only edition of the *Ormulum* ever made has at least 1,000
errors in it.[48] Even the short extracts from the *Ormulum* in Joseph
Hall's short *Selections* (1920) are full of introduced variants.[49] In

---

[44] Burchfield, 'Language and Orthography', 74–7.   [45] Ibid. 78.
[46] Turville-Petre, 'Studies in the *Ormulum* MS', 19.
[47] See Ker, 'Unpublished Parts of the *Ormulum*', 2.
[48] See Sigurd Holm, *Corrections and Additions in the Ormulum Manuscript*
(Uppsala: Almqvist & Wiksells, 1922). Burchfield includes an appendix listing the
many misreadings missed in Holm's 'corrections' ('Language and Orthography',
84–7).
[49] Ibid. 59 and 59 n. 1.

fact, given the difficulties in making out the shapes on the pages of MS Junius 1, it may be that the forms of the *Ormulum* simply *cannot* be reproduced accurately—even though we continue to try. In this way, the most startling form in which this poem knows that its writing is 'right' is the very invitation it endlessly extends to other writers to involve themselves in its trouble.

UT PICTURA, ORTHOGRAPHIA

Because such knowledge in the *Ormulum* is coextensive with what we more naturally see as the unravelling of a project or the blighting of a life, it is far easier to see how Orm was passionate than to see that he was wise. It is therefore perhaps hardest of all to believe that the *Ormulum* knows something from which we may benefit. The extraordinary contribution this poem makes, not only to the history of writing, but to the history of ideas, becomes a little clearer, however, when we compare its shape to the form of the text which regularly usurps its rightful place as the 'first' attempt to reform 'spelling' in English, the *De recta emendata linguae Anglicae scriptione dialogus* (1568) by Thomas Smith (1513–77).[50] Like Orm, Smith was led to make his text by a certain equation, in his case, not between 'words' and 'deeds', but between sound and pictures, as if writing were a mimesis of speech ('ut pictura corporis'), a reflection of what is said in the perfect mirror of letters:

Now writing is an imitation of utterance, as a painting is of a person. For as we sometimes see a man's face so well painted that a man who had never seen him can recognize by means of the lifeless picture the form of the living person the artist has chosen to paint: so in writing, the uttered words, speech, syllables, and letters are recognized, and writing takes the place of a picture, so that writing may be truly described as a picture of speech.[51]

---

[50] E. J. Dobson, *English Prononuciation: 1500–1700*, 2 vols., 2nd edn. (Oxford: Clarendon Press, 1968; 1st edn. 1957), 1: 62. Dobson provides a helpful summary of Smith's system as well as a careful analysis of its successes and failures (1: 46–62). Goldberg also mentions this text, but only in passing (see *Writing Matter*, 190 and 196).

[51] 'Est autem scriptura, imitatio sermonis, ut pictura corporis: nam ut videmus ita faciem hominis aliquando depictam, ut is qui nunquam ante viderit, agnoscere possit per inanimem tabellam, vivi figuram hominis quem voluit artifex delineare: ita per scripturam verba, voces, syllabae, literaeque prolatae agnoscuntur, subitque scriptura in picturae locum, ut vere possit dici scriptionem esse vocum picturam', Thomas

Smith also wants a writing that is 'right' [recta] by means of exact rectilinear relations—in this case between 'a particular sign' and a 'particular sound'—and, also like Orm, try as he might, he can never make his writing perfect by this means: he introduces many unphonetic spellings into his examples (because of the 'influence of conventional spelling'),[52] and the new alphabet he proposes at the end of his treatise provides a plethora of symbols to represent the same sound ([ð], as in *th*at, is represented ð or Δ, and [þ] as in '*th*in' is represented by either þ or θ).[53]

Smith's writing is unlike Orm's, however, in the way that its form anticipates errors, interposing a frame narrative between the writing of the text and the system it recommends, and, therefore, a vantage from which to pronounce on the whole reforming project from out-side it. In fact, the text we call the *De recta emendata scriptione* is not a manual for spelling reform but a dialogue in which one char-acter ('Smith') reads out such a manual, which he wrote earlier, to a companion ('Quintus'). 'Smith' distances himself from his own text from the start, forgetting exactly what he called it (it is probably the *Orthographia linguae Anglicae* 'or something like that' ['aut tale aliquid']), and, even though it is his own work, he also has trouble reading it since it is 'so spoiled by deletions and interlineations'.[54] It is, in fact, as if 'Smith' were Orm, reading out the *Ormulum* after having lost the courage of his conviction, since the shape given the author-function in this case makes spelling reform the project of a now-vanished person ('Smith' when he cared about orthography) and a book that we only know through this person's careless read-ing. In this way Smith converts his passion into ironic detachment,

Smith, *Literary and Linguistic Works*, Part III (*De recta emendata linguae Anglicae scriptione dialogus*), ed. Bror Danielsson, Stockholm Studies in English 56 (Stockholm, 1983), fo. 5ᵛ (pp. 30–1). The translation here and throughout is from this edition. Latin abbreviations have been silently expanded.

[52] Dobson, *English Prononuciation*, 1: 53–6.

[53] Because Smith has a variety of symbols for marking vowel length it could also be said that each vowel sound is represented by a variety of symbols (e.g. what Smith calls 'long ë' can be represented as E^, ë, ē, or e–). For these alternatives see the 'Alphabetum Anglicum' at the end of the *De recta emendata scriptione* (fos. 41ʳ–41ᵛ (pp. 172–5)).

[54] 'I shall have to read it to you, for as you can see, it is so spoiled by deletions and interlineations that I am not sure whether I can guess what I have written in a good many places' [Necesse est ut eum tibi legam, nam, ut vides, tam est deformatus lituris et expunctionibus, ut nescio an possim ipsemet divinare multis in locis quid scipserim], ibid., fo. 4ᵛ (pp. 26–7).

deflecting any criticism from himself by refusing ever properly to advance his method.

Such irony is wisdom too, and it is precisely the wry self-awareness (even self-mockery) that characterizes our own relationship to writing and the possibilities of its improvement or perfection; Smith's wit is, in other words, what we take to be truth in this sphere. Where Orm presses on before any problem he finds, Smith makes clear in his frame that he shares our belief that writing never can be perfect, that if we want a mimetic spelling, we had better give up at precisely the moment we start:

Not that writing represents speech to us as obviously and clearly as a picture represents bodies and their shadows, which the most ignorant of men recognizes at first sight; but because by agreement and consent between educated people, particular signs correspond to particular sounds.[55]

Like us, Smith concludes by suggesting that a phonetic alphabet is only worth crafting as a way of understanding the kinds of relation that obtain between words and letters, but the point of such craft is study, not a general change in writing procedures:

If these characters appear awkward, more convenient ones can be devised. I am content with my work if I have explained the difference of the sounds and the nature and force of the letters, so that they can be distinguished.[56]

But also inevitably—and, therefore, for us as much for Smith—such concessions draw a line under the possibilities of transparency in order to preserve them for writing in general, setting the limits to a particular system ('if these characters appear awkward) in order to suggest that a slightly better spelling may lie just around the corner ('more convenient ones can be devised'). For the perspicuity that knows that *this* writing is not right is necessarily the alibi (or the warrant, or the inversion) which permits both Smith and all of us never to have to think that *all* writing is never right—that what writing is, is never to be right.

---

[55] 'Non quod tam evidenter et apparenter voces nobis repraesentat, quam corpora et umbras corporum tabella depicta, quae vel ignorantissimus quisque primo aspectu cognoscit; sed quia pactione quadam et consensu inter doctos certa nota certo sono respondeat', ibid., fo. 5^v (pp. 30–1).

[56] 'Et characteres hi, si quidem rudiores videantur, poterunt excogitari faciliores. Satis est factum nostro labori si differentiam sonorum et naturas ac vires harum literarum explicuerimus, ut internosci possint', ibid., fos. 38^v–38^r (pp. 160–3).

What Smith's anticipation of our own knowledge helps us to see, in other words, is that it is precisely Orm's understanding that writing *is* all those forms of signifying failure I have described which make his writing more perspicuous than any other writing we know. It is actually all those attributes of the *Ormulum* which we have complained most about—its imperfections (and imperfectibility), its sprawling illogic and circularity—which make it the closest to 'right writing' English has ever had, or is ever likely to get. But this is perhaps exactly why its form seems so repugnant. In fact, in so far as it recognizes the troubles that constitute writing in its every line the *Ormulum* exists to see clearly what we must not see if we are ever to put finger to keypad in the belief that writing will succeed. It is in this sense that what the *Ormulum* knows, in every twist and turn of its form, is what we must *forget* if we are ever to believe that our own writing is 'right'.

4

The Meaning of Life:
The Owl and the Nightingale

To inquire into the effective force of speech and to investigate
the truth and meaning of what is said are precisely or practically
the same. A word's force consists in its meaning. Without the
latter it is empty, useless, and (so to speak) dead. Just as the soul
animates the body, so, in a way, meaning breathes life into a word.

[Cum examinare locutionis vim et eius quod dicitur veritatem
et sensum, idem aut fere idem sit; vis enim verbi sensus est;
quo si destituatur, sermo cassus et inutilis est et (ut sic dixerim)
mortuus; ut quodammodo, sicut corpus ad vitam vegetatur ab
anima, sic ad vitam quandam verbi sensus proficiat.]

(John of Salisbury, *Metalogicon*)

One of the stranger effects of the form of *The Owl and the Nightingale*
(*c.*1216) is its capacity to shape attempts to describe it, as if it were
at once so striking and so mystifying that the only way for criticism
to apprehend it was to retrace it. This effect can be detected in the
way that normally subtle readers choose to oppose the poem as if
they were one of the disputants within it, greeting all the complexity
of its statements with the blunt declaration that it 'has no message'.[1]
The effect is evident as well in the way even such an improbable
reading can breed opposition, and a complex and nuanced understanding of the poem's accomplishments will be brandished as if it
were a 'key' to the poem's 'significance as a whole'.[2] The effect may

---

[1] Geoffrey Shepherd, 'Early Middle English', 81–117 in *The Middle Ages*, ed.
W. F. Bolton (London: Sphere, 1970), 105.

[2] Janet Coleman, '*The Owl and the Nightingale* and Papal Theories of Marriage',
Journal of Ecclesiastical History 38 (1987), 517–68. 'By making use of recent
researches of Duby, Helmholz, Sheehan, C. N. L. Brooke and C. R. and M. G. Cheney,
the historian may well provide the key to this poem, a key that has thus far proved
elusive to students of early English literature, many of whom argue that the poem does
not seem to be written in support of any "cause"' (517–18).

even be detected in that 'curious transformation', diagnosed by Jay Schleusener, whereby 'the impulse to say something serious about the poem becomes an attempt to say something about the poem's seriousness', as if the poem somehow had the capacity to make criticism fight with itself.[3] All these phenomena may be explained by the recent insight that 'jurisdiction' is itself at issue in this poem, and, therefore, that one of the less obvious 'modes of social and institutional performance' it calls into question is literary criticism and its belief that it can determine what a text means.[4] On these grounds the meanings of this poem remain more elusive than that of most others because they involve any attempt at critical determination in some imitation of the owl and the nightingale's fight, as if to know anything about this poem required that one disagree with all that had ever been said about it before.

I want to propose in this chapter, however, that these effects and the scholarly irresolution they produce are not so much successive failures at critical understanding as nearly perfect readings of a form whose most characteristic gesture is the *feint*—a final turn away from the course that has been most fully followed and the destination that has been most carefully marked out. We have therefore been most likely to mistake this poem when we have been the most careful, and our interpretations have seemed to disagree most fully when they are, in fact, very nearly in accord. It is our near perception of this fact that also explains why our most characteristic mode of enjoyment of this poem is bemusement or surprise (we call it a 'marvel' or describe it as 'miraculous' because cheek-by-jowl with some certainty about meaning or method is the certainty that we have been gulled).[5] For all these reasons, too, we can see *The Owl and the Nightingale*'s form whole only if we invert our critical priorities and look for determinate principles in those tenets that seem to be the most casually held, if we take as wisdom those points the poem seems to press most lightly.

[3] Jay Schleusener, '*The Owl and the Nightingale*: A Matter of Judgment', *Modern Philology* 70 (1972–3), 185–9 (quotation from 185).

[4] Bruce Holsinger, 'Vernacular Legality: The English Jurisdictions of *The Owl and the Nightingale*', 154–184 in *The Letter of the Law: Legal Practice and Literary Production in Medieval England*, ed. Emily Steiner and Candace Barrington (Ithaca, NY: Cornell University Press, 2002), 156.

[5] For the first characterization see Derek Pearsall, *Old English and Middle English Poetry* (London: Routledge & Kegan Paul, 1977), 91, and, for the second, see J. A. W. Bennett, *Middle English Literature* (Oxford: Clarendon Press, 1986), 1.

All of these formal qualities and attributes are modelled by the poem's very first lines, which may therefore be understood as a kind of reading lesson for all that follows:

> Ich was in one sumere dale,
> In one suþe diȝele hale:
> Iherde ich holde grete tale
> An hule and one niȝtingale.
> Þat plait was stif & starc & strong,
> Sumwile softe & lud among;
> An aiþer aȝen oþer sval,
> & let þat vole mod ut al;
> & eiþer seide of oþeres custe
> Þat alre worste þat hi wuste;
> & hure & hure of oþeres songe
> Hi holde plaiding suþe stronge.

[I was in a summer-valley, in a really out-of-the-way retreat, when I heard an owl and a nightingale having a huge dispute. This controversy was fierce and ferocious and furious, sometimes calm and sometimes noisy; and each of them swelled up against the other and vented all her malicious feelings, saying the very worst thing they could think of about their antagonist's character; and about their songs, especially, they had a vehement debate.][6]

The scene, as it is initially set, is a simple one, a typical English field, containing typical English birds, making noise and puffing up their chests as birds do. And even if it soon emerges that these birds speak—that they even 'plead', as if in a court of law[7]—the narrator's insouciance in the face of such anthropomorphism is itself reassuring, a way of gathering everyday realities into a *locus amoenus*: this field is 'out-of-the-way' [diȝele], we must realize, because it is a territory in some mind, and, soon, in a slightly different way, this scene is also typical in so far as it satisfies all the generic conditions of a dream vision. And yet, to precisely the extent that we match the narrator's equanimity with our own in these ways we have been immediately and completely beguiled by the poem's candour—*for no one has fallen asleep*. The absence of this crucial predicate for a

---

[6] *The Owl and the Nightingale: Text and Translation*, ed. Neil Cartlidge (Exeter: University of Exeter Press, 2001), lines 1–12. Hereafter I quote this poem and its translation from this edition and citations will be given by line number in the text.

[7] On the legal lexicon of the poem see Holsinger, 'English Jurisdictions', 162–3 and 172–6.

dream vision also means that this poem not only presents bird speech as unremarkable, but it insists that an owl and a nightingale actually have something to say.

When we notice that a truth claim has been lodged in this scene we may also follow it to the intellectual context in which bird sounds were more generally accorded such consequence. The theories of language and nature (both human and avian) in question are spread wide in medieval learning, but I will also suggest in what follows that a good place to relearn many of these theories—not least because it was doubtless the place where the author of this poem found them—is the encyclopedia. It will take the first half of this chapter to reconstruct the salient parts of this thinking, but its governing premise is that words adequate the world, that, particularly in the case of living things, language is as animate as the objects it describes. Not only do two birds speak at the beginning of the poem, then, but two nouns, *hule* and *niʒtingale*, and it is therefore from the aliveness posited in these words that much of the rest of the poem's form is extrapolated. The task in the second half of this chapter will be to describe how such a form culminates in an even more dramatic feint, an undermining of such inaugurating ideas as complete as the thoroughness with which they are generally embraced. That manoeuvre allows *The Owl and the Nightingale* to proclaim its own form to be truer to the meaning of certain kinds of life than any of the forms from which these meanings have been derived, a set of words that adequate the world by understanding that world better than it has been understood before.

THE LIVING THING

The idea that words have some inherent attachment to the things they describe has sometimes been called *cratylism* after the foundational dialogue by Plato in which a speaker called Cratylus advances the view that words are 'natural and not conventional'.[8] This dialogue is playful, not least when Socrates proposes a variety of improbable connections between nature and word sounds ('α [is] assigned

---

[8] Plato, *Cratylus*, 421–74 in *The Collected Dialogues*, ed. Edith Hamilton and Huntington Cairns, Bollingen Series 71 (Princeton: Princeton University Press, 1961), 383b (p. 422). Hereafter citations to this dialogue will be given in the text.

to the expression of size, and η of length, because they are great letters' (427c)). Our modern sense that signs are arbitrary is strongly advocated by Cratylus's opponent, Hermogenes, and Socrates, who is soon enlisted to arbitrate this dispute, clearly favours this view, but, as has been observed, in such a way as to leave Cratylus's premises in place.[9] Socrates says that 'names have by nature a truth' (391b), and that, if not in all cases in many, 'imitation of the essence is made by syllables and letters' (424b). The dialogue finally allows that there is some correctness in many names and a few are precisely correct, and it is this weak cratylism that becomes the foundation of medieval attempts to explore the nature of signification. Although Augustine could hardly be considered a proponent of the naturalness of signs, the *De dialectica*, often ascribed to him, holds that 'a word is congruent with the thing that is signified' [verbum rei quam significat congruit].[10] The influence of such a view is also documented in the period and place of *The Owl and the Nightingale* by the *Metalogicon* of John of Salisbury (1115–80). For John, language is 'mainly an invention of man' [ex maxima parte ab hominum institutione], but also something that 'still imitates nature from which it partly derives its origin' [naturam tamen imitatur, et pro parte ab ipsa originem ducit].[11]

The encyclopedia is not conventionally connected to views such as these. The model for almost all medieval examples was Pliny's *Historia naturalis* (AD 23–79) whose project purports to be purely descriptive—to capture 'the countless figures of animals and objects of all kinds' [innumeras effigies animalium rerumque cunctarum]

---

[9] See Gerard Genette, *Mimologics*, trans. Thaïs E. Morgan (Lincoln: University of Nebraska Press, 1995), 26.

[10] Augustine, *De dialectica*, ed. Jan Pinborg, trans B. Darrell Jackson (Dördrecht, Holland: D. Reidel, 1975), vi (98–9). The *De dialectica* also qualifies this view by suggesting that words were not only 'affected by nature' but also 'by custom' ('sensus aut natura movetur aut consuetudine', vii (100–1)). See also Genette's chapter on the *De dialectica*, 'De ratione verborum' (*Mimologics*, 29–35).

[11] John of Salisbury, *Metalogicon*, ed. Clemens C. I. Webb (Oxford: Clarendon Press, 1929), I.14 (32); *The Metalogicon of John of Salisbury*, trans. Daniel D. McGarry (Berkeley: University of California Press, 1955), 39. For a very useful discussion of 'linguistic determinism' (which also cites this passage from the *Metalogicon*) see R. Howard Bloch, *Etymologies and Genealogies: A Literary Anthropology of the French Middle Ages* (Chicago: University of Chicago Press, 1983), 46–9. On the general topic of medieval cratylism see Jean Jolivet, 'Quelques cas de "platonisme grammatical" du viie au xiie siècle', 93–9 in *Mélanges offerts a René Crozet*, vol. 1 (of 2), ed. Pierre Gallais and Yves-Jean Riou (Poitiers: Société d'Études Médiévales, 1966).

which are in the 'world' [mundus].[12] But inasmuch as a profusion of
words is the only product of such an ambition, the encyclopedia is
itself a cratylist form, an attempt to adequate the world in words. For
this reason, the most influential medieval encyclopedia, what Isidore
of Seville (*c.*560–630) called his *Etymologiae*, does not begin with a
description of the world and its regions like the *Historia naturalis*,
but rather with grammar (book 1). As Isidore explains in this opening section, 'unless you know the name, you have no knowledge of
the thing' [nisi enim nomen scieris, cognitio rerum perit].[13] This statement is itself only a repetition of the name Isidore has given the thing
he has made, since etymology means to investigate the 'truth' (*etymos*)
by 'speaking about' it (*logos*).[14] To conduct natural history according
to such principles is in fact to believe that philology can substitute for
natural science. Isidore assumes, for example, that birds 'do not have
known paths' and 'travel outside their usual routes' because he believes
the word for 'path' (*via*) and the word meaning 'out of the way, remote,
untrodden' (*avia*) are condensed in the name he gives to birds, *avis*.[15]

   This last example is particularly important in what might now
be called encyclopedic thought, since cratylism in such cases was
supplemented by a medieval theory of language which held that
words were also alive. As John of Salisbury put this view, 'just as the
soul animates the body, so, in a way, meaning breathes life into a
word' [sicut corpus ad vitam vegetatur ab anima, sic ad vitam quandam verbi sensus proficiat].[16] This conflation inhered in the word *vox*
itself which was used to refer to both the 'voice, sound, tone, cry, [or]
call' of a living thing, and 'a word, saying, speech, [or] sentence'.[17] As

---

[12] Pliny, *Natural History*, 10 vols., ed. and trans. H. Rackham (London: William
Heinemann, 1940–67), II, iii.7 (1: 174–5). On Pliny's *Historia* in the period in question here see Marjorie Chibnall, 'Pliny's *Natural History* and the Middle Ages', 57–78
in *Empire and Aftermath: Silver Latin II*, ed. T. A. Dorey (London: Routledge &
Kegan Paul, 1975).

[13] Isidore of Seville, *Etymologiarum sive originum libri XX*, ed. W. M. Lindsay
(Oxford: Clarendon Press, 1911), I.vii.2.

[14] See *OED*, s.vv. 'etymology', 'etymon', and '-logy'.

[15] '*Aves* are so called because they do not have known paths, and they travel outside
their usual routes' [Aves dictae eo quod vias certas non habeant, sed per avia quaque
discurrunt], Isidore, *Etymologiae*, ed. Lindsay, II.vii. See also Isidore of Seville,
Étymologies: Livre XII (Des animaux), ed. and trans. Jacques André (Paris: Les
Belles Lettres, 1986), 227.

[16] John of Salibury, *Metalogicon*, ed. Webb, II.4 (66); *The Metalogicon of John of
Salisbury*, trans. McGarry, 81.

[17] Charlton T. Lewis and Charles Short, *A Latin Dictionary* (Oxford: Clarendon
Press, 1879), s.v. 'vox'.

Probus explained such usage in the *Instituta artium* (*c*.300), *vox* was
the 'sound' [sonus] any living thing produced by the 'striking of air'
[aer ictus], but that striking could result in either the 'articulate voice'
[vox articulata] expressed in letters ('qua homines locuntur et litteris
conprehendi potest'), or the 'confused voice' [vox confusa] made by
animals.[18] The conflation was further reinforced by definitions of
'life' which relied upon Aristotle's claim in the *De anima* that what
'displays life' is 'what has soul in it'[19]—or, as Bartholomaeus Anglicus
put the view more potently in his encyclopedia, the *De proprietatibus
rerum* (*c*.1245), the 'soul' [anima] is that part of the body which gives
it the 'capacity for being alive' [potenciam vitae habentis].[20] Such
definitions also followed Aristotle in believing that a thing had a soul
only if it had a voice ('voice is a kind of sound characteristic of what
has soul in it; nothing that is without soul utters voice'), and therefore
that 'voice' was the sign of life.[21] As Aristotle was translated in the

[18] 'Vox sive sonus est aer ictus, id est percussus, sensibilis auditu, quantum in ipso
est, hoc est quam diu resonat. Nunc omnis vox sive sonum aut articulata est aut confusa. Articulata est, qua homines locuntur et litteris conprehendi potest ut puta "scribe
Cicero", "Vergili lege" et cetera talia; confusa vero aut animalium aut inanimalium
est, quae litteris conprehendi non potest. Animalium est ut puta equorum hinnitus,
rabies canum, rugitus ferarum, serpentum sibilus, avium cantus et cetera talia; inanimalium autem est ut puta cymbalorum tinnitus, flagellorum strepitus, undarum
pulsus, ruinae casus, fistulae auditus et cetera talia. Est et confusa vox sive sonus
hominum, quae litteris conprehendi non potest, ut puta oris risus vel sibilatus, pectoris
mugitus et cetera talia. De voce sive sono, quantum ratio poscebat, tractavimus',
Grammatici Latini, ed. Heinrich Keil, 7 vols. (Leipzig: B. G. Teubner, 1857–80),
4: 47. Priscian (*c*.500) offers finer but similar distinctions in his *Institutiones gram-
maticae*. See *Grammatici Latini*, 2: 5–6. On the general topic see Vivien Law,
Grammar and Grammarians in the Early Middle Ages (London: Longman, 1997),
esp. 262–3.
[19] Aristotle, 'On the Soul', 1: 641–92 in *The Complete Works of Aristotle*, ed.
Jonathan Barnes, 2 vols., rev. edn. (Princeton: Princeton University Press, 1984),
413a22–23 (1: 658).
[20] Bartholomaeus, *De proprietatibus rerum* (Basel: Ruppel, *c*.1468), fos. 8ᵛ–9ʳ
(III.ii–iv). This incunabulum is not dated, but see R. Proctor, *An Index to the Early
Printed Books in the British Museum*, 2 vols. (London: Kegan Paul, 1898), 2: 538 (no.
7452). In the section from which I quote, Bartholomaeus cites Aristotle in order to
define the *anima rationalis* thus: 'Anima est *endilechia*, id est, actus primus siue per-
fectio corporis phisici organici potenciam vitae habentis' (III.iii, fo. 9ʳ). I have had to
emend the grammar here slightly for sense, but there is as yet no modern edition of this
encyclopedia (I thank Jill Mann for her advice in this matter). For a recent account of
the text see M. C. Seymour and colleagues, *Bartholomaeus Anglicus and his Encyclopedia* (Aldershot: Variorum, 1992). This encyclopedia is readily available in the modern
edition of John of Trevisa's 14th-c. English translation: Bartholomaeus Anglicus, *On
the Properties of Things*, 2 vols., ed. M. C. Seymour (Oxford: Clarendon Press, 1975).
[21] Aristotle, 'On the Soul', *Complete Works*, 420b5–10 (1: 641–92).

twelfth century by James of Venice (fl. 1125–50),[22] 'voice' was simply
'the sound of a living thing' [vox sonus quidam est animati].[23]

It might even be said, then, that the encyclopedia made no distinction between words and living things, as is made clear by the very
examples Bartholomaeus gives in his definition of *vox*:

And every voice is a sound [omnis enim vox est sonus], but not vice-versa. For
sound is the object of hearing, because all that is perceived by hearing is called
'sound', such as the breaking of trees, the striking together of stones, the
rushing of waves and of wind, the chattering of birds, the lowing of animals,
the cries and the calls of the voices of men, and the beating of instruments.
But the voice is properly the sound that comes from the mouth of an animal.
And sound is made from a striking of air against a hard body, the sound of
which is more quickly and easily seen than its sound is heard, as lightning is
seen more quickly than the ears of men are filled with the sound of thunder.
A voice is the thinnest air, struck by the instrument of the tongue. And some
kinds of voice signify naturally, such as the chattering of birds and the groan-
ing of the sick; and others signify by agreement, such as the voice of men
shaped into certain words by the order of reason, fashioned by the organ of
the tongue. For voice is the vehicle of a word, nor can the thought of a word
in the mind be expressed outwardly except with the assistance of the voice.
Whence the intellect first conceives the word in thought, and afterward it is
brought forth from the mouth by the voice. Whence the word is generated
and conceived in the mind and shows itself outwardly, as if by an instrument,
through the voice.[24]

---

[22] On James of Venice see Bernard G. Dod, 'Aristoteles latinus', 45–79 in *The
Cambridge History of Later Medieval Philosophy*, ed. Norman Kretzmann, Anthony
Kenny, and Jan Pinborg (Cambridge: Cambridge University Press, 1982), 54–5.
[23] I cite James's translation from Oxford, Corpus Christi College, MS 114, fo. 154ʳ.
On James of Venice and this manuscript see L. Minio-Paluello, 'Iacobus Veneticus
Grecus: Canonist and Translator of Aristotle', *Traditio* 8 (1952), 265–304. The
importance of James's translation of the *De anima* is attested by its 144 surviving
manuscripts. The popularity of the *De anima* in the 13th c. is further illustrated
by the two additional Latin translations made in this period, one by Michael Scot
(*c*.1220–35) surviving in 62 manuscripts, and the other by William of Moerbeke
(*c*.1268), surviving in 268 manuscripts. On these translations see *The Cambridge
History of Later Medieval Philosophy*, ed. Kretzmann, Kenny, and Pinborg, 76; and
Dod, 'Aristoteles latinus', 58–64 and 73–8. For the text of Michael Scot's translation
see *Averrois Cordubensis commentarium magnum in Aristotelis de anima libros*, ed.
F. Stuart Crawford (Cambridge, Mass.: The Medieval Academy of America, 1953).
For the text by William of Moerbeke see *Aristotle's De anima in the Version of William
of Moerbeke*, trans. Kenelm Foster and Silvester Humphries (London: Routledge,
1951).
[24] 'Omnis enim vox est sonus, sed non e converso. Nam sonus est obiectum auditus
quia quidquid auditu percipitur, sonus dicitur, ut fragor arborum et collisio lapidum,
strepitus fluctuum et ventorum, garritus avium, mugitus animalium, voces clamores

Vox here includes everything from 'the voice of men shaped into certain words' to the 'chattering of birds'. It is true that, in the course of this conflation, Bartholomaeus explicitly retreats from the major premise of cratylism (he notes that 'some kinds of voice signify naturally . . . and others signify by agreement'), but the retreat also isolates those (rarer) cases in which language *is* natural in its signification. As the last sentence of the passage makes clear, moreover, this specification occurs not only by finding that class of representable objects which most resemble words (the living things which have a 'voice'), but by understanding words to be created in the same way as new life, 'conceived' [conceptum] or even 'generated' [genitum].

A poet who wished to trace or test such thinking might well think about the 'chattering of birds', and in particular, the chattering of an 'owl' and 'nightingale', for encyclopedias also held that the names for these birds were not only alive like the voices of the things that they named, but that they were derived directly from the sounds they made—that the *vox* of the word, in these cases, essentially *was* the life of the bird. Pliny is already making something like this point when he describes these birds in terms of their voices alone: the 'eagle-owl' [bubo], he writes, has a particularly startling voice ('its cry is not a musical note but a moan'),[25] while 'nightingales' [luscinis] 'pour out a ceaseless gush of song for fifteen days and nights on end when the

et clangores hominum, et percussiones organorum. Vox autem proprie dicitur sonus ab ore animalis prolatus. Ex aëre autem percusso et ad superficiem duri corporis alliso generatur sonus. Cuius allisionis percussio citius et facilius visu percipitur quam eius sonitus audiatur, et ideo citius videtur procedens coruscatio quam tonitruo aures hominis perfundantur. Vox autem est aër tenuissimus ictus, plectro linguae formatus. Et est quaedam vox significativa naturaliter, ut garritus avium et gemitus infirmorum; et alia est significativa ad placitum, ut vox hominis articulata et ad aliquod verbum proferendum rationis imperio linguae organo informata. Vox enim verbi vehiculum est nec potest conceptum verbum in mente exterius exprimi nisi vocis adminiculo mediante proferatur. Unde intellectus primo verbum in mente gignit, quod per vocem postea ore promit. Unde verbum a mente genitum et conceptum per vocem quasi per organum se exterius ostendit', Herman Müller, 'Der Musiktraktat in dem Werke des Bartholomaeus Anglicus *De proprietatibus rerum*', 241–55 in *Riemann-Festschrift: Gesammelte Studien* (Leipzig: Max Hesses, 1909), 247 (cap. 132). This passage can also be found in *On the Properties of Things*, ed. Seymour as XIX, 131 ('de musica').

On the patristic origins of the connection between music and the flesh underwriting the equation here see Bruce W. Holsinger, *Music, Body, and Desire in Medieval Culture: Hildegard of Bingen to Chaucer* (Stanford, Calif.: Stanford University Press, 2001), 27–60 (chapter 1: 'The Resonance of the Flesh').

[25] 'Nec cantu aliquo vocalis sed gemitu', Pliny, *Natural History*, X.xvi (2: 314–15).

buds of the leaves are swelling'.[26] But it is Isidore who again sees most clearly how philology recapitulates ontology in such cases: he notices that *bubo* is imitative ('the owl has been given her name by the sound of her voice' [bubo a sono vocis conpositum nomen habet],[27] and that *luscinia* is a name which 'derives' from the fact that 'the nightingale indicates daybreak with her song' [luscinia auis inde nomen sumpsit quia cantu suo significare solet diei surgentis exortum].[28]

For a medieval poet writing in English, these encyclopaedic under-standings would have been further reinforced by two different sites where the nature of these particular birds was more or less reduced to the sound of their voices. The first is Ovid's *Metamorphoses* which posited the origins of both birds in a particularly memorable speech act. In this version of natural history the *bubo* is always a 'prophet of woe' [nuntia luctus] because he was once that Ascalaphus who saw Persephone eat the pomegranate and by his 'cruel tattling' [indicio crudelis] ensured that she would have to return yearly to Hades.[29] *Philomela* functioned as a common Latin noun for 'nightingale' because Ovid's tale of Philomela's transformation was so striking, not only because of its violence, but because it represented Philomela *as* speech—first as rape left her with no remedy but her cries ('I will fill the woods with my story and move the very rocks to pity'),[30] and, then, as her protestations provoked Tereus to take her voice from her: '[Tereus] seized her tongue with pincers, as it protested against the outrage calling ever on the name of her father and struggling to

---

[26] 'Luscinis diebus ac noctibus continuis xv garrulas sine intermissu cantus densante se fondium germine', Pliny, *Natural History*, X.xliii (344–5).

[27] Isidore also mentions two other words for 'owl', *noctua*, which is so named 'because it flies at night' ('noctua dicitur pro eo quod nocte circumuolat') and *noctico-rax*, which is also so named because it 'loves the night' ('nocticorax ipsa est noctua, quia noctem amat'), Isidore, *Étymologies: Livre XII (Des animaux)*, ed. and trans. André, XII.40–1 (254–5). Bartholomaeus repeats and cites Isidore's explanation of the word *bubo* ('bubo a sono vocis nomen habet'), *De proprietatibus rerum*, XII.v. He also extends it to the synonym for owl, *ulula*, which he says is also a name given to a bird because of its 'cry' ('ulula est avis a planctu ululatu nominata'). *De proprietatibus rerum* (XII.36). See also the description of the *nicticorax* (XII.27).

[28] Isidore, *Étymologies: Livre XII (Des animaux)*, ed. and trans André, XII.37 (252–3); on this etymology see 252–3 n. 502. There is a slightly different but similar etymology in the *Oxford Latin Dictionary* (Oxford: Clarendon Press, 1968–82) s.v. 'luscinia' (perh. <*lusci- cinia, 'singing in the twilight' Luscus + Cano). For 'lucinus' as 'light-bringing' see Lewis and Short, *Latin Dictionary*, s.v. 'lucinus'.

[29] Ovid, *Metamorphoses*, 2 vols., trans. F. J. Miller (London: Heinemann, 1966–8), V.533–52 (1: 274–7).

[30] 'Inplebo silvas et conscia saxa movebo', Ovid, *Metamorphoses*, VI.547 (1: 326–7).

speak, and cut it off with his merciless blade.'[31] Against this dramatic literary background, a poet writing in English would also have felt the etymological pressures from those words habitually used to replace *bubo* or *luscinia* or *philomela*. 'Hule' is a word that the attentive ear can still hear as a derivation from (as the *OED* puts it) the 'voice of the bird' (or, more precisely, from an 'echoic' Old Teutonic root, **uwwû*).[32] 'Niȝtingale' compounds Middle English elements for the making of a loud sound by a living thing (*galan* meaning 'cry' or 'shout') with the time of day (albeit a different time than the Latin etymology specifies) at which this bird's *vox* is typically heard.[33]

All such connections between voices and names are so fully absorbed to the form of *The Owl and the Nightingale* that the equation is made in the poem's second couplet: bird sounds precede bird names ('Iherde ich holde grete tale') but to hear those sounds is immediately to have produced those names ('an hule and one niȝtingale'). Nature therefore follows immediately from name ('eiþer seide of oþeres custe' [character, 9]), and the most significant attribute of character for each bird is its song: the nightingale begins by condemning the owl's 'hooting' or 'shrieking' ('me luste bet speten þane singe | Of þine fule ȝoȝelinge' (39–40)), while the owl hears the nightingale's song as equally obnoxious ('þu chaterest so doþ an Irish prost' (322)). But the form of *The Owl and the Nightingale* posits a natural relation between words and the world most extensively as grammatical gender is everywhere allowed to determine the natural gender of every living thing the poem mentions. Although there are exceptions to the general rule, the pressure of grammatical gender is particularly clear in the most minor cases: because they are historically masculine, the 'crowe' (304–5), 'faukun' (101–2), 'haueck' ('hawk' (303–4)), 'hare' (373–4), 'kat' (810) and 'fox' (812–13) are all male figures, taking dependent masculine forms; because they are grammatically feminine even lilies ('Þe lilie mid hire faire wlite' (439)) and roses ('Þe rose also, mid hire rude' (443)) are feminine presences in the poem.[34] And the equation is also most consistent where it is most

---

[31] 'Ille indignantem et nomen patris usque vocantem | luctantemque loqui conprensam forcipe linguam | abstulit ense fero', Ovid, *Metamorphoses*, VI.555–7 (1: 326–7).

[32] *OED*, s.v. 'owl sb.'.

[33] *OED*, s.v. 'nightgale obs.' See also *MED*, s.v. 'galen'.

[34] Cartlidge notes a few other exceptions, which he understands as evidence that grammatical gender is in 'competition' with natural gender in the poem (see *The Owl and the Nightingale*, ed. Cartlidge, p. xlvi).

consequential, in the case of the 'hule', the 'niȝtingale', and, finally,
the 'wrenne': each bird is a female figure whose name governs dependent feminine forms (demonstratives and pronouns) because these
words were grammatically feminine.[35]

The conflation of grammatical and natural gender is also particularly visible as a cratylist gesture in this case (a more obviously meaningful part of a poetic form rather than a transparent condition of
language) because it was hardly necessary. While the moment when
grammatical gender died out in Middle English is open to debate (and
this poem's prominence in the record necessarily confuses the issue),
it is generally accepted that the change occurred before the beginning
of the thirteenth century when we conventionally date *The Owl and
the Nightingale*.[36] Certainly by the time *The Thrush and the Nightingale*
(1272–1307) was written it is possible to have a poem in which two
birds speak (and which is therefore cratylist to that extent), without
equating grammatical and natural gender: while the 'niȝtingale' in
that poem is also female, the thrush is male even though 'þrysce' was,
historically, a feminine noun.[37] In at least one of the many traditions
on which the author of *The Owl and the Nightingale* relies, moreover, each of the birds who speaks in this poem is a masculine figure.
Although *philomela* and *luscinia* are both grammatically feminine,
bubo was grammatically masculine (which is why Ovid's owl is a

---

[35] On the grammatical gender of 'owl' see, again, *OED*, s.v. 'owl sb.'. For 'nightingale' and 'wren' the *OED* gives only the Old English etymons 'nightgale' and 'wrenna'
(s.vv. 'nightgale Obs.' and 'wren1'), but for the feminine gender of these roots in Old
English see *An Anglo-Saxon Dictionary*, ed. Joseph Bosworth and T. Northcote Toller
(Oxford: Oxford University Press, 1972; 1st published 1878), s.vv. 'nihtegale' and
'wrenna'. The mistaken view that Middle English 'niȝtingale' and 'wren' are derived
from Old English words which were grammatically masculine was advanced by Henry
Barret Hinckley ('Science and Folk-Lore in *The Owl and the Nightingale*', *PMLA* 47
(1932), 312). The problem is pointed out in Alexandra Barratt, 'Flying in the Face
of Tradition: A New View of the *Owl and the Nightingale*', *University of Toronto
Quarterly* 56 (1987), 471–85 (484, n. 31).
[36] See T. F. Mustanoja, *A Middle English Syntax: Part 1 (Parts of Speech)*, Mémoires
de la Société de Helsinki 23 (Helsinki, 1960), 43–52 (esp. 43–4). For the arguments
behind the conventional dating of *The Owl and the Nightingale* at the beginning of
the 13th c., as well as a persuasive argument placing the poem much later (and, for the
purposes of my argument, that much further from obligatory grammatical gender in
English), see Neil Cartlidge, 'The Date of *The Owl and the Nightingale*', *MÆ* 65
(1996), 230–47.
[37] For this poem see *Middle English Debate Poetry: A Critical Anthology*, ed.
John W. Conlee (East Lansing, Mich.: Colleagues Press, 1991), 237–48. For the grammatical gender of 'thrush' see *OED*, s.v. 'thrush 1', and *An Anglo-Saxon Dictionary*,
ed. Bosworth and Toller, s.v. 'þrysce'.

transformed boy). In the *lai* called 'Laustic' by Marie de France—a text the owl seems to have some knowledge of (1043–66)—the *russignol* (as the nightingale is first called there) as well as the *laüstic* (as it is subsequently described by Marie) are also masculine.[38] Since the common Latin term for the 'wren' is the masculine *regulus*, this 'royal' bird was often represented as a 'king' (a tradition *The Owl and the Nightingale* even acknowledges when it says the wren is a bird worthy to speak 'touore þe king' (1728)).[39]

Of course animal gender would only put light pressure on the relationship of words to lives if it governed no more than pronouns and declensions, were femininity not thought to have such determinate effects on the sound and the typical uses of the female voice. To medieval ears, in fact, the owl and the nightingale not only sound like birds when they make a noise that is 'stif & starc & strong' (5) they sound female, since such stridency was thought to be the essential mark of feminine speaking. The view is as old as the pseudo-Aristotelian *Problems* (where a 'shrill voice' is connected to 'persons without generative power, such as boys, women, men grown old, and eunuchs'),[40] but it was most fully and influentially developed in treatises on rhetoric. The author of the *Ad Herennium* (86–82 BC) cautions, for example, that 'sharp exclamation injures the voice and likewise jars the hearer, for it has about it something ignoble, suited rather to feminine outcry [muliebrem vociferationem] than to manly dignity in speaking'.[41] In the *Institutio oratoria* (*c*.100), Quintilian

---

[38] 'Une aventure vus dirae, | Dunt li Breton firent un lai; | Laüstic ad nun, ceo m'est vis, | Si l'apelent en lur païs; | Ceo est russignol en franceis | E nihtegale en dreit anglais', Marie de France, 'Laüstic', 97–101 in *Lais*, ed. Alfred Ewert, intro. Glyn S. Burgess (London: Duckworth, 1995; 1st published 1944), 97–101, lines 1–6. See also *Altfranzösisches Wörterbuch*, ed. Adolf Tobler and Erhard Lommatzsch, 10 vols. (Stuttgart: Steiner, 1915–), s.v. 'rosseignol'.

[39] On the 'royal wren', see *The Owl and the Nightingale*, ed. Eric Gerald Stanley (Manchester: Manchester University Press, 1960; rev. 1972), 167; and, as cited by Stanley, Alexander Neckam, *De naturis rerum libri duo*, 2 vols., ed. Thomas Wright, Rolls Series 34 (London, 1863), 1: 122–3. The Old French term for wren, *roitelet*, was also masculine. See Tobler and Lommatzsch, *Altfranzösisches Wörterbuch*, s.v. 'roitelet'.

[40] Aristotle, *Problems*, 2: 1319–527 in *Complete Works*, ed. Barnes, 903b30–3 (2: 1402).

[41] 'Acuta exclamatio vocem vulnerat; eadem laedit auditorem, habet enim quiddam inliberale et ad muliebrem potius vociferationem quam ad virilem dignitatem in dicendo adcommodatum', Pseudo-Cicero, *Ad Herennium*, ed. and trans. Harry Caplan, Loeb Classical Library (Cambridge, Mass.: Harvard University Press, 1976; 1st printed 1942), III.xii.22 (pp. 194–5).

writes of the 'feeble shrillness' [exilitas] that characterizes the voices
of 'eunuchs, women and invalids',[42] and also derogates the voice
that is 'thin, empty, grating, feeble, soft or effeminate' [tenuis, inanis,
acerba, pusilla, mollis, effeminata].[43] These observations were also
absorbed to that genre of writing which Howard Bloch has called
'medieval misogyny', whose various forms were united in the general attempt to vilify women by learned argument.[44] That absorption
is already occurring in Juvenal (second century AD) who sees the unpleasantness of a woman's voice as a reification of her bad character:
'The grammarians make way before her; the rhetoricians give in; the
whole crowd is silenced: no lawyer, no auctioneer will get a word in,
no nor any other woman; so torrential is her speech that you would
think that all the pots and bells were being clashed together.'[45] And
it was just this view which Jerome developed in the immensely influential *Adversus Jovinianum* (c.393) where garrulity not only represented, but constituted, women's badness (she 'floods [a man's] house
with her constant nagging and daily chatter').[46] In the equally influential *De amore* (c.1185) by Andreas Capellanus, noise is not only
the sound that women are, but the weapon they brandish in order to
spread discord throughout society: 'All women are also free with
their tongues, for not one of them can restrain her tongue from revil-
ing people, or from crying out all day long like a barking dog over the

[42] 'Sed cura non eadem oratoribus quae phonascis convenit tamen multa sunt
utrisque communia, firmitas corporis, ne ad spadonum et mulierum et aegrorum exil-
itatem vox nostra tenuetur', Quintilian, *Institutio oratoria*, ed. and trans. Donald
A. Russell, 5 vols., Loeb Classical Library (Cambridge, Mass.: Harvard University
Press, 2001), XI.iii.19 (5: 94–5).
[43] 'Deinde non subsurda rudis immanis dura rigida rauca praepinguis, aut tenuis
inanis acerba pusilla mollis effeminata, spiritus nec brevis nec parum durabilis nec in
receptu difficilis', Quintilian, *Institutio oratoria*, XI.3.32 (5: 100–1).
[44] R. Howard Bloch, *Medieval Misogyny and the Invention of Western Romantic
Love* (Chicago: University of Chicago Press, 1991).
[45] 'Cedunt grammatici, vincuntor rhetores, omnis | turba tacet, nec causidicus nec
praeco loquetur, | altera nec mulier; verborum tanta cadit vis | tot pariter pelves
ac tintinnabula dicas | pulsari', 'Satire VI', lines 438–43 in *Juvenal and Persius*, ed.
G. G. Ramsay (London: Harvard University Press, 1918; repr. 1990).
[46] 'Assiduis quippe jurgiis et quotidiana garrulitate facit perfluere domum eius
. . .', J.-P. Migne, *Patrologiae cursus completus, series latina* (Paris, 1844–64), vol. 23,
col. 250. I take my translation from *Woman Defamed and Woman Defended*, ed.
Alcuin Blamires (Oxford: Oxford University Press, 1992), 67 which is, in turn, taken
from W. H. Fremantle, *The Principal Works of St Jerome*, Select Library of Nicene
and Post-Nicene Fathers, vi (Oxford: James Parker, 1893). In this and the following
paragraph, I have been greatly assisted in my research by Blamires's comprehensive
anthology.

loss of a single egg, disturbing the whole neighbourhood for a trifle.'[47] We might say that the nightingale thinks the owl's sound is 'grislich' (224), or that the owl thinks the nightingale sings with an aggravating 'whistle' ['pipe', 319] according to that standard joke of beast fable in which species difference becomes ethical difference, but since that ethical difference maps so completely onto medieval misogyny, we can also say that these birds dislike each other because they hear each other as women.[48]

The connection between this owl and nightingale and medieval misogyny is further intensified by what these birds actually say, for there was also a more moralistic (less forensic, and, inevitably, more clerkly) strain of medieval misogyny in which the unpleasantness of women's voices was not so much a question of quality, but of content, not least as that content gave women's statements a characteristic stance and shape. As Jacques de Vitry (1170–1240) makes the relevant observation in a sermon (where he is citing Juvenal): 'the marital bed is always a place of dispute and mutual bickering',[49] because, as he continues (citing Ovid), 'a wife's dowry is quarrelling'.[50] According to this thinking it is not simply that women quarrel because they are inherently unkind or unreasonable, but because femininity can be defined *as* opposition. Women's noise is, as the popular poem *De coniuge non ducenda* (1222–50) had it, a kind of 'tongue' or 'sword',[51] not simply because it is generally harmful, but because it turns all conversation into a kind of combat:

[47] 'Est et omnis femina virlingosa, quia nulla est quae suam noverit a maledictis, compescere linguam, et quae pro unius ovi amissione die tota velut canis latrando non clamaret et totam pro re modica viciniam non turbaret', *Andreas Capellanus on Love*, ed. and trans. P. G. Walsh (London: Duckworth, 1982), Book III.100 (316–17).

[48] My point in this paragraph was anticipated by Hinckley, who also noticed the implicit claim of such a conflation of grammatical and natural gender in the context of an argument: 'Is it too much to fancy that the poet thought of his birds as scolding women?' ('Science and Folklore', 312).

[49] 'Semper habet lites alternaque iurgia lectus | in quo nupta iacet', Sermon 66 in *Sermones Vulgares* as excerpted and translated in *Woman Defamed, and Woman Defended*, 145. See also 'Satire VI', lines 268–9 in *Juvenal and Persius*, ed. Ramsay.

[50] 'Dos est uxoria lites', Ovid, *Ars amatoria*, II.155 in *The Art of Love and Other Poems*, ed. J. H. Mozley, rev. G. P. Goold (London: William Heinemann, 1979). I cite the English from Blamires's translation of Jacques de Vitry's *Sermones vulgares* in *Woman Defamed and Woman Defended* (145).

[51] 'Est lingua gladius in ore femine | Quo vir percutitur tanquam a fulmine | Per hanc ilaritas fugit ab homine; | Domus subuertitur ut austri turbine', *De coniuge non ducenda: Gawain on Marriage: The Textual Tradition of the De coniuge non ducenda with Critical Edition and Translation*, by A. G. Rigg (Toronto: Pontifical Institute of Mediaeval Studies, 1986), J.12.

> The wife's demands are always met;
> If not, she'll quarrel, rage and fret.
> The noise defeats the patient spouse;
> He yields to her and quits the house.[52]

In this view, female noise is a mode of being in language which only exists in so far as there is a position for it to attack. This is also what bird noise is when the owl and the nightingale employ oaths or imperatives that signify nothing more than their disagreement ('Unwiȝt! awei þu flo!' [33]; 'Nay, nay, [543]; 'Abid! Abid' [837]; 'Hwat!' [1730]). It is also a mode of speaking embraced by the nightingale when she entirely abandons statement near the end of the poem, vowing to 'plaide na more' (1639) and offering, instead, a 'song so schrille & so brihte' (1656) that her voice occupies all the aural space in which the owl might speak. As Andreas Capellanus describes this feminine technique in the *De amore*, 'A woman gossiping with other women would never willingly give another a chance to speak; she always tries to dominate the conversation with her own opinions, and to go on talking longest.'[53] According to Helen Solterer, the very extent of clerical investment in the figure of the 'women responding both iteratively and antagonistically' was self-perpetuating, a 'system' which itself furnished 'reasons' for the 'exclusion and progressive objectification' in which it was itself engaged.[54]

It is therefore one of the poem's best and most significant jokes that the owl and the nightingale immediately agree about the efficacy and necessity of disagreeing, that, after they have first crossed swords, the nightingale proposes that they continue to argue, but with more 'decorum' ('mid fayre worde' (182)), and the owl readily assents ('Ich granti wel' (201)). This joke is also the form's second and most significant feint, for, even as this agreement itself quickly sinks beneath the onslaught of renewed (and, again, ever more insistent) quarrelling, such disagreement has been reclassified by the poem as a recognizable procedure, what the owl later names 'disputinge' (875) or 'sputinge'

---

[52] 'Voluntas coniugis semper efficitur; | Sin autem, litigat, flet et irascitur | Maritus paciens clamore vincitur; | Et cedens coniugi domum egreditur', *De coniuge non ducenda*, J.14.

[53] 'Immo mulier cum aliis commorando nunquam alicui ad loquendum vellet cedere locum, sed suis semper dictis nititur dicenda committere et in suo diutius sermone durare', *Andreas Capellanus on Love*, ed. and trans. P. G. Walsh III.100 (316–17).

[54] Helen Solterer, *The Master and Minerva: Disputing Women in French Medieval Culture* (Berkeley: University of California Press, 1995), 100.

(1574). As Peter Cantor understood this particular form of intellectual aggressivity it was the method by which received ideas were
transformed into understanding (nothing can be 'fully understood
or properly preached', he said, unless it 'has been chewed by the teeth
of disputation').[55] But the name the Middle Ages gave to 'the science
of disputing well' was *dialectic*.[56] Therefore, as the birds pursue this
science so fully that it finally fills out the bulk of the poem, their disagreement gives this whole poem the shape which the Middle Ages
most valued for words, a shape that was often taken to be equivalent
to understanding itself. In fact, since it was itself proverbial in the
same clerkly milieu that gave this owl and the nightingale their female
identities and voices that 'the business of dialectic is to discern the
truth' [veritas diiudicanda . . . dialectica profitetur] the narrator's
encounter with precisely two birds is the poem's most important
cratylist gesture: as *The Owl and the Nightingale* is itself no more
than the qualities and structures inherent in this dyad, it adequates
the world most fully as its form approaches what the Middle Ages
often understood to be the form of truth.[57]

THE TRUTH ABOUT WOMEN

We have long known that *The Owl and the Nightingale* is dialectical,
of course, but this awareness has rarely prevented this poem from

[55] 'In tribus igitur consistit exercitium sacrae Scripturae: circa lectionem, disputa-
tionem et praedicationem. Cuilibet istorum mater oblivionis et noverca memoriae est
nimia prolixitas. Lectio autem est quasi fundamentum, et substratorium sequentium;
quia per eam caeterae utilitates comparantur. Disputatio quasi paries est in hoc ex-
ercitio et aedificio; quia nihil plene intelligitur, fideliterve praedicatur, nisi prius dente
disputationis frangatur', Petrus Cantor, *Verbum abbreviatum*, ed. Migne, *Patrologia
Latina*, 205, col. 25. Cited in James J. Murphy, 'Rhetoric and Dialectic in *The Owl and
the Nightingale*', 198–230 in James J. Murphy, *Medieval Eloquence: Studies in the
Theory and Practice of Medieval Rhetoric* (Berkeley: University of California Press,
1978), 201.
[56] 'Dialectica est bene disputandi scientia', Augustine, *De dialectica*, ed. Pinborg,
trans. Jackson, ch. 1 (82–3). Citing this definition Catherine Brown calls it a 'medieval
commonplace', *Contrary Things: Exegesis, Dialectic, and the Poetics of Didacticism*
(Stanford, Calif.: Stanford University Press, 1998), 160 n. 2.
[57] Augustine, *De dialectica*, ed. Pinborg, trans. Jackson, ch. 8 (102–3). The common medieval mnemonic for the liberal arts also understood 'truths' to be the province
of dialectic: 'Gram. loquitur; Dia. vera docet; Rhe. verba ministrat; Mus. canit; Ar.
numerat; Geo. ponderat', Ernst Robert Curtius, *European Literature and the Latin
Middle Ages*, trans. Willard R. Trask, Bollingen Series 36 (Princeton: Princeton
University Press, 1953), 37.

causing us to forget what dialectic is or why it might ever have been highly valued.[58] What Schleusener has described as an 'overly stringent balance of contradictory positions' leads us to expect that this particular debate '*must* have a winner' as well as disappoints or confuses us when, in the end, it does not.[59] Our sense that this owl and this nightingale present viable alternatives that the poem finally fails to choose between ('which of the two (solemn or serious) is the better way of life')[60] effectively produces our sense that this poem cannot be serious about the alternatives it seems to consider (that it is 'mock-debate', a 'burlesque-satire on human contentiousness').[61] It is certainly true that medieval thinkers were themselves often disappointed by dialectic's results, and even John of Salisbury wrote the *Metalogicon* as 'a moderate and moderating critique of the excesses of contemporary dialectical teaching and reading'.[62] But, as John also knew, dialectic was an indispensable instrument precisely because it absorbed inconclusiveness to its cognitive procedures, because it counted uncertainty as a form of knowledge (as John put this point, 'of a truth, there is no dearth of questions, which present themselves everywhere, although they are by no means everywhere solved').[63] However sure we now are that (as Isidore put this point) dialectic was 'the discipline established to explain the reasons for things . . . in several kinds of questions' [dialectica est disciplina ad disserendas rerum causas inuenta . . . in pluribus generibus quaestionum], it is yet

[58] See Murphy, 'Rhetoric and Dialectic' and, also, Douglas L. Peterson, '*The Owl and the Nightingale* and Christian Dialectic', *Journal of English and Germanic Philology* 55 (1956), 13–26. Michael Swanton says the birds speak in the 'reflective mode of medieval disputation' or 'demonstrative dialectic', a form of 'enquiry' whose form may make us expect a 'decisive outcome' but which seeks, rather, to provide a 'balanced tension' (*English Literature Before Chaucer* (London: Longman, 1987), 279–80).

[59] Schleusener, ' "The Owl and the Nightingale" ', 185; the emphasis is Schleusener's.

[60] *The Owl and the Nightingale*, ed. Stanley, 22.

[61] Constance Hieatt, 'The Subject of the Mock-Debate Between the Owl and the Nightingale', *Studia Neophilologica* 40 (1968): 159; and Kathryn Hume, *The Owl and the Nightingale: the Poem and its Critics* (Toronto: University of Toronto Press, 1975), 100.

[62] Brown, *Contrary Things*, 40. In her second chapter, Brown describes these criticisms (many lodged by John of Salisbury himself in the *Metalogicon*) as well as the positive role dialectic was thought to play ('Contradiction in the City: John of Salisbury and the Practice of Dialectic', 36–62).

[63] 'Siquidem undique emergunt questiones, sed non undique absoluuntur', John of Salibury, *Metalogicon*, ed. Webb, II.12 (84); *Metalogicon*, trans. McGarry, 102.

another of the extraordinary powers of *The Owl and the Nightingale* to make us expect dialectic to provide answers.[64]

Criticism's forgetfulness in this regard has also been assisted by its failure to care enough about the kinds of questions and truths important in this poem; we had, in short, to wait for our own feminism to catch up with *The Owl and the Nightingale* before we could notice that these birds are not only represented as women, but that what they actually talk most *about* is women (lines 1043–1111 and again lines 1336–1603).[65] What such a feminism must also find is that these birds generally accept medieval misogyny's major premises. For the nightingale, a woman is frail (of 'nesche flesche' (1387)) and for the owl she is 'soft and delicate' ('wel nesche and softe' (1546)), and it is on these grounds that the nightingale also says women fall 'by nature' ('falþ icundeliche' (1424)). But it is also because they agree on these points of departure that these two birds can bring the interrogative energy of their disputation to bear so powerfully on these particular tenets. In so far as grammar produces femininity as a subject for debate in this poem, the ideas associated with the feminine become available to the corrosive questioning of dialectic; as John of Salisbury described this crucial relation, 'while grammar chiefly examines the words that express meanings, dialectic investigates the meanings expressed by words'.[66]

Since the unfolding of that dialectic is also the elaboration of a poetic structure, this interrogation is inevitably structuralist, and it does not dismantle misogyny by counter-example or argument, but by noticing some of the ignored implications and consequences forced out of a structure by the positions it otherwise forces its makers to adopt (the poem's feminism consists of what misogyny knows but refuses to acknowledge). This procedure ensures that the misogyny which confects the poem emerges from a shared ethic, a common grid for orienting behaviours with respect to the 'good'. That this ethic is misogynistic is itself one of the poem's jokes, for

---

[64] Isidore of Seville, *Etymologies Book II, Rhetoric*, ed. and trans. Peter K. Marshall (Paris: Les Belles Lettres, 1983), 96–9.

[65] Barratt was the first to notice this poem's extended interest in the 'sufferings of women' and to connect this interest to the 'extended treatment of the Owl and the Nightingale as female' ('Flying in the Face of Tradition', 476–7).

[66] 'Illa verba sensuum principaliter: sed hec examinat sensus verborum', John of Salisbury, *Metalogicon*, ed. Webb, II.4 (66); *The Metalogicon of John of Salisbury*, trans. McGarry, 81.

both birds are true Aristotelians in defining goodness not only as that which helps people (rather than birds or any other kind of animal), but as that which helps *men*.[67] This means, however, that the birds' first observations about women are morally neutral with respect to them, mapping out a field of social possibility in which women are never actually the point. When the owl complains that the nightingale once 'tried to entice a lady into a disgraceful love' ('woldst lere | Þe lefdi to an uuel luue' (1051–2)), for example, it is clear that woman never actually did anything wrong. Similarly, when the nightingale replies that this woman only had the capacity to make her husband unhappy because he was so jealous ('he was so gelus of his wive' (1077)), the obstruction to goodness in the case turns out to be the man himself. Even though these examples focus on women, in other words, the birds do not even bother to blame them. And it is in precisely this way that they also make clear that women 'always' oppose men because they are only visible when they stand athwart them— because human ethics defines the 'good' from a male point of view.

   Although the birds make this important discovery almost as soon as they take up this subject, they soon seem to abandon it altogether (the nightingale tells us at some length about the owl's capacity to frighten and portend doom (1111–74), then the owl describes the accuracy of her prognostications (1175–1290), then the nightingale accuses the owl of practising witchcraft (1291–1336)). But the importance of women to this poem is also demonstrated by the way these movements return to this topic, as if there was no other place the speech of these birds could lead. And if, at that point, the birds still understand themselves to be in complete disagreement, they have both clearly learned the same thing from their earlier investigation, and now, they think about both men and women, carrying their schematic analysis forward by means of this wider perspective. Although this is the moment when the nightingale says that women sin 'naturally', it is also when she makes clear that to possess such a nature is to have an equivalent potential for behaving well:

> 3ef maide luueþ dernliche,
> Heo stumpeþ & falþ icundeliche:
> For þah heo sumhwile pleie,

---

[67] See Aristotle, *Nichomachean Ethics*, 2: 1729–867 in *Complete Works*, 1097a15–1098a21 (2: 1734–5).

Heo nis nout feor ut of þe weie.
Heo mai hire guld atwende
A rihte weie þurþ chirche bende;
An mai eft habbe to make
Hire leofmon wiþute sake,
An go to him bi daies lihte,
Þat er stal to bi þeostre nihte.
An ȝunling not hwat swuch þing is:
His ȝunge blod hit draȝeþ amis
An sum sot mon hit tihþ þarto,
Mid alle þan þat he mai do:
He comeþ & fareþ, & beod & bid,
An heo bistant & ouersid,
An bisehþ ilome & longe—
Hwat mai þat chil þah hit misfonge?
Hit nuste neauer hwat hit was.

[If (a maid) loves secretly, she trips and falls because of her nature: for
although she plays around for a while, she isn't far off course. She can turn
away from guilt and onto the right track by making use of the bonds of
marriage. Then she can make her lover her partner again without any dispute, and go to him by the light of day, instead of creeping there in the dead
of night as before. A youngster doesn't understand about this business. Her
young blood leads her astray and some foolish man entices her towards it in
every way that he can: he comes and goes, pleading and demanding; he
stands up close to her or sits right next to her, beseeching her often and at
length—how is a young girl to blame if she does wrong? She never knew
anything about the matter.]

(1423–41)

A woman may require institutional assistance to turn from bad to
good—'through church' ('þurþ chirche') or marriage—but her error
is reparable according to a much larger positional truth: to be 'out of
the way' ('ut of þe weie') is still to be close enough to the 'right way'
('rihte weie') to get back into it. In fact, the very inevitability with
which a woman finds herself in the track opposite to good is itself the
assurance that she can return to the track opposite to bad whenever
she wants. This enlarged ethical grid also makes clear that, in so far as
women move between the positions available to them, under certain
social pressure they are not even responsible for the wrong they do:
'how is a young girl to blame if she does wrong?' ('Hwat mai þat
chil þah hit misfonge?'). In fact, to the extent that a woman tends to
behave badly because a man who pressures her (drawing her toward

wrong 'in any way he can' ['mid alle þan þat he mai do']), it is not women who oppose men, but men who oppose women.

Once this observation has been made the owl insists that she has caught the nightingale caring for the wrong kind of women ('maidens' rather than 'ladies'), but this technicality is a thin disguise for what would otherwise have to be entered as an overwhelming endorsement of the nightingale's view. In fact, the analysis in train has now so fully defined women as a position in a structure that the direction from which that structure is viewed no longer matters. Although the owl offers a very different example here (what happens when a husband returns home after having been with his lover) that difference only proves the nightingale's point to be more generally true. In fact, the only real departure in the owl's example is that it actually succeeds in making the case against men more compelling:

> Wan he comeþ ham eft to his wiue,
> Ne dar heo noʒt a word ischire.
> He chid & gred swuch he beo wod
> An ne bringþ hom non oþer god.
> Al þat heo deþ him is unwille;
> Al þat heo spekeþ hit is him ille;
> An oft hwan heo noʒt ne misdeþ,
> Heo haueþ þe fust in hire teþ.
> Nis nan mon þat ne mai ibringe
> His wif amis mid swucche þinge.
> Me hire mai so ofte misbeode,
> þat heo do wule hire ahene neode.
> La, Godd hit wot! heo nah iweld,
> Þah heo hine makie kukeweld.
> For hit itit lome & ofte,
> Þat his wif is wel nesche & softe,
> Of faire bleo & wel idiht—
> Þi hit is þe more unriht
> Þat he his luue spene on þare,
> Þat nis wurþ one of hire heare!

[When he comes home again to his wife, she dare not utter a word. He shouts and rails as if he were mad, but that's all the good he brings home with him. Everything she does is an annoyance to him; and everything that she says is an irritation; and often, even when she hasn't done anything wrong, she gets a fist in her teeth. There's no man who can't drive his wife astray by behaving like this. She might be abused so often, that she'll want to satisfy her own needs. Oh she can't help it, God knows!—even if she makes him a cuckold.

For it's very often the case that a man's wife is soft and delicate, pretty and well brought-up—therefore it's all the more wrong that he should expend his love upon a woman not worth one of her hairs!]

(1531–50)

Addressed to something like the misogyny of the *De coniuge non ducenda*, this example makes clear that 'quarrelling' and 'raging', the 'noise which defeats the patient spouse', are as native to male as to female behaviour. And the owl's startlingly frank and naturalistic description of spousal abuse in this instance is also the poem's most overt advocacy of the position of women (if any further evidence is needed for characterizing its views as feminist). Even if the owl's condemnation of such behaviour is still tied to the misogyny from which it emerges (so, for the owl, this is where it is appropriate to describe women as 'wel nesche & softe'), female weakness is here rooted in the overwhelming physical strength of men: what a woman is less likely to prevent than going astray, it turns out, is being punched in the face. As the owl continues, moreover, her more graphic genealogy of morals leads to a rare instance of medieval misandry:

> An swucche men beoþ wel manifolde
> Þat wif ne kunne noþt ariʒt holde:
> Ne mot non mon wiþ hire speke—
> He ueneð heo wule anon tobreke
> Hire spusing ʒef heo lokeþ
> Oþer wiþ manne faire spekeþ.
> He hire biluþ mid keie & loke;
> Þarþurh is spusing ofte tobroke,
> For ʒef heo is þarto ibroht,
> He deþ þat heo nadde ear iþoht.
> Dahet þat to swuþe hit bispeke,
> Þah swucche wiues heom awreke!

[And there are numerous men of this sort, who are unable to treat a wife properly: no other man is allowed to speak to her—he thinks she'll immediately break her vows if she even looks at any other men, or just talks politely to them. He shuts her away under lock and key; and because of this a marriage is often destroyed, for if she's driven that far, she'll do what she would never previously have considered. To hell with anybody who grumbles very much about it if such women take their revenge!]

(1551–62)

It is not really the owl's point that the bad behaviour of a woman is somehow right given what a man has done but, rather, that the wrong she does cannot be her moral responsibility since it is a wrong a man has actually committed, something his action has 'driven' her to ('þarto ibroht'), which 'she would never previously have considered' ['He deþ þat heo nadde ear iþoht']. Although it has only unfolded from all the other observations which precede it, this last claim reverses the view of women on which misogyny necessarily depends: for if female badness is ever a projection of male badness—and particularly if it is such a projection generally—then women are neither as bad as they have been thought to be, and certainly not (or never) as bad as men. This different view of the structure of male and female living also makes clear that a change in female behaviour could only come about by some improvement in the conduct of men. Women's *nature* could only be altered (but it therefore could be altered) were women's behaviour simply viewed from a different vantage, were the ethics so pleased to condemn women finally able to turn (as here) and view men from a woman's perspective.

Neither the owl nor the nightingale carry this analysis forward to any such statement, but since the principles out of which their voices are confected have now been undermined, the point can now be made as it is absorbed to those voices—as these birds are now allowed to agree, not implicitly, but overtly. Since initiating principles have themselves been overturned by showing that they are not what they initially seem (not by contradiction but by a greater clarity of vision) the change also highlights this form's most important and substantial feint. For if the owl and the nightingale are soon prepared to acknowledge their agreement, this is not only a repetition (for, as I noted, they agreed to argue at the poem's beginning), but the opportunity they take (and which we may take as well) to notice that, in most ways large and small, they have *always* agreed. Aspects of this surprising convergence have been noticed before. According to Schleusener, the very stringency of the contradictions established throughout the poem depends upon the extent to which these birds 'accuse each other and flatter themselves on almost identical grounds' ('their songs are, respectively, gay and solemn, their dwellings suffer from questionable sanitation, their diets are unsavoury, and their value to mankind, however crucial to the debate, is generally slight').[68] It has also been noticed that 'the substance of the poem's central marriage debate' is no more than a collective summary of 'the ecclesiastical

---

[68] Schleusener, ' "The Owl and the Nightingale" ', 189.

views of love and marriage as they were discussed in the English church courts during the late twelfth and early thirteenth centuries'.[69] This poem *looks* like a debate, of course, and there is much that is very important in that appearance (which is why the poem is appropriately grouped with other debate literature), but considering what these birds generally say, a debate is finally what this poem is *not*.[70]

THIS DEBATE WHICH IS NOT ONE

That this owl and this nightingale should finally discover that the very traditions which have made them are mistaken also allows *The Owl and the Nightingale* to adequate the world better than any of the wisdom it inherits. In fact, the last movements of the poem make this discovery by completely absorbing it to the poem's very form, not only presenting a new understanding of women and their lives as if it were this poem's last and brightest idea—the truth (not the answer) which such an enquiry into the relation between these words and the world must discover—but in this way demonstrating that the whole of this poem has a more truthful structure than it initially appeared to. The crucial part of this revisionary coda is the entry of the wren, and, along with her, the cessation of all debate at line 1717. This articulation hides beneath yet another feint, for the wren's appearance actually heralds an intensification rather than a truce in hostilities. She appears to be partisan—there to 'helpe' (1719) the nightingale since both are songbirds—and therefore likely to widen the ambit of the quarrel. True to such anticipation, the wren begins to speak with a voice like the owl's and the nightingale's, all unpleasantness and argument:

> 'Lusteþ!' heo cwaþ. 'Lateþ me speke!
> Hwat! Wulle ʒe þis pes tobreke
> An do þanne kinge swuch schame?
> ʒe, nis he nouþer ded ne lame!
> ʒunke schal itide harm & schonde,
> ʒef ʒe doþ griþbruche on his londe.
> Lateþ beo & beoþ isome,

[69] Coleman, '*The Owl and the Nightingale*', 535 (see also 547).
[70] For the consensual classification of the poem (as a 'bird-debate' in the larger category of 'debates on love and women') see Francis Lee Utley, 'Dialogues, Debates, and Catechisms' in *MWME* 3: 669–7 (esp. 3: 716–20).

> An fareþ riht to ower dome:
> An lateþ dom þis plaid tobreke
> Al swo hit was erur bispeke!'

['Now listen!' she said. 'Let me speak! What!—do you want to break this peace and so then disgrace the King? Indeed, you won't find him dead or crippled! If you commit a breach of the peace in his land, you'll both suffer injury and dishonour. Now stop all this, call a truce and go straight off to hear the verdict upon you: and let arbitration bring this dispute to an end, just as it was previously agreed!']

(1729–38)

But, in fact, the wren does not argue—if she speaks stridently, the other birds also assent quiescently to her commands. Her presence may therefore be understood as a reification of the position the other birds discovered within the structures of misogyny as they progressively undermined it: what the wren in fact opposes is *opposition*, and therefore what she represents (the social form her presence makes) is concord. In this she is not only an ally of both the owl and the nightingale, but a figure for that more open view of female possibility that each of these other birds has always represented, even if that has only now become clear. Her role is to sit athwart neither bird but alongside each of them, mediating not so much by keeping disputation from growing too heated (it has already done that), but by eliminating the possibility of confrontation. Her tripling presence itself models the kind of structures in which women actually exist, not always oppositional because never just a dyad, not always confrontational because as easily (and differently) joined together as they are parted.

In this last sense—but in all the others which predict it—*The Owl and the Nightingale* adequates the world by insisting that it knows the things it cares about better than they have been known before. This accomplishment is substantial enough for the poem to seek a slight lightening of tone as it trumpets this claim, and so we also get the fawning praise for 'Maister Nichole' and a complaint about the assignment of ecclesiastical revenues, which (because of their near-terminal position) criticism has often mistaken for the poem's real concerns.[71] This triviality itself prepares the poem's concluding joke:

---

[71] For a helpful summary of those who have, as a result of this praise, 'fathered the poem' on 'Nicholas of Guildford' see *The Owl and the Nightingale*, ed. Stanley, 20–1. For a few more recent examples, see *The Owl and the Nightingale*, ed. Cartlidge, xiv n. 8.

the delightful recursion in which the narrator declares that he cannot
reveal what happened after the story he is telling because there is no
more story in which it has been told ('her nis na more of þis spelle'
(1794)). Like the rest of the poem's humour, this last line also makes
a crucial point: this explicit reference to all the living that lies beyond
the poem's bounds acknowledges that this very boundary is at issue.
But the mention of Master Nicholas and this joke also constitute the
poem's last and most delicate feint, for the conclusion actually sits
between these two gestures (and is therefore easily assimilated to
this lightness of tone), when the owl offers to repeat both sides of
the debate that has just taken place, and she asks the nightingale to
correct her if she should go 'astray':

> 'Þarof ich schal þe wel icweme',
> Cwaþ þe Houle, 'for al ende of orde
> Telle ich con word after worde:
> An ȝef þe þincþ þat ich misrempe
> Þu stond aȝein & do me crempe'.

['On that point I can easily satisfy you', said the Owl, 'since I can recite every
word from beginning to end: and if you think that I go astray, you stand up
and stop me'.]

$$(1784-8)$$

The owl's vision of a consensual future that actually includes the
contents of this poem not only acknowledges that there never was a
disagreement, but also envisions a wider world in which women's
speech is not harmful but useful, an indispensable means of knowing.
Thus, the ethical language applied by the owl to herself is also the
positional language that both birds have applied to human lives all
through the poem, but now this language has been turned to valuing
every position, to envisioning a collection of voices able to assist each
other toward a general betterment. So, even though the birds began
by agreeing to disagree, the final action of these birds is not (cannot
be) the opposite of such a strange deal, but the aggregate of its result:
they agree to preserve the *whole* of their debate, and, in that agreement, they embrace the view that all of it matters.

Such a view is so unusual in the larger context of medieval misogyny
that it may seem like the largest feint of all, impossible to believe precisely because so wise by modern measure. It is therefore important
to make clear that, while I also believe that *any* prolepsis of feminism
is significant and had the potential to ameliorate lives (by creating the

possibility for transformative action and thought), the only thing I
here claim for this poem and the owl and the nightingale's political
precocity is that their discourse is as opportunistic as every view which
emerges in the poem. The nightingale's sympathy for 'maidens' is, of
course, no more than a provocation designed to induce maximum
rage in the owl. The owl's overwhelming sympathy for married
women is no more than an attempt to outflank the nightingale's prior
acts of compassion. The wisdom of the poem is therefore itself an
outgrowth of the *richness* of its form—truths a poem which knows
so very much simply could not avoid—but it is only stumbled upon
by the very insistence with which these birds go after their respective
'natures'—and therefore the principles which confect those natures
—with hammer and tongs. Such opportunism is dialectic's normal
procedure for discovering truth, an intellectual aggressivity which
produces the thinking in which keenly held positions can be reviewed,
revised, and transformed. *The Owl and the Nightingale* is not a feminist poem, then, but the truths it finds latent in certain structures of
belief are exactly those which feminism will later embrace. A final
question this may raise is why, if these structures governed female
lives, should a poem be required for such discoveries? If the thought
I have discerned in this poem is right, however, the properties of
things can only be fully known when they are converted into words,
and that knowledge can only be used to transform or alter mistaken
assumptions and traditions as those properties are revealed in their
truthfulness by the investigative pressures of philology and argument.
It is therefore *only* because *The Owl and the Nightingale* is a poem—
because its words can and do adequate the world—that the speech
of this owl and this nightingale (and, finally, this wren) is the best
instrument for subjecting life to the kinds of scrutiny which will
truly yield up its meaning.

5

The Place of the Self: *Ancrene Wisse* and the *Katherine*-group

Each of the levels in which we successively live makes its appearance when we cast anchor in some 'setting' which is offered to us.

[Chacun des niveaux dans lesquels nous vivons tour à tour apparaît lorsque nous jetons l'ancre dans quelque 'milieu' qui se propose à nous.]

(Merleau-Ponty)

One of the more dramatic moments in Middle English scholarship was E. J. Dobson's claim in 1976 that he had not only identified the author of *Ancrene Wisse* (Brian of Lingen, a canon of Wigmore Abbey) as well as the three women for whom this anchoritic rule had been written, but that he could precisely locate the place in which those women had lived, the site of modern-day Chapel Farm, then called the 'Deerfold' [La Derefaud]—'1¼ miles WSW of Wigmore' at 'grid reference 395685' on the Ordnance Survey map of Britain (Fig. 6).[1] At first, the 'massiveness of the documentation' and Dobson's 'meticulous attention to the details of the argument' were persuasive enough to sweep all scepticism aside.[2] But the annals of Middle English scholarship are so full of attempts to specify the origins of *Ancrene Wisse* (even Dobson's title was an echo of an equally meticulous article by Hope Emily Allen, who had, nonetheless, attached this text to a different author and audience) that literary historians might be forgiven their reluctance to attribute *Ancrene Wisse* to

---

[1] E. J. Dobson, *The Origins of Ancrene Wisse* (Oxford: Clarendon Press 1976), 218–22. Dobson cites the 1: 25,000 series of the Ordnance Survey, Sheet SO 36 (Presteigne) (*Origins*, 220 n.1).

[2] Derek Pearsall, Review of *The Origins of Ancrene Wisse*, by E. J. Dobson, *Review of English Studies* 28 (1977), 316–18.

FIG. 6 The portion of the March in which Dobson places the origins of *Ancrene Wisse* (he locates the anchorhouse of the three sisters to whom it is addressed at what is here labeled 'Chapel Fm').

Brian of Lingen.[3] The predictable queries and disagreements have subsequently emerged,[4] and, these days, Dobson's particulars serve as little more than another demonstration of the power of early Middle English forms to conscript critical response: just as the stringency of the debate in *The Owl and the Nightingale* forces its readers to pick a side, a work that is 'deliberately anonymous', written in order to help its readers hide from the world, seems to propose itself as a mystery requiring solution, as if it were (in Dobson's phrasing), a 'code [which] can be broken'.[5]

What I wish to demonstrate here, however, is that the origins Dobson fixed upon are less important than the concerns which guided his investigation, that the place Dobson proposed for *Ancrene Wisse* actually matters much less than the degree to which he insisted on the importance of *some* place. While, as I have said, many have tried to identify the 'origins' of *Ancrene Wisse* in the past, Dobson was unusual in plumping for geographical precision at all costs, abandoning the very meticulousness which had generated his entire argument up until that point in order to manufacture the fact that most firmly associated this text with the Deerfold: the charter in which he reported the crucial mention of 'sisters' living in this valley, at the right time, in the right circumstances (next to that chapel which gives modern-day Chapel Farm its name) actually mentions '*brothers*' (Dobson seems to have seen—or allowed himself to see—an 'f' as a long 's' and, as a result, expanded the abbreviation 'frib3' into 'sororibus').[6] There was already general consensus about the area

---

[3] See Hope Emily Allen, 'The Origin of the *Ancrene Riwle*', PMLA 33 (1918), 474–546. For a strong refutation of Allen's argument see *Ancrene Wisse: Parts Six and Seven*, ed. Geoffrey Shepherd (Exeter: Short Run Press, 1985; 1st published 1959), pp. xxi–xxiii. For a general history of attempts to assign *Ancrene Wisse* to a particular location and author see Roger Dahood, '*Ancrene Wisse*, the Katherine Group and the *Wohunge* Group', 1–33 in *Middle English Prose: A Critical Guide to Major Authors and Genres* (New Brunswick, NJ: Rutgers University Press, 1984), 8–11.

The only instance I know in which Dobson's attribution was actually adopted is John Burrow, *Medieval Writers and Their Work: Middle English Literature and its Background, 1100–1500* (Oxford: Oxford University Press, 1982), 28, although Burrow originally ascribed the text to 'John of Lingen' (an error corrected in the revised edition).

[4] Bella Millett has recently suggested that 'Dobson's identifications of author and audience . . . need to be reconsidered', 'The Origins of *Ancrene Wisse*: New Answers, New Questions', MÆ 61 (1992), 206–28 (quotation from p. 219).

[5] Dobson, *Origins of Ancrene Wisse*, 1 ('deliberately') and 344 ('code').

[6] The charter in question is preserved in 'The Black Book of Wigmore' [Liber Niger de Wigmore], London, British Library, MS Harley 1240. It locates 'the church of the

in which Dobson had been hunting of course: in 1929 Tolkien demonstrated convincingly that the accidence and orthography of Cambridge, Corpus Christi College, MS 402 (which contains the final revision of *Ancrene Wisse*) and Oxford, Bodley MS 34 (which contains *Katerine, Margarete, Iuliene, Hali Meidhad, Sawles Warde*, the so-called *Katherine*-group of texts) are consistent enough to be 'in close touch with a good living speech—a soil somewhere in England'.[7] The careful phonological argument whereby Dobson narrowed the origins of 'AB language' (so named after the standard sigla for the Corpus and Bodley manuscripts) to that part of the Welsh March that lies in northern Herefordshire and southern Shropshire remains convincing to this day.[8] Moreover, even if the Deerfold is one degree of precision too far, it has the distinction of being that place whose contours seemed so appropriate to *Ancrene Wisse* that they were capable of sweeping all of *Dobson's* scepticism aside.[9]

In what follows I want to suggest that Dobson's embrace of the Deerfold is, in fact, a different sort of accuracy, and, furthermore,

Blessed Mary and of St Leonard of Sutelsford' ('ecclesia beate marie et sancti leonardi de Sutelesford') in the 'valley' [valles] called 'the Deerfold'. For Dobson's text and his translation see *Origins of Ancrene Wisse*, 218 and n. 1. The error Dobson makes is particularly strange because the word 'sororibus' appears, unabbreviated, several times in the charter (referring to benefactors rather than people who lived in the Deerfold). This mistake was first pointed out by Sally Thompson, *Women Religious: The Founding of English Nunneries after the Norman Conquest* (Oxford: Clarendon Press, 1991), 34 n. 126.

[7] J. R. R. Tolkien, '*Ancrene Wisse* and *Hali Meiðhad*', *Essays and Studies* 14 (1929), 104–26 (quotation from p. 106). Dobson also showed that the part of the earliest manuscript of *Ancrene Wisse* (London, British Library, MS Cleopatra C.vi) which was written by its 'corrector and reviser', and therefore 'the author' of *Ancrene Wisse*, also used AB language. See *The English Text of the Ancrene Riwle (edited from B. M. Cotton MS Cleopatra C.vi)*, ed. E. J. Dobson, EETS os 267 (1972), pp. xciii–cxl (esp. pp. cxxvii–cxl).

[8] See Dobson, *Origins*, 114–26. Millet confirms Dobson's localization ('Origins of *Ancrene Wisse*, 223–4 n. 15), as does Richard Dance ('The AB Language: the Recluse, the Gossip and the Language Historian', 57–82 in *A Companion to Ancrene Wisse*, ed. Yoko Wada (Cambridge: D. S. Brewer, 2003), 71).

[9] It is only by means of the most literal reading of the modes of address employed in *Ancrene Wisse* that it can be assumed that it was not written for the 'brothers' who lived in the old Deerfold. Anchoritic rules were so commonly addressed to women that the pose was already traditional by *Ancrene Wisse*'s day. As Elizabeth Robertson has recently noted, there is clear evidence that manuscripts of *Ancrene Wisse* were read by men. In fact, the various modes of address in *Ancrene Wisse* presume a surprising array of 'reader functions' and, therefore, an equal variety of readers. See Elizabeth Robertson, ' "This Living Hand": Thirteenth-Century Female Literacy, Materialist Immanence, and the Reader of the *Ancrene Wisse*', *Speculum* 78 (2003), 1–36 (esp. 25–8).

that it will seem like the right place of origin for *Ancrene Wisse* and all of the *Katherine*-group to anyone who thinks equally hard about the role of place in these texts. In fact, what may have drawn Dobson to the Deerfold in ways that the details of a charter should not have is its distinctive topography, for it has precisely those contours which these texts repeatedly trace, and which *Ancrene Wisse* actually traces as its very form. As I shall argue in the first section of this chapter, by narrowing the 'somewhere' of AB language to the Welsh March, Dobson correctly aligned the AB texts with a territory whose general conditions resemble those they represent, a place where the anxieties about bodily boundaries and their penetration which fill the AB texts was not only a practical consideration but a function of geography, the general condition of life in a borderland so constantly subject to war. The Deerfold has particular importance within these general conditions because it is one of those elevated valleys which ensured that the March constituted an effective border: it was a natural enclosure that was extraordinarily difficult to penetrate, but which, for this very reason, was subject to frequent attack. In both of these senses, Dobson found a place where people certainly lived *like* anchorites, not only next to a church, but sheltered from their immediate surroundings by the high woodland rising to the north, east, and south, generally cut off from the wider world by the broad highland in which this narrow declivity was set (again, see Fig. 6).[10] In fact, in *Ancrene Wisse*'s day it is clear that the term Deerfold clung to this valley (rather than to the whole of the two-mile mile ridge to its west and south-west where it has now been generalized), because it was a stretch of ground that was effectively 'folded', if not a 'deer-park' in function (as the term 'deerfold' could mean) then land that would be ideal for such a purpose because it formed a natural 'enclosure' (as 'fold' in such usage has always meant).[11]

[10] The use of 'anchoress' to describe women anchorites is traditional in translations and discussions of *Ancrene Wisse*, but this usage is unsupported by Middle English grammar where the form *ancre* was 'of common gender' (see *OED*, s.v. 'anchor n2'). I have therefore avoided the term here.

[11] For these meanings see *MED*, s.v. 'fold n1' and *OED*, s.v. 'fold n2'. As Dobson explains 'the name Deerfold evidently belongs properly to the whole of [a] two-mile-long ridge', but 'in the charter . . . the name *La Derefaud* is given a more specialized application' (*Origins*, 220–1). The valley identified in the charter was not in fact a deer park (since 'no medieval noble would have granted away his deer-park'), but, it would appear, a place to which this term seemed particularly apt (*Origins of Ancrene Wisse*, 223 n.1).

Even if he had recognized their importance to his own argument, however, such connections would have been difficult for Dobson to articulate because the idea that *Ancrene Wisse* and the *Katherine*-group formulate by means of such materialities is what we now tend to think of as an abstraction, the idea that *Ancrene Wisse* is already describing as the 'self' [þe seolf].[12] The role of the anchoritic life in elaborating the self in the context of twelfth- and thirteenth-century intellectual concerns has already received extensive treatment,[13] but, since it has also been shown that the self is an idea that emerges by 'drain[ing] . . . away' its more 'grossly structural features', certain more solid determinates have yet to be recovered.[14] What I wish to focus on here, then, are all those ways that the self can be regarded not only as a form, but as Charles Taylor has suggested, a kind of 'moral topography' or 'solid . . . localization', a shape that has all the characteristics of the kind of place one might actually visit in the physical world.[15] As I shall suggest in the second section of this chapter, placement is so important to the procedures of self-fashioning articulated by the AB texts that they also spend a great deal of time exploring the concept of place as such.

It is also important that Dobson should have specified the origins of *Ancrene Wisse* in a place one might actually go to because, as will become clear in the conclusion of this chapter, the self finally emerges in AB thinking as if *it* were a thing. If, as I have just suggested, it is common to most theories of the self to try to hide such materiality, the AB theory—and its particular perspicuity—is characterized by the embrace of a defining tension. In fact, although it produces many apparent contradictions on the surface of these texts,

---

[12] *Ancrene Wisse: Guide for Anchoresses*, trans. Hugh White (Harmondsworth: Penguin, 1993), 129; *The English Text of the Ancrene Riwle: Ancrene Wisse (edited from MS Corpus Christi College Cambridge 402)*, ed. J. R. R. Tolkien, EETS, os 249 (London, 1962), 142. Subsequent citations from *Ancrene Wisse* will be cited by page number from this translation (abbreviated 'W') and this edition of the Corpus manuscript (abbreviated 'T'). For the sake of consistency I have emended White's use of 'anchoress' to 'anchorite' in quotations throughout. I have also occasionally added punctuation and expanded abbreviations silently to Tolkien's diplomatic edition.

[13] Linda Georgianna, *The Solitary Self: Individuality in the Ancrene Wisse* (Cambridge, Mass.: Harvard University Press, 1981).

[14] Francis Barker, *The Tremulous Private Body: Essays on Subjection*, 2nd edn. (Ann Arbor: University of Michigan Press, 1995), 8.

[15] Charles Taylor, *Sources of the Self: The Making of Modern Identity* (Cambridge: Cambridge University Press, 1989), 111.

the tension between thought and thing serves as an opportunity for these texts to locate selfhood right *on* a boundary, as the very precipitate of the attempt to separate the locus of thinking from the world in which it is enmeshed. As the most thoughtful and exploratory of all the AB texts it is *Ancrene Wisse* which is most precocious in its description of this fundamental relation, anticipating the language of modern phenomenology by describing selfhood as a kind of *anchorage*, that separation which results from a carefully secured attachment.

THE PLACE OF AB LANGUAGE

'March' is a term used to designate a 'boundary, frontier, [or] border', but since it divides two territories, not with a line, but with still more territory, it is one of the most unstable of locations, what the *OED* calls a 'tract of debatable land'.[16] The March of Wales was 'a historical rather than a geographical category', a place whose identity was as fluid as the politics and warfare which determined it.[17] This March had a secure centre after 1071, when William I created the earldoms of Chester, Shrewsbury, and Hereford as bulwarks against Welsh incursion, so that 'by 1200 it had acquired a broad measure of definition which it was to retain until the final conquest of Wales in 1277–83'.[18] For the whole span of time that Dobson presumed for the composition of *Ancrene Wisse* (1215–22), the later dates more recently urged for this text (1221–36), and the larger span possible for the *Katherine*-group texts (1190–1220), the March thus included what could be described as AB territory.[19] The identity of this territory was bound up with, rather than distinct from, the two places it divided: it was not precisely 'England' but what *Ancrene Wisse* describes as its 'end' [englondes ende] (W 119/T 130). AB language shows itself to be native to such a territory not only in so far as it can be localized to this border area, but in so far as its English absorbs

[16] See *OED*, s.v. 'march n3'.
[17] R. R. Davies, *Conquest, Coexistence and Change, Wales, 1063–1415* (Oxford: Clarendon Press, 1987), 272.
[18] Ibid. 272.
[19] For Dobson's datings of *Ancrene Wisse* and the *Katherine*-group texts see *Origins of Ancrene Wisse*, 163–6. The later date for *Ancrene Wisse* is proposed in Millett, 'Origins of *Ancrene Wisse*', 219.

Welsh words such as *cader* [cradle], *keis* [henchman], and *genou* [mouth].[20]

Words for 'cradle' and 'mouth' moved across the linguistic boundary because there was necessarily close contact in an area where both Welsh and English speakers lived, but the exchange of the word for 'henchman' was doubtless the result of the kinds of contact that were more typical of this place. In fact, in the period from the Norman Conquest until the conquest of Wales, the March was under English control but, also, constantly overrun by Welsh invaders (the Lord Rhys nearly overran the whole of the territory in 1196, and smaller raids were frequent until Llywelyn ab Iorwerth overran the whole of the territory in 1231 and again in 1233).[21] It has been said that a Marcher lordship was 'a military lordship or it was no lordship at all',[22] not least because a Marcher lord lacked standard crown protections ('the king's writ did not run in the March, and the area thereby lay beyond the reach of royal justice and of the common law of England'), and the king of England himself often preyed upon Marcher territories.[23] William de Braose's career was exemplary in this respect: he had to defend himself vigorously against incursions into the March by Llywelyn in 1201 only to find his lands confiscated by King John in 1207.[24] Although William's lands were eventually restored, his grandson (also William) was forced into an alliance

[20] These words are identified as Welsh borrowings in Dobson, *Origins of Ancrene Wisse*, 115–16. For the history of each see *MED*, s.vv. 'cader n.', 'keis n. pl.', 'genou n.'. 'Genou' is a *hapax legomenon* in Middle English, and the other two words are attested on only one other occasion in the 14th or 15th c. For the words themselves see T 192 ('cader') and *The Katherine-Group edited from MS Bodley 34*, ed. S. T. R. O. d'Ardenne, Bibliothèque de la Faculté de Philosophie et Lettres de l'Université de Liège, Fascicule 215 (Paris: Les Belles Lettres, 1977), 69 ('genow' in *Margarete*), 155–6 ('cader', twice, in *Hali Meiðhad*), 167 ('keis' in *Sawles Warde*). Hereafter citations to the AB texts other than *Ancrene Wisse* will be to the page number in this edition, abbreviated 'd'A'. Translations will be taken from *Anchoritic Spirituality: Ancrene Wisse and Associated Works*, trans. Anne Savage and Nicholas Watson (New York: Paulist Press, 1991), abbreviated 'S&W', and cited by page number in the text.

[21] Davies, *Conquest, Coexistence and Change*, 274. On this period generally see also Austin Lane Poole, *From Domesday Book to Magna Carta, 1087–1216*, 2nd edn. (Oxford: Clarendon Press, 1955; 1st edn. 1951), 298–301; and *A History of Herefordshire*, 4 vols. in *The Victoria History of the Counties of England*, ed. William Page (London: Eyre & Spottiswoode, 1908; repr. 1975) 1: 360–3.

[22] R. R. Davies, *Lordship and Society in the March of Wales, 1282–1400* (Oxford: Clarendon Press, 1978), 69–70.

[23] Ibid. 3.

[24] See Poole, *From Domesday Book to Magna Carta*, 298–9; and Davies, *Conquest, Coexistence and Change*, 277.

with the Welsh (in 1228 this William de Braose was made to marry his daughter Isabel to Llywelyn's son Dafydd), although Llywelyn then executed this William in 1230, and the crown (in this case, in the person of Henry III) once again confiscated the Braose lands.[25] The March of this period was, in fact, 'a land of war, interrupted on occasion by peace',[26] and so documents were often dated 'by reference to Welsh raids or to the siege of a castle'.[27]

Although the AB texts do not make specific references to such incursions, for texts on devotional subjects they show a surprising awareness of the methods and tactics of Marcher warfare. For example, in a passage which describes the 'eyes' [eien] as 'the arrows and the first weapons of lechery's pricks' [þe earewen & te ereste armes of lecheries pricches] *Ancrene Wisse* observes that lechery attacks 'just as men fight with three kinds of weapons—with shot, with spear-point, and with sword-edge' [also ase men weorreð mid þreo cunes wepnen, mid scheotung, mid speres ord, & mid sweordes egge].[28] Another passage likens 'the love of Jesus our Lord' [þe luue of iesu ure lauerd] to the incendiary devices employed during siege: 'People throw Greek fire on their foes and so overcome them' [Me warpeð grickisch fur upon his famen & swa ouerkimeð ham] (W 185–6/T 205–6).[29] Yet another passage expands an image from *Lamentations*, which refers to the 'shield of the heart' [scutum cordis], into a lesson in the techniques of combat: 'A shield has to be held up above the head in combat, or against the breast, not dragged behind' [Me schal halden scheld i feht up abuuen heaued, oðer aȝein þe breoste, nawt ne drahen hit bihinden] (W 136/T 151). In perhaps the most acute registration of the impact warfare could have on a solitary

---

[25] Davies, *Conquest, Coexistence and Change*, 248 (on William's forced alliance with Llywelyn) and 277 (on his execution and the confiscation of his lands). For a narrative of these events see also the *History of Herefordshire* 1: 363. For a convenient summary of the complex genealogy of the Braose family (and its entwining with Llywelyn's heirs) see *English Historical Documents*, vol. 3, ed. Henry Rothwell, gen. ed. David C. Douglas (London: Eyre & Spottiswoode, 1975), 1017.

[26] Davies, *Lordship and Society*, 68.

[27] Davies, *Conquest, Coexistence and Change*, 280.

[28] *Ancrene Wisse*, trans. White, 32. The Corpus manuscript is defective at this point so I quote the original here from the text in the Nero manuscript (*The English Text of the Ancrene Riwle (edited from Cotton Nero A.xiv)*, ed. Mabel Day, EETS os 225 (1952), 26) the manuscript to which White also turns at this point.

[29] On 'Greek fire' as a weapon see the extensive notes for this passage in *Ancrene Wisse: Parts Six and Seven*, ed. Shepherd, 65. See also (as cited in Shepherd), Poole, *From Domesday Book to Magna Carta*, 480 n. 1.

life, *Ancrene Wisse* relaxes the injunction, common to anchoritic rules, forbidding the 'anchor-house' [ancre-hus] (W 195/T 217) to be used as a store for valuables:[30]

Nawt deore dehtren ne wite ȝe in ower hus of oðer monne þinges, ne ahte, ne claðes, ne boistes, ne chartres, scoren ne cyrograffes, ne ðe chirch uestemenz, ne þe calices, bute neode oðer strengðe hit makie, oðer muchel eie.

[Do not, dear daughters, keep other people's things in your house—not live-stock, or clothes, or boxes, or charters; no tallies or indentures, not the church vestments or the chalices, unless need or force make you, or great fear.]

(T 213–14/W 193)

Although it could be said that anchoritic enclosure always appro-ximated the conditions of siege since every anchorite vowed to main-tain 'fixity of place' [stude steaðeluestnesse'] (W 3/T 8), *Ancrene Wisse* betrays its anxieties about the more dangerous aspects of fixity when it relaxes this vow should the anchorite find herself afraid for her life ('she shall never more change that place, except out of neces-sity only [such as violence and fear of death]' [ha ne schal þet stude neauer mare changin bute for nede ane, as strengðe & deaðes dred]) (W3/T 8).

The identity of every Marcher resident was defined by such fears because, as *Ancrene Wisse* recognizes, the March did not simply lie along a border it *was* a border—a place identified by its liminality. It was also a 'frontier society' that everywhere mixed 'peoples of different languages, different cultures, different laws, [and] different customs'.[31] It constituted the line between two different territories, but it was also a place that it was possible to be from, as Walter Map (c.1130–1205) made clear when he described himself as a 'dweller on the marches of Wales' ('marchio sum Walensibus').[32] Documents from this period therefore differentiated Marcher lords from the lords of England and Wales (they were the 'barones de marchia'), and documents also distinguished the 'marchia Wallie' from 'Wallia' or

[30] On the general nature of this injunction see Ann K. Warren, *Anchorites and their Patrons in Medieval England* (Berkeley: University of California Press, 1985), 111–12. For evidence that the anchorhouse was often used as a place 'for local men to deposit money', see H. Mayr-Harting, 'Functions of a Twelfth-Century Recluse', *History* 60 (1975), 343.

[31] Davies, *Lordship and Society*, 2 ('peoples') and 9 ('frontier').

[32] Walter Map, *De nugis curialium* (*Courtiers' Trifles*), ed. and trans. M. R. James, rev. C. N. L. Brooke and R. A. B. Mynors (Oxford: Clarendon Press, 1983), Dist ii., 23 (pp. 194–5).

'pura Wallia'.[33] In fact, the Marcher lords were sufficiently independent from the king of England that, in a time when 'the making of war and the concluding of peace had come to be regarded as the exclusive prerogatives of the king', the Marcher lords assumed such prerogatives for themselves.[34] Magna Carta recognized this fact when it set the 'law of England' ('lex Angliae') and the 'law of Wales' ('lex Walliae') against the 'law of the March' ('lex Marchiae'), in this way, too, placing this borderland on a par with the places it separated.[35]

Marcher identity can also be understood as an abstraction from a topography that intermixed the two different kinds of land it separated, for the March was a stretch of land consisting both of the small hills and tightly packed valleys that characterized Wales to its west, and of the substantial expanses of flatland that characterized England to its east. In fact, social arrangements traced these geographic conditions with great consistency, with the Welsh so generally in the heights and the English so substantially on the lower slopes and in the valleys that, throughout the March, 'the 650 feet [198 metre] contour line' constituted 'the boundary between Welshry and Englishry'.[36] It was therefore possible to live well within the March and still live on a border: Wigmore Abbey for example (the place where Dobson suggests the author of *Ancrene Wisse* may have been a canon) sits firmly on the very low land where the English tended to live, but it is located at the edge of a plain, just beneath the kind of high hills on which the Welsh settled. On the other hand, the physical determinates of such inner borders meant that each one tended to provide a natural barrier between one Marcher place and another: for example, while the Deerfold may itself be lowland, this valley is in

---

[33] Davies, *Conquest, Coexistence and Change*, 272.   [34] Ibid. 285.

[35] Chapter 56 of the charter reads: 'If we have disseised or kept out Welshmen from lands or liberties or other things without the legal judgment of their peers in England or in Wales, they shall be immediately restored to them; and if a dispute arises over this, then let it be decided in the March by the judgment of their peers—for holdings in England according to the law of England, for holdings in Wales according to the law of Wales, and for holdings in the March according to the law of the March' [Si nos dissaisiviumus vel elongavimus Walenses de terris vel libertatibus vel rebus aliis, sine legali iudicio parium suorum, in Anglia vel in Wallia, eis statim reddantur; et si contentio super hoc orta fuerit, tunc inde fiat in Marchia per judicium parium suorum, de tenementis, Angliae secundum legem Angliae, de tenementis Walliae secundum legem Walliae, de tenementis Marchiae secundum legem Marchiae]. *English Historical Documents*, vol. 3, ed. Rothwell, 322. *Select Charters*, ed. William Stubbs, 9th edn. (Oxford: Clarendon Press, 1913), 300.

[36] Davies, *Lordship and Society*, 310.

fact set into a large plateau of generally high ground (rolling hills that fill almost the whole of the area mapped in Fig. 6), a collection of declivities and even higher elevations that tower over the much flatter land of England to the east (as, for example, at Wigmore). As a result the Deerfold was enclosed not only by the hills 'folded' around it to the north, east, and south, but by the warren of folds this highland interposed between it and the wider (flatter) world.

As in the case of the legal principles absorbed into Laȝamon's *Brut*, it is worth describing such protective topography as the land's idea, for these natural shapes provided models for the kinds of structures the inhabitants of the March built to supplement such natural defences. In fact, in their earliest form such fortifications were no more than man-made hills, mounds of earth or 'mottes' for which height alone was the method of keeping invaders at bay. Such hills soon acquired the kind of surrounding barriers that protected a raised valley like the Deerfold, ditches or 'ring-works' set around the motte's perimeter, or (a little later) wooden or stone enclosures set into the top of the mound, eventually elaborated into the entirely stone structures which were called 'castles'.[37] So characteristic did these structures become as a way of supplementing the natural topography of the March that this whole territory has been said to 'bristle' with them (260 mottes and 90 stone castles are known to have existed in the March before 1215).[38] In fact, as a map that conflates topography and this proliferation of castles shows, such construction extended the defensive potential of the Marcher upland into its eastern plains, effectively raising this territory by means of the barriers it added to it (Fig. 7).[39] It is in keeping with just such a mode of topographical extension that the river plain of Wigmore was effectively raised by a substantial stone castle built in just this period.[40]

The AB texts reflect their Marcher origins as they bristle with these structures too—for example, *Sawles Warde* understands the body to be a set of barriers so reinforced by Strength [strengðe] that it is

[37] On 'mottes' and their 'ring-works' generally see S. C. Stanford, *The Archaeology of the Welsh Marches* (London: William Collins Sons & Co., 1980), 209–10.

[38] On castles in this period see Davies, *Lordship and Society*, 70–6 (for the characterization I quote see p. 71). See also Davies, *Conquest, Coexistence and Change*, 280–1; and Stanford, *Archaeology of the Welsh Marches*, 214.

[39] For another map showing the distribution of castles across the March see Stanford, *Archaeology of the Welsh Marches*, 206.

[40] Ibid. 215–16.

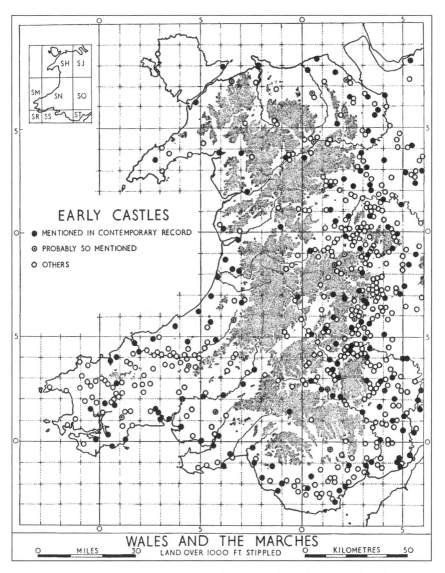

FIG. 7 A map of all castles known to have been in Wales and the March in the period 1066–1215.

also a 'castle' [castel] (S&W 216–17/ d'A 176–7), while the virtuous woman in *Hali Meiðhad* stands on a 'hill' so 'high' [hehe hul] (S&W 232/d'A 142) that she is effectively a 'tower' [tur] resisting 'the devil's army from hell' [deofles here of helle] (S&W 226/d'A 129). These imagined versions of the body draw heavily on traditions that go back as far as the *Timaeus*, but this legacy is always reinforced in the Marcher case by more specific knowledge of the way that castles functioned in war.[41] In *Ancrene Wisse*, for example, the 'castle' containing an anchoritic self is 'strong' because it is surrounded by the 'deep ditch' or ring-works of 'humility and wet tears' [ah habbe ʒe deop dich of deop eadmodnesse, & wete teares þerto, ʒe beoð strong castel] (W 115 / T 126). 'Scalding tears' [scaldinde teares] of desperation help the anchorite when the 'fiend attacks' [feond asaileð] because, in siege warfare, 'when towns or castles are attacked, those inside pour out scalding water and thus guard the walls' [hwen me asaleð burhes oðer castel, þeo wið innen healdeð scaldinde weater ut, & werieð swa þe walles] (W 114/T 125).

What the AB texts also know about such Marcher structures is that they protect the self simply by locating it, that, in so far as the body has a shape something like a house or a castle, it is, as *Ancrene Wisse* puts it, a 'place' [stude] (W 173/T 192). Marcher experience therefore brought to the securing of such an identity an acute understanding of how to keep vulnerable places safe. It knew, for example, that, as *Ancrene Wisse* puts it, 'two houses' [twa huses] (W 173/T 193) are better than one, that if a body is like a castle because its walls protect something that is 'always within' [eauer inwið] (W 1/T 5), then the body is even safer if its walls are placed within another structure, 'the outer house, which is like the outer wall around the castle' [þe uttre hus, þet is as þe uttre wah abute þe castel] (W 173/T 193). Marcher experience also taught that reinforcement could come, not only by nesting such structures inside one another, but by placing them *close* to one another—that, just as the Marcher hills made the whole of the March into a borderland by laying out barriers in staggered rows, any collection of fortified structures was more difficult to penetrate

[41] On this tradition see Roberta D. Cornelius, *The Figurative Castle: A Study in the Mediaeval Allegory of the Edifice with Especial Reference to Religious Writings* (Bryn Mawr: [no publisher], 1930). See also Plato, *Timaeus*, 1151–1211 in *The Collected Dialogues*, ed. Edith Hamilton and Huntington Cairns, Bollingen Series 71 (Princeton: Princeton University Press, 1961), 69c–72b (pp. 1193–5).

than one strong fortification on its own. Thus, there was 'a general policy of farmstead fortification' throughout the March whereby 'soldier-farmers' held title to their land 'in recognition of the duty of castle guard',[42] and, as a result, a 'close pattern' of castles 'extend[ed] itself without break' through most of AB territory 'creating a strong defensive *zone* some sixteen kilometres wide' in all those lowlands where natural protections were weak.[43] According to this structural logic, the self in *Ancrene Wisse* is not only sheltered by a castle, but it finds 'succour' [sucurs] in Christ because *he* is a 'castle', someone who helps the anchorite 'stand upright' [stonden upright] (W 124/T 137), not by surrounding her or holding her up, but by being a 'tower' or edifice of 'stone' standing strongly *next* to her [stan of help, tur of treowe sucurs, castel of strengðe] (W 135/T 123).

It is in fact as they state the need for density in the protection of any vulnerable place that the AB texts show themselves to have absorbed Marcher realities most fully. Indeed, they present their own forms as contributions to such a close pattern, fortifications to put next to the protections of the body, helping to form the self by the strength of cooperative resemblance. Thus, *Hali Meiðhad* not only understands the virtuous female self it describes as a tower secure in its virginity, but it understands *virginity* to be a 'tower' which lends its own strengths to any self that strives to possess it ('this tower signifies the sublimity of maidenhood' [bitacneð þis tur þe hehnesse of meiðhad] (S&W 225/d'A 128). *Sawles Warde* is not only a lengthy instruction in how to fortify the body as if it were a 'castle', but a set of instructions that are, by way of their allegory, yet another castle. It is *Ancrene Wisse*, however, which takes this structural logic the furthest, since the whole of its form is a 'body model' wherein the exterior parts (1 and 8) describe 'outer things' [uttre þinges], ruling 'the body and bodily deeds' [riwleð þe licome & licomliche deden], while the interior parts (2–7) 'rule the heart within' [riwlin þe heorte wiðinnen] (W 1–2/T 6–7).[44] Where such a body is also everywhere understood to be a fortification, *Ancrene Wisse*'s eight parts can be diagrammed

---

[42] Stanford, *Archaeology of the Welsh Marches*, 216.

[43] Ibid. 215. Emphasis mine.

[44] For the phrase 'body model' and a description of *Ancrene Wisse*'s form see Jocelyn Wogan-Browne, 'Chaste Bodies: Frames and Experiences', 24–42 in *Framing Medieval Bodies*, ed. Sarah Kay and Miri Rubin (Manchester: Manchester University Press, 1994), 27. The way the 'outer rule' surrounds the inner rule has also been noticed by Georgianna (*Solitary Self*, 22) and Warren (*Anchorites and Their Patrons*, 104).

so as to emphasize this analogy, as shown below, linking parts 1 and 8 with a line at the top (so as to indicate their common and protective purpose), thereby modelling the castle these outer parts provide for parts 2–7 (thus, huddling, in their fragility, 'within').

```
+-------------------------------------------+
|               Outer Rule                  |
|   +-----------------------------------+   |
|   |           Inner Rule              |   |
|   |                                   |   |
|   |   2. Five Wits                    |   |
|   |   3. Birds and Anchorites (the feelings) |
|   |   4. Outer Temptations and Inner  |   |
|   |      Temptations, Their Comforts  |   |
|   |      and Remedies                 |   |
|   |   5. Confession                   |   |
|   |   6. Penance                      |   |
|   |   7. Love of Christ               |   |
1. Service                          8. Food, Clothing
                                       Work, Servants
```

In fact, part 1 describes *Ancrene Wisse* as just such a fortification, one that not only guides but 'protects' [witeð] anyone who reads it 'pure and unspotted from the world' [from þe worlt . . . cleane & unwemmet] (W 5/T 10). In part 8, the whole of *Ancrene Wisse* is said to fortify the anchorite by the particularly Marcher logic of the 'close pattern', making her strong in so far as it is kept constantly next to her ('read from this book each day . . . [and] if you read it often, it will be very profitable to you' [of þis boc redeð . . . euche dei . . . [&] hit schal beon ow ȝef ȝe hit redeð ofte swiðe biheue] [W 199/T 221]).

PLACE ITSELF

Because Marcher life demanded such extensive attention to both natural and man-made boundaries it seems to have bred a certain precocity in understanding the nature of borders as such. The variety of forms the AB texts were capable of attributing to people meant, for example, that they were well on their way to realizing that, even where it seems most obdurate, the body is never more than an 'imaginary morphology', matter whose very givenness is always a function of 'regulatory schemas', a physical shape entirely determined by 'historically revisable criteria of intelligibility'.[45] The AB texts also recognize, therefore, that even the most ostensibly physical of deficiencies can be ameliorated by the care taken in thinking about them. Consequently, the peculiarly vulnerable condition of the March was a detailed schooling in how to secure borders by improving one's imaginative skills, resisting invasion and injury through more rigorous definition of the *concept* of place.[46]

Even in this more abstract sense thought about place is always thought about borders since, in physics, place is the concept that emerges from trying to explain what happens *between* rather than to material things. Although it is not properly a source for the AB texts, Aristotle's *Physics*, as it was widely disseminated in the Latin translation of James of Venice (1125–50), was the crucial site for such explanation in the Middle Ages.[47] Here the identity of 'place' [locus] as such is difficult to secure because rather than a thing it is a particular set of relations between 'bodies' [corpora].[48] On the one hand, place is 'something other than a body' [aliquid locus preter corpora] for, if it could be said to occupy space, this would put 'two bodies in the same place' [in eodem enim utique essent duo corpora].[49] On the other hand, there is no body without a place, and so

---

[45] Judith Butler, *Bodies that Matter: On the Discursive Limits of Sex* (London: Routledge, 1993), 13–14. For an important consideration of *Ancrene Wisse* in relation to such an imaginary see Sarah Beckwith, 'Passionate Regulation: Enclosure, Ascesis, and the Feminist Imaginary', *South Atlantic Quarterly* 93 (1994), 803–24.

[46] For the history of this concept I have relied in this secton on Edward S. Casey, *The Fate of Place: A Philosophical History* (Berkeley: University of California Press, 1997).

[47] On James of Venice generally see Bernard G. Dod, 'Aristoteles latinus', 45–79 in *The Cambridge History of Later Medieval Philosophy*, ed. Norman Kretzmann, Anthony Kenny, and Jan Pinborg (Cambridge: Cambridge University Press, 1982), 54–5. The 'table of translations' in this volume shows that James's translation survives in 139 copies (p. 75). I take my text of the *Physics* from the version of James's translation available in *Aristoteles Latinus, VII.1: Physica (translatio vetus)*, ed. Fernand Bossier and Jozef Brams (Leiden: Brill, 1990), citing page numbers in the text. Translations of this text are my own.

[48] 'Quoniam autem aliud quidem secundum se aliud vero secundum aliud dicitur, et locus alius quidem communis, in quo omnia corpora sunt, alius vero proprius, in quo primo', *Physica*, 140. See also Aristotle, *Physics*, 1: 315–446 in *The Complete Works of Aristotle*, ed. Jonathan Barnes, 2 vols, rev. edn. (Princeton: Princeton University Press, 1984), 209a31–3 (1: 356).

[49] *Physica*, 137–8 and Aristotle, *Physics*, 208b27–209a7 (1: 355–6).

place accompanies *every* body: 'all that is, is in a place' [omne quod est in loco est].[50] Place is neither the matter nor the form of the thing 'since form and matter are not separate from the thing, whereas the place can be separated' [species quidem enim et materia non separantur a re, locum autem contingit], but somehow a given place also *has* the form of the thing, for that place folds itself so tightly around any object that it effectively adopts that thing's form:[51] 'Because it contains something it seems to be form, for the extremities of what contains and of what is contained are identical. They are indeed both boundaries, but not of the same thing, for the form is the boundary of the thing, while place is the boundary of the containing body.'[52] Place may therefore be understood as a kind of March in abstraction, a line whose identity consists of the division it makes.

Since it is an idea, place also has its own form; it is not simply the shape of the individual objects it locates, but of the idea of so placing them. Even if it is an attempt to think about a space that lies just beyond matter, in other words, such a thought (like any thought) is capable of coalescing as some material shape, giving its own contours to some solid thing, even if this is itself no more than an imagined object. Accordingly, Aristotle's definition of place achieves its greatest clarity when the complexity of all its abstractions congeal in the kind of thing one might actually touch: 'Wherefore place is neither part nor the state of anything, but is separable from it. It therefore seems that place is something like a vessel—for a vessel is a transportable place; the vessel is, however, no part of the thing.'[53] This is also the form that the AB texts use to register their more theoretical interest in 'place', for, even though they tend to understand the place of the self as a 'castle' or some other dwelling, they acknowledge the inherent vulnerability which caused that place to be fortified by sometimes imagining it in all its delicacy, in such cases, not as an unassailable stone tower, but as something akin to a breakable vase. Thus, in *Hali Meiðhad* the body is a 'brittle vessel' [bruchele ueat]

---

[50] *Physica*, 139 and, also, Aristotle, *Physics* 209a24 (1: 356).

[51] *Physica*, 141 and, also, Aristotle, *Physics*, 209b22 (1: 357).

[52] 'Sed propter id quidem quod continet videtur forma esse; in eodem enim sunt extrema continentis et contenti. Sunt quidem utraque termini sed non eiusdem, sed species quidem rei locus autem continentis corporis', *Physica*, 147–8 and, also, Aristotle, *Physics*, 211b10–13 (1: 360).

[53] 'Quare neque pars neque habitus, sed separabilis est locus ab unoquoque. Et videtur enim huiusmodi aliquid esse locus ut vas; est enim vas locus transmutabilis; vas autem nichil rei est', *Physica*, 141, and, also, Aristotle, *Physics* 209b26–9 (1: 357).

(S&W 229/d'A 136), while in *Ancrene Wisse* this 'fragile vessel' [feble uetles] is said to be made of 'brittle glass' [ibruchel gles] (W 80/ T 85). Where *Ancrene Wisse* describes the body as fragile in these terms it can also be seen to understand its own form in terms of such fragility; its bodily shape can therefore also be diagrammed, as shown below, by linking parts 1 and 8 with a line at the bottom rather than the top (thereby indicating the vulnerability of the barriers these outer parts try to place between the self and the world), leaving the shelter that contains parts 2–7 open to invasion.

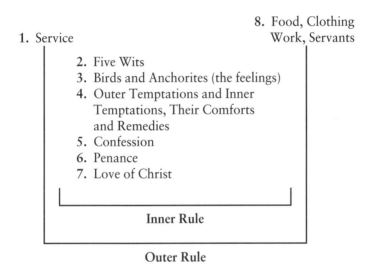

The similarities of this diagram to the previous one help to make clear that exterior fortifications are no more than an awareness of exterior dangers precisely proportionate to the strength of those fortifications —that what any castle's walls amount to is particularly solid knowledge of the extent to which the enclosure it provides is no more than an open vessel *in potentia*. In a place as war-torn as the March such knowledge would have also manifested itself in the development of castles from structures of earth to structures of stone; it would also have been clear in those shattered castles which siege had overcome —those towers of earth or stone which war had broken open to reveal the (fragile) vessel inside. The Deerfold's shape would itself have counted as such material knowledge of these structural relationships because it actually had the shape of *both* a castle and an open vessel: as an enclosure set high in a plateau, it was protected on every side by substantial, material barriers; on the other hand, if a person (or army) actually made it across these barriers and surmounted the protective heights around it, this enclosure was open on every side, a bowl-like shape which gravity itself would help anyone enter.

As they continually confront such vulnerabilities in the strongest places they know, the AB texts generally come to understand that place is defined by such fragility. This is true for Aristotle as well, since he refines his description of the 'vessel' constituted by each place so that it slowly seems less and less like a bowl with breakable sides (something that might be made of 'glass'), and more like a gossamer film, 'a kind of surface' [planum quoddam] that can cling to the outline of any shape ('just the size of a certain thing' [amplius simul cum re quodammodo]), like the thinnest—and weakest—sack or bag.[54] As Aristotle absorbs these structural properties to his idea of place, he says that it is fragile in its very specifications, 'hard to grasp' [videtur autem . . . difficile accipi locus].[55] This is the point the AB texts also make when they insist—particularly in the three saints' lives—that a body is secure as a place only in so far as it can be shown to be fragile. For example, Katherine is only a 'unique maiden' [anlepi meiden] (S&W 273/d'A 33), secure in her virginity, when her physical safety is threatened by a throng of fifty men, 'all of them fearsome fighters' [alle ferliche freken] (S&W 268/d'A 30));[56] she is only fully secure in her saintliness when her body is broken open by the utmost violence ('and, as [Katherine] had ordered him, he heaved up that hateful sword and struck off her head' [ant he as ha het him hef þet heatele sweord up & swipte hire of þet heaued] [S&W 283/d'A 52]). It is also by way of embracing this defining fragility that the 'treasure' [tresor] of the soul in *Sawles Warde* resides 'inside' [inne] a 'house' [hus] (S&W 212/d'A 167) that is repeatedly opened to the most dangerous visitors (for example, to 'Fear' [Fearlac], who comes straight 'from hell' [of helle] [S&W 212–13/d'A 169–70]).

---

[54] 'Propter hoc videtur planum quoddam esse et sicut vas locus continens. Amplius simul cum re quodammodo locus est; simul enim fines sunt et locus', *Physica*, 150, and, also, Aristotle, *Physics*, 212a28–31 (1: 361).

[55] *Physica*, 148, and, also, Aristotle, *Physics*, 212a8–9 (1: 360).

[56] Savage and Watson here translate 'anlepi' as 'single' and I have slightly pressed the point by altering this to 'unique'. For this definition see *MED*, s.v. 'on-lepi', b.

But recognizing that a certain vulnerability defines place is also a way of understanding that a particular place can be secured by conceptual clarity, that identifying fragilities is the most rigorous fortification of all. Such an insight is most apparent in the AB texts in part 7 of *Ancrene Wisse* where the castle is initially proffered as an image of the security of the body, but it slowly emerges that such a castle only provides protection in so far as its weaknesses are exposed, as it is *opened* rather than kept firmly closed. The general subject of this part of *Ancrene Wisse* is the 'pure heart', and it describes how the connection between selves usually called 'love' secures the integrity of each self (it is 'entirely about love, which makes the heart pure' [al of luue þe makeð schir heorte] [W 176/T 195]), and the most powerful illustration of this love and the resulting security occurs in the [tale] or 'parable' [forbisne] it tells about 'a lady' [leafdi], closed 'inside a castle of earth' [inwið an eorðene castel], 'closely besieged by her enemies' [biset al abuten], but also the object of 'a powerful king's love' [mihti kinges luue] (W 179/T 198). This king sends the lady many messages and gifts of 'wooing' [for wohlich] and, finally, 'the help of his fine army in holding her castle' [help of his hehe hird to halden hire castel], but the only moment in which the lady is in serious danger is when she *resists* this lover and his army, securing her boundaries against their help in so far as she is 'heard-hearted' [heard iheortet] (W 179/T 198). A story of this kind is, as Rosemary Woolf observed, 'one of the commonest allegories in medieval preaching books and manuals of instruction', for, as even *Ancrene Wisse* soon tells us, 'this king is Jesus, God's Son, who in just this way wooed our souls, which devils had besieged' [þes king is iesu godes sune, þet al o þisse wise wohede ure sawle þe deoflen hefden biset] (W 180/T 199), and the lady in the castle is a figure for every Christian soul held within a body.[57] But such an account of place also knows that the threat of invasion is to the fortification what difficulty is to the idea: a castle—like a body—is only as strong as its knowledge of the fragile vessel that it *also* is.

At its most acute, such knowledge extends to the recognition in all the AB texts that place comes into being not in relation to the object or objects it contains but in relation to every other thing—that, as in Aristotle's most concise definition of the concept, a given place is

---

[57] Rosemary Woolf, 'The Theme of Christ the Lover-Knight in Medieval English Literature', *Review of English Studies*, NS 13 (1962), 1–16 (p. 1).

brought into being by that which lies beyond it ('wherefore place is
the closest motionless boundary of that which is containing').[58] This
is to know, in other words, that the place of something like the self
cannot be secured in and of itself—solely by means of its isolation or
separation—since it only exists, in its autonomy, in relation to the
places outside it (as Aristotle put this point: 'if, therefore, a body is
contained in another body outside it, then it is in a place, and if not,
not').[59] Such wisdom is succinctly formulated in *Hali Meiðhad*, when
the maiden understands herself to be firmly placed within her body—
safe and secure in her chastity—only in so far as that body is related
to some other: 'just so I will guard myself truly unblemished, as I am
wedded to him' [al swuch ich chulle wite treowliche umwemmet as
ich am him iweddet] (S&W 243/d'A 163). But such wisdom is again
given its greatest emphasis in part 7 of *Ancrene Wisse*, when the inset
romance I have just described issues onto an image of the shield of
the victorious 'king' hung up, after his death, in a church. This image
also registers unpleasant Marcher realities, the kind of residue of
warfare that the anchorites for whom *Ancrene Wisse* was written
might have seen regularly through their 'church window' [chirche
þurl] (W 37/T37):[60]

Efter kene cnihtes deað, me hongeð hehe ichirche his scheld on his mun-
gunge, alswa is þis scheld, þet is þe crucifix, ichirche iset i swuch stude þer me
hit sonest seo, forte þenchen þer bi o iesu cristes cnihtschipe þet he dude o
rode. His leofmon bihalde þron hu he bohte hire luue, lette þurlin his scheld
openin his side to schawin hire his heorte, to schawin hire openliche hu
inwardliche he luuede hire, & to ofdrahen hire heorte.

[After the death of a brave knight his shield is hung up in church in his
memory; just so this shield—that is, the crucifix—is put in the church in a
place where it can most easily be seen, so through it people may think of the
knightliness of Jesus Christ on the cross. His beloved should look at it and see

---

[58] 'Quare continentis terminus inmobilis primum, hoc est locus', *Physica*, 150, and,
also, Aristotle, *Physics*, 212a20–1 (1: 361).

[59] 'Cui quidem igitur corpori inest aliquid extra corpus continens ipsum, hoc in loco
est, cui vero non, minime', *Physica*, 150, and, also, Aristotle, *Physics* 212a32 (1: 361).

[60] 'Purpose-built cells were positioned either next to the church, in order to view the
high altar, or within the churchyard . . . in order to view the Mass the cell was positioned most often to the north or south of the chancel and was provided with a hatch,
or squint, through which to view the high altar', Roberta Gilchrist, *Contemplation
and Action: The Other Monasticism* (London: Leicester University Press, 1995), 185.
On living arrangements in anchorhouses see Warren, *Anchorites and Their Patrons*,
29–41.

how he bought her love, let his shield be pierced, his side opened to show her his heart, to show her openly how fervently he loved her inwardly, and to draw her heart to him.]

(T 200/W 181)

The shield of this knight also represents a heroism that is quickly transformed into an allegory of Christ's sacrifice. In both of its meanings, however, this shield is governed by the proposition that a boundary may well be strengthened by its penetration, as the crossing of that boundary defines the singular place located within it. The Marcher knight, like Christ, is profoundly hurt when he is pierced, but, as a part of the fortification which seals some place, this 'opening' serves to make clear to all those who remain within that boundary but unpierced, that, at the very least, they are *placed*—also 'opened' to such danger, but, at least, until the moment they experience it (and their place truly is dissolved), separated from that danger *in* that place. Another way to put this is that a very Marcher sort of sacrifice allows traditional allegory to discover an Aristotelian physics: it shows place to be a division so thin and subtle, a distinction so dependent upon the delicacy and care of its formulation, that it is strengthened most by clear *thinking* about those objects and relations which bring it into being.

ANCHORAGE

It has long been known, of course, that there is no escaping what lies beyond the self even in the most inward explorations of the AB texts, that it is an 'organizing assumption' of *Ancrene Wisse* in particular that 'exterior and interior realities are inextricably bound'.[61] But an Aristotelian account of place uncovers the extent to which the self in all of these texts is actually *exterior* to all those boundaries that are thought to contain it. This is not only true because the place in

---

[61] Georgianna, *Solitary Self*, 5. Georgianna explores this assumption most fully in her second chapter, 'Self and Society' (32–78). Elizabeth Robertson calls the merging of interior and exterior in *Ancrene Wisse* 'quotidien psychological realism'. See *Early English Devotional Prose and the Female Audience* (Knoxville: University of Tennessee Press, 1990), 44–76 (for the phrase see p. 44). Robertson has more recently called this interrelationship 'materialist immanence'. See ' "This Living Hand" ', 3–4 and 34–6. As Sarah Beckwith notes, 'interiority' in *Ancrene Wisse* 'is not so much the opposite of exteriority as its complex co-product' ('Passionate Regulation', 808).

which this self was thought up was a topography particularly rich in modelling shapes, but because it turns out to be *other* selves that are indispensable to the procedures of self-fashioning. Because boundaries between selves are governed by conflict and aggression—because a self might be defined as that which tries to exist at the expense of another—these more personal relations have also been characterized by Emmanuel Levinas as 'the permanent possibility of war' [la possibilité permanente de la guerre].[62] Consequently, the thinking of the AB texts not only unfolds as a kind of physics in which one body is defined in relation to other bodies, but as a kind of Levinasian ethics in which each self is 'preserved as independent and self-sufficient but in some sense in relation with one another'.[63]

As I suggested at the beginning of this chapter, the formal facts which arise from such relations reveal themselves most broadly in a set of apparent contradictions, and these contradictions are, again, most clearly visible among the AB texts in *Ancrene Wisse*. It is there that an anchorite tries to dwell in the 'most solitary place of all' [anlukest stude of alle] (W 46/T 48) and may therefore 'make each spiritual gain better than in a crowd' [do betere þen i þrung euch gastelich biȝete] (W 85/T 91), but it is also there that the anchorite must care about the crowd if she is to galvanize her 'heart' to be appropriately charitable ('this rule is the charity of a pure heart' [þeos riwle is chearite of schir heorte] [W 1/T 6]). She is told to 'be afraid of each man . . . in case he draws you out—that is deceives you with sin and lies in wait to get you into his clutches' [beoð ofdred of euch mon alswa as þe þeof is leste he drahe ow utwart, þet is biswike wið sunne & weiti forte warpen up on ow his cleches] (W 85/T 90–1), but she must also do everything for God and 'for the good of another and for his advantage' [schir heorte . . . makieð twa þinges, þet tu al þet tu dest do hit oðer for luue ane of godd, oðer for oþres god & for his biheue] (W 178/T 196).[64] Of course charity need have neither a material result nor a material form; as we have just seen in relation to

[62] Emmanuel Levinas, *Totality and Infinity: An Essay on Exteriority*, trans. Alphonso Lingis (Pittsburgh: Duquesne University Press, 1969), 21; *Totalité et Infini: Essai sur l'extériorité* ([Paris]: Martinus Nijhoff, 1971), 5.

[63] This is how Colin Davis characterizes the 'central difficulty' the philosophy of Levinas confronts. See *Levinas: An Introduction* (Cambridge: Polity Press, 1996), 41.

[64] *Ancrene Wisse* is here citing Bernard, *Tractatus de moribus et officio episcoporum*, ch. 3, *Patrologia Latina* 182, col. 817. I take this reference from *Ancrene Wisse*, ed. Shepherd, 53.

the figure of Christ, the 'heart' may 'open' itself to the world by the act of thought or feeling we normally call 'love'. But *Ancrene Wisse* is alive to the ways that each such thought is a danger to the solitude designed to foster it, that among the things that thinking about the world can do is to reveal solitude in its most negative aspect, as a mode of withdrawal which amounts to imprisonment:

Bi dei sum time oder bi niht gederið in ower heorte . . . þe pinen þe prisuns þolieð & habbeð þer ha liggeð wið irn heuie ifeðeret, nomeliche of þe cristene þe beoð in heaðenesse. Summe i prisun, summe in ase muche þeowdom as oxe is oðer asse.

[During the day some time, or the night, gather in your heart . . . the pains that prisoners endure and feel where they lie, heavily fettered with iron, especially of the Christians who are in heathen parts, some in prison, some in as great servitude as an ox or an ass is.]

(T 19/W 16)

Moreover, where charity might extend even the smallest degree beyond the heart into some activity—where for example an anchorite might try to give food to others—the very worldliness of the action ensures that it is but a step down the slippery slope toward sin:

[Þe sweoke of helle] bringeð hire on to gederin & ʒeouen al earst to poure, forðre to oðer freond, aleast makien feaste & wurðen al worldlich, forschuppet of ancre to husewif of halle. Godd wat swuch feaste makeð sum hore. Weneð þet ha wel do, as dusie & adotede doð hire to understonden, flatrið hire of freolec, herieð & heoueð up þe ealmesse þet ha deð—hu wide ha is icnawen. Ant heo let wel of & leapeð in orhel. Sum seiðe inohreaðe þet ha gedereð hord, swa þet hire hus mei & heo ba beon irobbett.

[(The deceiver of hell) leads her on to gather and give all at first to the poor, later to other friends—lastly to hold feasts and become completely worldly, degenerating from an [anchorite] into a housewife in a hall. God knows, this sort of feast makes whores of some. She thinks she is doing right, as stupid and foolish people give her to understand: they flatter her for her generosity, praise and extol the alms-giving that she does—how widely she is known! And she thinks well of this and leaps into pride. Soon enough someone is saying that she is treasure-gathering, so that both her house and herself may get robbed.]

(T 115/W 105–6)

Some of what is dangerous here is an attitude toward charity (a self-congratulation which is a 'leap into pride'), but it is also clear that 'generosity' and 'alms-giving' are the positive names given to actions which defeat, rather than foster, the solitude otherwise equated with selfhood.

Ancrene Wisse also embeds this contradiction in aspects of its shape that propose some solution, and the most economical and revealing of these is a pun on the word *ancre*, the name this text generally uses to designate the kind of self it seeks to fashion. Because this word, in this period, could also refer to 'an appliance for holding a ship', it provided an opportunity for anticipating that modern phenomenology in which it has been argued that we can exist only when we 'cast anchor in some "setting"' [jetons l'ancre dans quelque 'milieu'].[65] As he develops this point in *The Phenomenology of Perception*, Merleau-Ponty explains that isolation is not the obverse of community or connection but its complement, a different perspective on the necessity of human relations:

Solitude and communication cannot be the two horns of a dilemma, but two 'moments' of one phenomenon, since in fact other people do exist for me . . . my experience must in some way present me with other people, since otherwise I should have no occasion to speak of solitude, and could not begin to pronounce other people inaccessible.[66]

According to this view, what appears to be an insistence on separation as a condition of selfhood in *Ancrene Wisse* is, in fact, a way of relating the self to others, and, as in the modern case, this entire principle can be found latent in the two meanings of *ancre*:

Recluses . . . wunieð . . . under chirche euesunges, þet ha understonden þet ha ahen to beon of se hali lif þet al hali chirche, þet is cristene folc leonie & wreoðie up on ham, ant heo halden hire up wið hare life halinesse & hare eadie bonen. For þi is ancre ancre icleopet, & under chirche iancret as ancre under schipes bord forte halden þet schip, þet uþen ant stormes hit ne ouerwarpen . . . Euch ancre haueð þis o foreward, ba þurh nome of ancre & þurh þet ha wuneð under þe chirche to understiprin hire ȝef ha walde fallen . . . Ancre wuninge & hire nome ȝeieð eauer þis foreward, ȝet hwen ha slepeð.

[65] For the definition I cite see *OED* s.v. 'anchor n1'. For the various forms this word took in Middle English see *MED*, s.vv. 'ancre n.', and 'anker n.'. For the phrase I quote see M. Merleau-Ponty, *Phenomenology of Perception*, trans. Colin Smith (London: Routledge, 1962), 253. For the original see *Phénoménologie de la perception* (Paris: Librairie Gallimard, 1942), 293. Elsewhere, Merleau-Ponty also describes the connection between the self and the world as a kind of '*anchorage*' [un ancrage]. Merleau-Ponty, *Phenomenology*, 280; *Phénoménologie de la perception*, 325.

[66] Merleau-Ponty, *Phenomenology of Perception*, 359. See also *Phénoménologie de la perception*, 412–13.

[Recluses . . . live under the church's eaves, because they understand that they ought to be of so holy a life that all Holy Church—that is, Christian people—may lean and support itself upon them, and they may hold it up with their holiness of life and their blessed prayers. For this reason the anchorite is called an anchorite and anchored under the church like an anchor under a ship's side to hold the ship, so that waves and storms do not overturn it . . . Each anchorite has agreed to do this, in virtue both of the name of anchorite and of her dwelling under the church to prop it up should it be going to fall. . . . The anchorite's dwelling and her name proclaim this agreement all the time, even when she is sleeping.]

(T 74–5 / W 70)

Although this image makes the anchor what the self is rather than that which the self projects (as in Merleau-Ponty's image), the point is the same: connections between selves are in fact the basis of— rather than any danger to—solitude. According to this image, those others who elsewhere threaten the anchorite by requiring her concern also require her solitude as a guarantor of *their* selfhood ('to prop it up should it be going to fall'). The anchorite secures other selves just by existing ('even when she is sleeping') and in this way is also shown to be theoretically prior to what she is elsewhere understood to have left behind—psychic 'support' for other Christians in so far as 'her dwelling and her name' show that separateness is a way of being *in* the world (as Levinas puts this point, 'to be separated is to dwell somewhere' [être séparé, c'est demeurer quelque part]).[67]

This complicated thought necessarily ramifies through the 142 other uses of *ancre* in *Ancrene Wisse*, and its more positive meanings are further underscored by a subtle but deeply momentous revision of the structure of the castle in part 4 of the rule.[68] The material for this change is the contradiction between separation and communication implicit in *Ancrene Wisse*'s implied audience, the fact that there were never fewer than 'three sisters' [þreo . . . sustren] in the anchorhouse envisioned in this text,[69] and (as the reference goes in

---

[67] Levinas, *Totality and Infinity*, 168; *Totalité et infini*, 182.

[68] For these uses see *A Concordance to Ancrene Wisse, MS Corpus Christi College Cambridge 402*, ed. Jennifer Potts, Lorna Stevenson, and Jocelyn Wogan-Browne (Cambridge: D. S. Brewer, 1993), s.v. 'ancre'. Related forms include *ancrehus* (used 13 times), *ancren* (19), *ancrene* (1), *ancres* (22), and *ancrewununge* (1).

[69] Three 'sisters' are mentioned at the end of part 2 of *Ancrene Wisse* in the Corpus manuscript (T 62) but White deletes the number from his translation (see W 58). In a passage not present in Corpus the Nero text of *Ancrene Wisse* also refers to the audience of the rule as 'three . . . sisters of one father and of one mother' ('þreo . . . sustren of one ueder & of one moder'), *Ancrene Riwle* (*Cotton Nero A.XIV*), ed. Day, 85.

the text's final revision), in the end, 'twenty . . . or more' [twenti . . .
oðer ma] (W 119/T 130).[70] The change incorporates this crowd into
the structure of the imagined castle, at the precise centre of *Ancrene
Wisse*'s 'body model', in its discussion of 'inner temptation' [inre
fondunge] (W 92/T 99). This image insists that communication is a
form of solitude, that not only is 'each good man that the devil wars
against' a 'castle' [castel is euch god mon þet te deouel weorred]
(W 115/T 125–6), but so too is any community of loving people —
even a community of anchorites:

ȝe beoð tur ow seoluen mine leoue sustren, ah ne drede ȝe nawt hwil ȝe beoð
se treoweliche & se feste ilimet wið lim of anred luue euch of ow to oþer, for
na deofles puf ne þurue ȝe dreden bute þet lim falsi, þet is to seggen, bute luue
bitweonen ow þurh þe feond wursi. Sone se ei unlimeð hire, ha bið sone
iswipt forð, bute ȝef þe oþre halden hire, ha bið sone ikeast adun as þe lowse
stan is from þe tures cop in to þe deope dich of sume suti sunne.

[You are a tower yourselves, my dear sisters, but do not fear while you are so
truly and firmly cemented with the cement of constant love, each of you to the
others. For the devil's blast need not be feared unless the cement fail, that is
to say, unless the love between you deteriorate because of the fiend. As soon
as anyone uncements herself, she is quickly swept off, unless the others hold
her; she is quickly pitched down, as the loose stone is from the top of the
tower, into the deep ditch of some filthy sin.]

(T 117/W 107)

This is not quite the self which appears in part 7 of *Ancrene Wisse* as
a 'lady' secure in her place to the extent that she is 'opened', nor is it
that self which is likened to a castle according to that structural logic
whereby fortifications are strengthened by multiplication and proximity. In this case, the danger that threatens the 'tower' does not come
from beyond its walls but from within it: at issue here is not an invasion, but the prospect of collapse, the disintegration of a structure
that had been firmly 'cemented'. Thus, this image argues that 'each'
person only *is* 'each' person (a 'castle' in herself) in so far as she is
linked by some 'love' to another person ('each of you to the others').

[70] Although one passage in the Corpus text suggests that each sister lived separately,
('when your sisters' maids come to you to comfort you, come to them at the window
. . .' [hwen ower sustres meidnes cumeð to ow to froure, cumeð to ham to þe þurl]
[W 199/T 221]), it is generally assumed that these three women 'lived together in a
single household' (Dobson, *Origins*, 169; for more general discussion of the community implied in *Ancrene Wisse* see this volume, 252–9 and 261–71). Wogan-Browne
imagines an anchorhold with 'at least three cells' ('Chaste Bodies', 34).

This may seem to suggest that a castle is lent its strength by the parts that comprise it, but, in fact, this image makes the opposite, counter-intuitive point: the strength of each part of this 'cemented' whole—'each' anchorite as she is a 'castle'—derives from the whole structure that 'holds her' firm, *as* a subsidiary part of it.

This surprising inversion of physical realities is the most general resolution the AB texts provide for the problem others pose to a given self, for this version of the castle is only one of many instances in which the AB self is not only autonomous and separate but effectively other *to* itself, not only a place that is isolated from the world, but that part of the world into which a person extends herself in order to fashion her identity. It is for precisely this reason that the AB texts continually imagine the self by means of exterior (and, in many ways, everyday) objects—castles, towers, houses, glass vessels, the bodies of injured knights. It would be appropriate to call each of these objects prosthetic—a way of capturing a complex thought that is in no way dependent upon that object—but it is inevitable that the consistent evocation of such things will imply the necessity of such materiality to the idea they refine. Merleau-Ponty has suggested that such prostheses are in fact essential to self-understanding, since the self must be envisioned as if it were an object in the larger world: 'Consciousness is removed from being, and from its own being, and at the same time united with them, by the thickness of the world. The true *cogito* is not intimate communing of thought with the thought of that thought: they meet only on passing through the world.'[71] This is to say that the topography of the March exerts pressure on self-fashioning in the AB texts not only because it is so generally life-shaping (forms constantly pressed upon the consciousness of dwellers on the March by wars and their aftermath), but because the self never has any choice but to fashion itself from the things most immediately to hand.

The AB texts also know that the prosthetic object that presses hardest on every instance of self-fashioning is the already fashioned other self. This other is the best possible prosthetic because it has already assumed the shape the self wants to have, but for precisely this reason it is intimidating (as that which has somehow formed itself better or more easily), even threatening (as that which has the power to stop the forming self in its tracks). This is of course

---

[71] Merleau-Ponty, *Phenomenology*, 297–8; *Phenoménologie de la Perception*, 344.

the model that Hegel advanced so influentially in the allegory of the
'lord' [der Herr] and his 'bondsman' [der Knecht] in the *Phenomenology of Spirit*. Although this allegory begins by suggesting that the
lord is the more successful of these two selves, its point is that the
bondsman actually has all the power in this relation because the lord
actually lacks a useful model for his own self-fashioning (the bondsman being inadequate for the task) while the bondsman has the
powerful and compelling shape of the lord who 'exists for him as his
object'.[72] In its own version of this allegory *Ancrene Wisse* constantly
asks the anchorite to imagine herself in relation to such a 'lord';
as part of her daily 'devotions' [seruise] (W 6 /T 11), she is asked to
internalize this powerful other as if he were her very heart:

Efter þe measse cos, hwen þe preost sacreð, þer forʒeoteð al þe world, þer
beoð al ut of bodi, þer i sperclinde luue bicluppeð ower leofmon þe in to ower
breostes bur is iliht of heouene, & haldeð him heteueste aþet he habbe iʒettet
ow al þet ʒe eauer easkið.

[After the mass-kiss, when the priest consecrates, there forget all the world,
there be entirely out of body, there in gleaming love embrace your beloved,
who has alighted into the bower of your breast from heaven, and hold him
tight until he has granted you all that ever you ask.]

                                                                    (T 21/W 18)

However, the inversion in this case does not consist of finding defining
power in the lord, but rather a useful exteriority, for, as the 'lord'
moves inside the anchorite, alighting in the 'bower' of her 'breast, her
very selfhood moves 'entirely out of body' and becomes equivalent to
'all the world'. This AB self is not troubled by the existence and power
of other selves, then, because it is effectively other to itself, a thought
protected from the insistence of the objective world because it can
itself be contemplated as its own object.

   It could therefore be said that the idea of the self in the AB texts
borrows the materiality of exterior objects in order to fashion an
interiority that is a made thing. Hegel makes something like this point
in the *Phenomenology of Spirit* when he notes that the 'truth' of the
bondsman's selfhood is only perceptible to him by means of the

[72] G. W. F. Hegel, *Phenomenology of Spirit*, trans. A. V. Miller (Oxford: Oxford
University Press, 1977), 111–19 (quotations here from p. 117). For the original of the
passage see Georg Wilhelm Friedrich Hegel, *Phänomenologie des Geistes*, ed. Wolfgang
Bonsiepen and Reinhard Heede, vol. 9 in *Gesammelte Werke* (Hamburg: Felix
Meiner, 1980), 109–16.
   On the importance of this passage in Hegel see Charles Taylor, *Hegel* (Cambridge:
Cambridge University Press, 1975), 153–7.

objects he makes for his lord, since it is in such things that he can see evidence of his own consciousness added to the compulsions that caused him to make them (in those aspects of these objects that were not expressly demanded). Once the bondsman's thought has been rendered 'permanent' in such things, in other words, the very obduracy of these objects models the 'individuality' of his thought:

> Work on the other hand, is desire held in check, fleetingness staved off; in other words, work forms and shapes the thing. The negative relation to the object becomes its form and something permanent, because it is precisely for the worker that the object has independence. This negative middle term or the formative activity is at the same time the individuality or pure-being-for-self of consciousness which now, in the work outside of it, acquires an element of permanence. It is in this way, therefore, that consciousness, qua worker, comes to see in the independent being [of the object] its own independence. (p. 118)[73]

In *Ancrene Wisse* the 'devotions' or 'work' done at the behest of a 'lord' are equally 'formative' of an 'independent being', in part because *all* of the work the anchorite does holds her 'desire . . . in check'. But, rather than discovering her own 'consciousness' in the things she makes, what the anchorite makes is in fact 'pure-being-for-self'. Moreover, she is both made to recognize that this is her work as well as assisted in its accomplishment by the made thing she routinely holds in her hands, since *Ancrene Wisse* not only contains all the injunctions that constitute lordship in her daily life (as if this book were a more powerful person), but it asks her to make herself as if *she* were a book. It may seem odd to think of *Ancrene Wisse* as the most important object the anchorite has to hand for her self-imagining, but, as I have been suggesting throughout this chapter, it is the extraordinary achievement of *Ancrene Wisse* to *be* as well as to describe an anchorite.

In fact, it is as it understands itself to be an instance of the self it urges upon the anchorite that *Ancrene Wisse* most fully resolves the contradiction whereby the self is, at once, an idea and a thing.

---

[73] 'Die Arbeit hingegen ist gehemmte Begierde, aufgehaltenes Verschwinden, oder sie bildet. Die negative Beziehung auf den Gegenstand wird zur Form desselben, und zu einem bleibenden; weil eben dem arbeitenden der Gegenstand Selbstständigkeit hat. Diese negative Mitte oder das formirende Thun, ist zugleich die Einzelnheit oder das reine Fürsichseyn des Bewußtseyns, welches nun in der Arbeit außer es in das Element des Bleibens tritt; das arbeitende Bewußtseyn kommt also hierdurch zur Anschauung des selbständigen Seyns, als seiner selbst', Hegel, *Phänomenologie des Geistes*, ed. Bonsiepen and Heede, 115.

As I have already suggested, it helps that *Ancrene Wisse* everywhere likens its own form to exterior objects such as castles or vessels, but it is particularly important that *Ancrene Wisse* also insists at both its beginning and its end that it is, above all other things, a '*book*' [boc] (W 4/T 8; W 6/T 11 and W 199/T 221). When it does so, *Ancrene Wisse* not only envisions itself as a collection of words, but it envisions the self as such a thing, a set of thoughts unspooling themselves into the world, across a page, from left to right, down a page's length, across however many pages comprise a given version of this text. Since the 'outer rule' of *Ancrene Wisse* describes that kind of person who encounters such thoughts in an 'inner rule'—since it is that body whose comforts, privations and actions are described in parts 1 and 8 who is actually looking *out* at parts 2–7—to notice this more obvious aspect of this text's form is to discover that its version of the 'inner' self actually sits *outside* whatever body holds this book in its hands, and opens its pages before it. The most precise diagram of the form of *Ancrene Wisse* would therefore account for this text's physicality by placing parts 1 and 8 *inside* parts 2–7, as shown below.

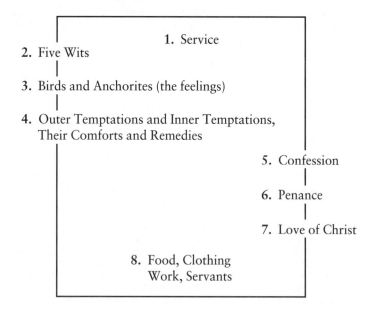

It is appropriate to connect parts 2–7 with lines that completely surround parts 1 and 8 in a diagram because the 'book' of *Ancrene Wisse* is the one prosthesis offered by the AB texts in which the self is actually enclosed on every side, a dwelling whose walls consist, not of earthworks or stone, but the carapace of the self's own imaginings. In fact, it could even be said that this is the version of the AB self which most powerfully demonstrates how to transform a threatening world into that self's very substance: as it opens the self out like some prospect in this outer world—as if it were the kind of place the anchorite looked out of her body and saw—*Ancrene Wisse* suggests that the self is most accurately and safely understood as just such a prospect.

Because Dobson's scholarship gives so firmly onto such a prospect this form of *Ancrene Wisse* can also help us to see how his discoveries were most topographically right where they were most paleographically wrong. In fact, to look deeply into such a book and find its 'origins', not in some idea or doctrine, but, rather, 'on the bank of a stream' beneath 'high wooded ground (Burnt Coppice and Barnett Wood) . . . which rises steeply on the other side' is not only to see *exactly* where this book came from, but how it became the kind of thing it is and what it urged every anchorite (indeed, every Christian) to be.[74] Whether the Deerfold was the place that the author of *Ancrene Wisse* or his anchorites knew is itself immaterial. Dobson's extraordinary misprision shows us that to locate *Ancrene Wisse* correctly but more approximately would be to know very much less about the material from which this text is made—and, therefore, what this text exists to say.

[74] Dobson, *Origins of Ancrene Wisse*, 221.

6

The Spirit of Romance:
King Horn, *Havelok the Dane*,
and *Floris and Blancheflour*

The spirit itself is not a body, but may be said to be analogous to the body.

[Nec ipse spiritus corpus est, sed corpori similis]
(*De spiritu et anima*, c.1170)

This chapter is the story of the closing down of formal possibilities that marked the end of the early part of Middle English, a description of the consolidation of a general idea of literature which reined in both the boldness and experimentation that had characterized English writing after the Conquest until the fourteenth century. It is no accident, therefore, that the texts in which I attempt to specify this new idea have been denigrated for making a poor beginning (they are 'crude ore') but are, at the same time, part of a mode of literary making which has been described as 'a record of decadence'.[1] This is not to say that the impoverishment that concerns me is in any way an attribute of these forms—that they are in some way worse than the forms I have so far been describing—but that it is an important effect of the figures romances cut that they *can* be taken for granted.

---

[1] The first phrase is from Derek Pearsall's description of *King Horn* ('*Horn* seems to us of crucial importance, for it embodies, partly by derivation from Laȝamon, a conventional technique and conventional phraseology in unalloyed form, like crude ore, from which later romances such as *Guy* or *Richard* drew extensively'), 'The Development of Middle English Romance', *Mediaeval Studies* 27 (1965), 91–116 (pp. 106–7). The second phrase is from Gillian Beer's history of the genre ('Any history of the romance will in one sense be a record of decadence. The works now popularly called "romances" are usually sub-literature, magazines like *True Romances* or lightweight commercial fiction deliberately written to flatter day dreams. Such "romances" batten on the emotionally impoverished. Sub-literary romances are not new'), *The Romance* (London: Methuen, 1970), 1.

Of the forms so far discussed in this book, only the three saints' lives of the *Katherine*-group can be said to share a form, but, toward the end of the thirteenth century, there are suddenly many texts that can be (and have been) called 'romance'. And yet Middle English romances are not only undervalued because there are so many of them, but because, for the first time after the Conquest, some writing in English actually knows of such multiplicity. It is not only that an audience faced with this sudden surfeit is suddenly in a position to take its constituents for granted, but that *every* audience does so because it is in the nature of such written forms to undervalue them*selves*.

As I suggested at the beginning of this book, English romance can therefore be described as revolutionary in a classically Marxist sense; in this period, English romances are the 'ideological forms' in which a more 'material transformation' is making itself available for scrutiny. The language of Marxism is particularly appropriate in this case because the quantity of texts which brings about this change is itself a product of a substantial change in underlying 'economic conditions': there is a general increase in demand for, and a consequent elaboration of, the means for producing writing in English. But a Marxist description is also particularly helpful here because it makes visible the extent to which a broader social and political change has been absorbed directly into made forms, how the treatment of a certain class of objects has commodified them, with the result that the ideas embedded in individual things become devalued in favour of a more general 'surplus'—as, in other words, value in this sphere (the cultural capital of 'literature') comes to reside, not in the ideas designing particular things, but in the metaphysical subtlety attributed to the aggregation of those things. In this sense it is actually crucial that such a change be described as a 'revolution' for it is only in such terms that it is possible to say how romance form emerged, not as an innovation, but as a *reversal* (the transformation of what had been 'productive forces' into 'fetters'): it is in this way that the very isolation which had been the grounds of English literature up until that point—the source of the continuous and rich invention of English literary forms —became the condition which made what had passed for literature look like anything *but* (as, under this new regime, formal difference came to seem like eccentricity or ignorance). A Marxist account also helps us to understand why this reversal should have been so little remarked upon ('we [can] not judge of such a period of transformation by its own consciousness'), and, therefore, why this change is only visible in the 'material life' of objects, and only recoverable in the careful description of these new and radically different forms.[2]

Romance form is not the only kind of English writing that the thirteenth century begins to produce in quantity, of course, and it is true that many of the points made in this chapter could be made about saint's life. In fact, *Katerine*, *Iuliene* and *Margarete* were probably written earlier than any English romance, and the frequent production of other saints' lives over the rest of the thirteenth century means that there may even have been more English lives than romances in circulation by 1300. Romance form and saint's life are also similar: Oxford, Bodleian Library, MS Laud misc. 108 (*c*.1300) not only contains the growing collection of saints' lives which was eventually described as *The South English Legendary*, but its compiler seems to have included *King Horn* and *Havelok the Dane* as well because he thought them to be such lives.[3] Saint's life was also more quickly recognized than romance *as* a form; what we now term romance was still known in Middle English by a variety of names, while *Katherine*, *Iuliene* and *Margarete* were each described in their earliest manuscripts as a 'lyf'.[4]

Even if its importance was not immediately clear, however, romance form is more in need of description because of its subsequent consequence, the extent to which later English writers and, finally, literary scholarship came to regard it as foundational. It matters very much, in other words, that Chaucer is thought to have 'started a tradition',

---

[2] The quotations in this paragraph are taken from Marx's summary of the 'guiding thread' of his 'studies' in the preface to *A Critique of Political Economy*, 388–92 in *Selected Writings* (Oxford: Oxford University Press, 1977), 389–90. On the importance of 'creative practice' in Marxist thinking see, in particular, Raymond Williams, *Marxism and Literature* (Oxford: Oxford University Press, 1977), 206–12. For a materialist account of English romance see Stephen Knight, 'The Social Function of the Middle English Romances', 99–122 in *Medieval Literature: Criticism, Ideology and History*, ed. David Aers (Brighton, Sussex: Harvester, 1986).

[3] This observation is made in Gisela Guddat-Figge, *Catalogue of Manuscripts Containing Middle English Romances*, Texte und Untersuchungen zur Englischen Philologie, vol. 4 (Munich: Wilhelm Fink, 1976), 282–3. For a list of the saints' lives in Laud 108 see *The Early South-English Legendary*, ed. Carl Horstmann, EETS OS 87 (London, 1887), xiii (contents of the other major manuscripts of the *Legendary* are also given in this volume, pp. xiv–xxiv). For a description of the relationship between the manuscripts of the *Legendary* see Manfred Görlach, *The Textual Tradition of the South English Legendary*, Leeds Studies in English Texts and Monographs, NS 6 (University of Leeds: School of English, 1974).

[4] Paul Strohm, '*Passioun, Lyf, Miracle, Legende*: Some Generic Terms in Middle English Hagiographical Narrative', *Chaucer Review* 10 (1975), 62–75 and 154–71 (esp. 156–7).

and the one tradition in English he can be shown to have relied upon is the 'plain and easy verse style' in romance narrative.[5] This is not to say that there is necessarily a through-line from romance to what was later called English literature via Chaucer, not least because Chaucer's centrality in such matters has always accomplished most for the writer or scholar who posited it (in every case, the need to create a 'Father of English Poetry' has always exceeded the possibility that any one figure could have been so influential). On the other hand, the misapprehension is an indication of the general importance of romance: the extent to which its form reflects a general cultural change ensures that it can become grounds for the English literature in later periods. Nor is it irrelevant that the nature of romance should always be wrongly estimated, since it is also in the nature of these forms—like that of the commodities they resemble—to seem to be something they are not.

The main task of this chapter is to trace the complexity of this seeming, to show how the idea born by romance forms—what I shall tend to call, for reasons that will become clear, the 'spirit' of romance —can be so vivid and compelling that it substitutes itself for the very objects which bear it. The result is that one of the ideas early Middle English writing conveys functions as if it were a material, and, therefore, despite its immateriality, becomes a ground for further literary making. Although this ground appeared first in French, not English, I am only concerned here with its effects in English, particularly as they are manifested in the texts normally described as the earliest English romances, *King Horn* (*c.*1240), *Floris and Blancheflour* (*c.*1250), and *Havelok the Dane* (*c.*1280).[6] The distinction between 'text' and 'romance' turns out to be crucial in this case because, as the first section of this chapter will show, romance form is not the set of words found in any particular manuscript or printed book, but rather the thought which seems to be projected—as if into the ether itself—by the aggregation of all such texts (as it is edited to become—or simply regarded as—a 'romance'). In the second section of the chapter I will

[5] Manfred Görlach, 'Chaucer's English: What Remains to Be Done', *Arbeiten aus Anglistik und Amerikanistik* 3 (1978), 61–79 ('started a tradition', 74). P. M. Kean, *Chaucer and the Making of English Poetry*, 2 vols. (London: Routledge & Kegan Paul, 1972) ('plain and easy verse style', 1: 9).

[6] For the conventional dates of these texts see the chronological table of the ninety-four surviving verse romances identified in *MWME* 1: 13–16. *King Horn* and *Floris and Blancheflour* survive in 'one of the oldest romance [manuscripts] we have', Cambridge, University Library MS G.4.27 (2), Guddat-Figge, *Catalogue of Manuscripts Containing Middle English Romances*, 99.

try to explain how such a transformation is less native to particular texts than to a method of regarding them, that romance form is actually the result of the kind of perceptual error routinely made within a certain species of metaphysics. In the third section of this chapter I shall suggest that this perceptual error is also responsible for creating the kind of literary thing I described in Chapter 1, that chain Chambers demanded of early Middle English but could scarcely find, 'the form of . . . English literature' that Eliot called 'tradition', the category of 'literature' we still invoke even though we are not quite sure what resides in it. While romance was only one of the many ways in which this thing was produced, I shall argue in conclusion that Middle English romance is responsible for the set of metaphysical pretensions that made English literature what it remains today. Although the older form did not in any sense *cause* the other, the relation can be put most simply by saying that the spirit of English romance became the spirit of English literature.

ROMANCE FORM

One of the more curious features of the shapes we call romance is that, however sure we are that this category exists, it turns out to be 'practically impossible to generalize about . . . because there is so little [that romances] all have in common'.[7] W. P. Ker famously complained that what romances lacked most was the quality that named them ('almost the last thing that is produced in [the] "romantic school" is the infallible and indescribable touch of romance').[8] Ker was being wilfully anachronistic in this view of course, but the

---

[7] Dieter Mehl, *The Middle English Romances of the Thirteenth and Fourteenth Centuries* (London: Routledge & Kegan Paul, 1968), p. 28. [This volume was first published as *Die mittelenglischen Romanzen des 13. und 14. Jahrhunderts* (Heidelberg: Carl Winter, 1967).] On the 'absence of generic commonplaces' in romance see Kathryn Hume, 'The Formal Nature of Middle English Romance', *Philological Quarterly* 53 (1974), 158–80 (p. 159). Ad Putter also describes the 'category of "romance"' as 'loose and fuzzy at the edges' in his 'Historical Introduction', 1–15 in *The Spirit of Medieval English Popular Romance*, ed. Ad Putter and Jane Gilbert (Harlow: Longman, 2000), 1. Although the title of this collection shares a key term with the title of this chapter, 'popular' is both the term and category pressed most firmly in its definitions and observations (see, in particular, Jane Gilbert's 'Theoretical Introduction', 16–20).

[8] W. P. Ker, *Epic and Romance: Essays on Medieval Literature*, 2nd edn. (London: Macmillan & Co., 1908; 1st edn. 1896), 325.

inappropriate pressure was possible because the term *romance* has always had astonishingly wide reference. In its earliest uses in English it referred to any text derived from some French source.[9] On the other hand, such texts were not always called by this name (they were often called *tale* or *spell*, although, for their part, these terms were not themselves limited to texts which originated in French).[10] Over time there was 'a growing acceptance of *romance* as a characterization of works with a certain kind of subject matter',[11] and this resulted in the habit of subdividing these subjects according to the 'three matters of France, of Britain, and of Rome' [trois materes . . . De France et de Bretaigne et de Ronme la grant].[12] Even such divisions needed continuous expansion, however (to the 'matter of England', for example), since another defining feature of romance was that its 'range of stories . . . was continually widening'.[13]

It has therefore long been said that, while there is a clear 'corpus of romance', it has 'no inviolate identity', and that an account of romance form or 'morphology' can never be more than a 'classification' of 'broad divisions' or 'types'.[14] According to such a division *King Horn*, *Havelok the Dane*, and *Floris and Blancheflour* are each important for having founded (or first articulated in English) one type. *King Horn* is first in the 'tradition of "lyric romance" . . . the first narrative outgrowth from song or lay';[15] *Havelok the Dane* represents 'the first growth of couplet-romance', a kind of romance generally characterized by 'vigorously professional adaptations of French poems of the *chanson de geste* type';[16] and *Floris and Blancheflour*

---

[9] Paul Strohm, 'The Origin and Meaning of Middle English *Romaunce*', *Genre* 10 (1977), 7.

[10] See Paul Strohm, 'Middle English Narrative Genres', *Genre* 13 (1980), 381–3.

[11] Strohm, 'Origin and Meaning of Middle English *Romaunce*', 7–8.

[12] Jehan Bodel, *La Chanson des Saisnes*, ed. Annette Brasseur, 2 vols., Textes Littéraires Français 369 (Geneva: Librairie Droz, 1989), lines 6–7. Bodel does not understand these three categories to be subdivisions of 'romance' (he calls his own text a 'bonne chançon' and is only explicitly considering the possible subjects for 'les vers' or 'le chant'). But, as Derek Pearsall observed in 1965, 'this classification is used in virtually all the standard textbooks and bibliographies', 'Development of Middle English Romance', 96 n. 10. For this categorization in relation to the period I am describing see e.g. R. M. Wilson, *Early Middle English Literature* (London: Methuen, 1939), 198–9. For a more recent and wide-ranging example of the categorization see Mehl, *Middle English Romances*, 268 n. 3.

[13] Ibid. 31. On the 'problem of classification' generally see this volume, 30–8.

[14] Pearsall, 'Development of Middle English Romance', 93–6. By this means, Pearsall identifies 50 such texts in his study (93–5 n. 7)

[15] Ibid. 105.   [16] Ibid. 97.

represents the earliest English 'ventur[e] into French love-romance'.[17] It is as they differ from one another, however—the extent to which each of these romances is like none of the others—that these different types are most representative of the form as such. As George Kane described medieval romance, it was most fully characterized by its 'refusal to run true to form'.[18]

If romances do share any concern, it is with an attribute that is perhaps the most difficult to give form to, those aspects of the person which are untouchable or ethereal—that which has long been called the 'spirit'. It is therefore no accident, as R. W. Southern suggested, that the Troyes of Chrétien 'is only about thirty miles from Clairvaux', the home of Bernard and Cistercian spirituality.[19] It is therefore equally predictable that a rule such as *Ancrene Wisse*, which derives from such spirituality and teaches its readers to live life in flight from the world, should turn to romance form at a climactic point.[20] The earliest manifestation of this tendency in English romance—the first significant event in *King Horn*—is when Horn's mother, Godhild, shorn of all her rank and possessions, must go to live her life as a recluse:

> Ut he wente of halle,
> Fram hire Maidenes alle,
> Under a roche of stone;
> Þer heo wonede alone:
> Þer heo seruede Gode
> Aȝenes payn forbode.

[She went out of the hall, away from all her attendants. She lived under a rock of stone, all alone, where she served God against the pagans' command.][21]

Horn's mother is forced to live this life because her kingdom has been conquered, but even if she does not choose to live 'all alone', her solitude isolates her more extraordinary qualities (in this case her

[17] Pearsall, 'Development of Middle English Romance', 102.

[18] George Kane, *Middle English Literature: A Critical Study of the Romances, the Religious Lyrics, Piers Plowman* (London: Methuen, 1951; repr. 1970), 9.

[19] R. W. Southern, *The Making of the Middle Ages* (London: Random Century, 1967), 234.

[20] See Chapter 5, above, 159.

[21] *King Horn: An Edition Based on Cambridge University Library MS Gg.4.27 (2)*, ed. Rosamund Allen (London: Garland Publishing, 1984), lines 73–82. Subsequent quotations from *King Horn* will be taken from this edition and cited by line number in my text. Translations are my own.

native piety) since those qualities are all that she is left with. In fact, isolation of this kind is the common condition of many romance heroes. In *Havelok the Dane*, for example, Havelok moves through the early parts of the narrative as a person characterized by what he lacks:

> 'I ne haue none kines þinge—
> I ne haue hws, Y ne haue cote,
> Ne I ne haue stikke, Y ne haue sprote,
> I ne haue neyþer bred ne sowel,
> Ne cloth but of an hold with couel.
> Þis cloþes þat Ich onne-haue
> Aren þe kokes and Ich his knaue!'

['I have nothing: I have no house, nor coat; I have no stick, nor twig; I have neither bread nor sauce, nor cloth, except for an old white cloak. These clothes that I have on are the cook's, and I am his knave!']²²

Although romance stories generally posit such misfortune in order to reverse it, the isolation of persons is important enough that Floris and Blancheflour are never fully relieved from it; even at the end of *Floris and Blancheflour*, while the lovers are reunited and safe, they are still in a foreign land, still about to 'return home' [wende hoom].²³

If dispossession can generally be understood as the opportunity for romance heroes and heroines to demonstrate their excellence in an almost infinite variety of arenas (ethical, martial, physical, intellectual), every one of these accomplishments is the sign of an equally immaterial exceptionality, that which can manifest itself in any or all of a person's physical conditions and activities because it is confined to none of them. This is demonstrated most clearly in early Middle English romance in the opportunity Havelok's poverty gives him to *shine*—to reveal that he is extraordinary in a variety of ways because he has the capacity to emit light. Havelok's luminescence is, in fact, a very schematic representation of the exceptionality that marks

---

²² *Havelok*, ed. G. V. Smithers (Oxford: Clarendon Press, 1987), lines 1141–7. Subsequent quotations from *Havelok the Dane* will be taken from this edition and cited by line number in my text. Translations are my own.
²³ Throughout I cite *Floris and Blancheflour* from London, British Library, MS Egerton 2862, often referred to as the 'Trentham MS', 71–110 in *King Horn, Floriz and Blauncheflur, The Assumption of Our Lady*, ed. J. Rawson Lumby, rev. George H. McKnight, EETS OS 14 (London, 1901). I quote from line 1078 here. Translations are my own.

out all romance heroes; it resides 'within' the body but it has no obvious bodily source; it is always present as part of that person (even
when, say, he is not himself aware of such a capacity), but it is often
entirely invisible. Havelok's light can also be equated with a material
determinant, and it is in this sense that Goldboru recognizes it as an
indication that Havelok is nobly born:

> On þe nith als Goldeborw lay,
> Sory and sorwful was she ay,
> For she wende she were biswike,
> Þat she were yeuen unkyndelike.
> O nith saw she þer-inne a lith,
> A swiþe fayr, a swiþe bryth—
> Als so brith, al so shir,
> So it were a blase of fir.
> She lokede norþ and ek south,
> And saw it comen ut of his mouth
> Þat lay bi hire in þe bed.
> No ferlike þou she were adred!
> Þouthe she 'Wat may þis bimene?
> He beth heyman yet, als Y wene—
> He beth heyman er he be ded!'

[In the night, as Goldboru lay down, she was sad and sorrowful as ever,
for she thought she had been deceived, in having been married to someone
less noble than she; at night she saw a light within, a very beautiful and
very bright light, shining as if it were a blaze of fire. She looked north and
south, and saw it coming out of the mouth of the person lying beside her. No
wonder she was afraid! She thought, 'What can this mean? He shall be a
nobleman yet, I think; he will be a nobleman before he is dead.']

(1248–62)

Havelok's high birth is also sometimes indicated by a more physical
sign, usually called a 'kin-mark' [kynemark (605); kunrik (2144)],
that is tattooed on Havelok's shoulder. But even this tattoo seems
to signify more than high birth since it is remarkably luminescent,
shining so brightly at times that it is said you could find a penny in the
dark by its light ('Þat men mouthe se by þe lith/A peni chesen, so was
it brith!' (2147–8)).

Havelok's luminescence necessarily marks him out even among
the poem's aristocrats, and some indication of how is given by
Dame Leve who shouts 'Jesus Christ!' (596) when she sees Havelok
shining. A similar indication is provided by the cross-like shape of the

mark on Havelok's shoulder, as well as the angelic voice that explains
the meaning of that shape to Goldboru on her wedding night:

> On hise shuldre, of gold red
> She saw a swithe noble croiz.
> Of an angel she herde a voyz:
> 'Goldeborw, lat þi sorwe be!
> For Hauelok, that haueth spuset þe,
> He is kinges sone and kinges eyr—
> Þat bikenneth þat croiz so fayr.
> It bekenneth more—þat he shal
> Denemark hauen and Englond al.
> He shal ben king strong and stark,
> Of Engelond and Denemark—
> Þat shal þu wit þin eyne sen,
> And þou shalt quen and leuedi ben.'

[On his shoulder, she saw an extraordinary cross. She heard the voice of an
angel: 'Goldboru, put your sadness aside, for Havelok, who has wed you, is
the son of a king and his heir; that is what the beautiful cross means. And it
means more: he will possess Denmark and all of England. He shall be a strong
and powerful king of England and Denmark—that you will see with your
own eyes, and you will be queen and lady.']

(1263–75)

What Havelok possesses, in short, is an exceptionality of *spirit*, and
every time his mouth fills with fire he has been marked out with a
version of those 'cloven tongues like as of fire' ('dispertitae linguae
tamquam ignis') which indicated that Christ's apostles were inhabited by the *spiritus sanctus* at Pentecost.[24] In this biblical event, as
on all such occasions in Havelok, the resident spirit is only known
by some material manifestation, and yet that materiality marks a
spiritual presence by being itself impossible to touch (a shining light
or fire). In this way the 'nothing' that Havelok possesses is filled with
neither excellent thing nor even excellent circumstance, but with

---

[24] 'And when the day of Pentecost was fully come, they were all with one accord in
one place. And suddenly there came a sound from heaven as of a rushing mighty wind,
and it filled all the house where they were sitting. And there appeared unto them cloven
tongues like as of fire, and it sat upon each of them. And they were all filled with the
Holy Ghost, and began to speak with other tongues, as the Spirit gave them utterance'
[Et cum conplerentur dies pentecostes errant, omnes pariter in eodem loco, et factus est
repente de caelo sonus tamquam advenientis spiritus vehementis, et replevit totam
domum ubi erant sedentes, et apparuerunt illis dispertitae linguae tamquam ignis
seditque supra singulos eorum, et repleti sunt omnes Spiritu Sancto, et coeperunt loqui
aliis linguis prout Spiritus Sanctus dabat eloqui illis], Acts 2: 1–4.

excellence itself—that which is immanent in Havelok and exceeds
the quality (or value) of *any* thing.

Although its signifying methods are unusually explicit, *Havelok* is
typical of every romance in so far as it is not really 'about' a person,
nor even those transferable virtues or behaviours that this person
possesses (his or her 'honour', or 'courtesy' however much it is
praised), but, rather, the *extent* to which that person exceeds the
bounds of personhood, that which is in him or her which exceeds
what any person *could* be. As a result, the relationship between the
bodies and acts that the romance describes and the idea its form is
committed to tracing is exactly the relation Marx posited between
the commodity and the ideas this haughty form is capable of 'having'.
It could be said, in other words, that the person a romance is about is
so puffed up by his or her extraordinary spirit that they are effectively
persons with surplus value, a bodily shape and all its potential actions
so enriched by a greater (and knowable) idea that its form actually
knows more than it *is*. Not incidentally, then, a much more common
method for marking such excellence in romance is not luminescence,
but some process of exchange, the measuring of a kind of excess of
spirit in the metric of a more general equivalent such as gold. In one
of the most schematic instances of this procedure, Blancheflour is
said to exceed the value of her own body by a factor of seven: she can
be 'bouȝt' (482) for 'seven times her weight in gold' [seuen sithes of
gold hur wyȝt] (484). Elsewhere her extraordinariness is marked, not
by money, but as it can be measured in objects that are themselves
held to be worth a great deal of money:

> Þer haue þey for þat maide ȝolde
> xx Mark of reed golde,
> And a Coupe good and ryche,
> In al þe world was non it lyche
>
> .   .   .   .   .   .
>
> And in þe Pomel þerone
> Stood a Charbuncle stoone.
> In þe world was not so depe soler,
> Þat it nold lyȝt þe Botlere,
> To fylle boþ ale and wyne
> Of syluer and golde boþ good and fine.

[There they have given twenty marks of red gold for that young woman, and
a good and valuable cup; there was none other like it in all the world . . . and
in the base a carbuncle-stone had been placed; there was not a cellar so deep

in all the world where it would not provide light enough for a bottler to fill both ale and wine bottles, of both silver and gold, good and fine.]

(161–4, 171–6)

As in commodity exchange Blancheflour's value is actually created by the presumption that two incommensurable things (a woman and a cup) *could* have equal worth. Since the resplendence of the cup already marks it with a kind of immaterial excess—since, like Havelok and his tattoo, it shines with a preternatural light—the nature of this excess is also spiritual. But the cup's excess of spirit is most fully marked in its rarity ('there was none other like it in all the world'), as if the value of the cup was not only surplus to itself but surplus to that of every cup that could be made. Although such value only exists in the way a given cup is commodified by a system of exchange, one of the most important results of such exchange is to insist that such value inheres in the cup, and, therefore, in Blancheflour. Although she is never described in these terms herself, the importance of such rarity to romance is indicated by one version of *King Horn* which says of Horn that 'there was no knight like him' [Þer nas no kniȝt hym ilik].[25]

As I suggested in the preface, it is historically interesting that commodification should play such an important part in a literary form that is being produced at roughly the moment Marx identified as that of 'primitive accumulation', but commodification is only one of the many procedures romances use to isolate a hero or heroine's defining spirit. In fact, the most common method is to describe the hero or heroine as if his or her *body* signified an inherent excess, to suggest, as in the first lines of *King Horn*, that a person's value was marked in his or her physique:

> Non fairer nere born,
> No rein ne birine
> Ne no sunne bischine
> Fairer þane he was.
> He was briȝt so glas
> Also whit so flur
> Rose red was his colur.

---

[25] The reading is actually in Allen's base text (Cambridge UL MS Gg.4.27 (2)), but emended according to readings in MS Laud 108 and Harley 2253. See the variants for *Horn*, ed. Allen, line 508 (p. 164). See also the parallel text edition, *King Horn: A Middle English Romance*, ed. Joseph Hall (Oxford: Clarendon Press, 1901), 'C', line 502.

[None fairer had been born, nor had rain fallen upon, nor sun shined upon, anyone who was fairer than he was. He was as bright as glass, and also as white as a flower, and his colour was rose-red.]

(10–16)²⁶

The name we now tend to give to such markings is 'beauty', a surplus to a given form that is sometimes coinable in exchange (something might be worth more than something else because it is more beautiful), but which may be defined, even within capitalism, as that which cannot be measured (the quality that makes something priceless). In fact, although such beauty is usually held to be a specific part of some physical form, it is often identified in attributes of that form which are impossible to touch (in this case Horn's brightness and whiteness), or with reference to the absence of some material ('nor had rain fallen upon . . .'). In this sense, beauty is the extent to which the physical form approximates spirit; the qualities *in which* that person or thing seems to shine.

   The most general method for marking such exceptionality in romance is the exceptionality of event that attends a given person's life, the extraordinary nature of a given 'plot' or 'story'. It is an indication of just how extraordinary the romance hero is, in other words, that, for example, Horn, exiled in the very first lines of his story, 'comes back to Suddene' [com to Suddene] (1553) as king at the end of it; or Havelok, defined from the start by his dispossession, ends up with so much that he may endow all his 'Danish men . . . with rich lands and goods' [Denshe men . . . wit riche landes and catel] (2939–40); or Floris, far from home, in a foreign land, only recently sentenced to death, 'sits at the side' [setteþ next his syde] (1055) of his sworn enemy, 'dubbed knight' [dubbed . . . knyȝt] (1057) by him at the end of his romance. This aspect of romance form is more, however, than an extremely happy ending, for, where outcomes in life are normally in a reciprocal relation with a person's identity (instilling certain qualities as often as they manifest inherent capacities), in romance events are always *cognitive*, a way for both the reader (and sometimes the hero himself) to know just how extraordinary the hero

²⁶ The other romances discussed in this chapter include similar descriptions. The first surviving lines of *Floris and Blancheflour* say, 'no one ever had occasion to look after fairer children' ('Ne thurst men neuer in lond | After feirer Children fonde' (1–2)). In *Havelok*, Goldboru is described as 'the fairest woman alive' ('þe fayrest wman on liue' (281)).

is, 'proof', as the language romances use for this process have it, of an excellence that success simply discovers.[27] *Havelok the Dane* offers one of the better examples of this relation early on, when Havelok has been expressly reduced to no more than his body (he is 'almost naked') (963), and can therefore only indicate his worth by doing something:

> Ful sone it was ful loude kid
> Of Havelok, hw he warp þe ston
> Ouer þe laddes euerilkon,
> Hw he was fayr, hw he was long,
> Hw he was with, hw he was strong.
> Þoruth England yede þe speke
> Hw he was strong and ek meke.

[It was very soon made known all over how Havelok threw the stone further than every one of the young men. Word went all over England about how handsome he was and tall, and brave as well as strong, how powerful he was and gentle.]

(1061–7)

Havelok's nobility is proved in his success, and the truth of this relation is further emphasized by the way that the malicious regent in England, Godrich, initially misses the typical point (thereby proving his own bad character). Although Godrich has promised to marry the king's daughter, Goldboru, to the 'highest man alive, the best and most beautiful' [þe hexte man þat mithe liue | Þe beste, þe fairest] (1081–2), he believes he can keep to the letter of this promise, and disparage Goldboru, by marrying her to a man who is *only* high in height and 'no more than a churl's son' [sum cherles sone and no more] (1093). What this romance knows, however—and will itself quickly 'prove'—is that the man who is highest in height is high in *every* sense; he is, above all, certainly the man destined to be king.

Of course, even though romance form pretends that such excellence is marked in a set of events that really occurred, or in a body that actually existed, the material object which actually bears the idea of that excellence is the set of words to which we point when we say 'Horn', 'Havelok', or 'Floris and Blancheflour' (and mean these texts rather than even a fictional person). And so, one of the ways that romances insist that they are finally about an immateriality rather

---

[27] For such language see e.g. *King Horn*: 'And kniȝthod haue proue' (1298).

than a person is to recognize this fact, to understand themselves to be objects. This curious perspicuity is typically lodged in a narrative frame where the voice of some 'minstrel-narrator' describes the romance of which he is a part as an object, often, as in *King Horn*, as an object of considerable value ('May all be happy who listen to my song!' [Alle beon he bliþe | Þat to my song ylyþe!, 1–2]), even, as in *Havelok*, an object worth enough to buy its teller a drink:[28]

> Þat ye mowen nou yhere,
> And þe tale ye mowen ylere.
> At þe beginning of vre tale,
> Fil me a cuppe of ful god ale.

[So that you might now hear, and so that you might learn, at the beginning of our story, fill me a cup of very good ale.]

(11–14)

Where a commodity knows that it is a commodity it also knows that it is a thing whose form bears a certain value in excess of its physical shape. Since this value in a romance is necessarily equivalent to the excellent spirit born by the bodies and acts that romance describes —since the 'song' or 'tale' that knows itself to be a commodity also knows itself to be 'horn*es* song', 'þe tale *of* horn', or 'þe tale . . . *of* Hauelok' (5)—a romance is a form also aware that it knows *more* than it is, that it is a shape capable of providing some idea in excess of its own design.[29]

In other words, even as they distinguish the material forms that they are (the shape traced by their words) from the material forms that they know (the spirit of heroes like Horn and Havelok), romance form knows that its matter posits, but never fully grasps, an ideal. Such a form also marks this capacity in so far as it contains itself, for where a variety of material versions of a given idea will do, it is

---

[28] On minstrel-narration in romance as it can be related to the surviving accounts of performance practice see Andrew Taylor, 'Fragmentation, Corruption and Minstrel Narration: The Question of Middle English Romances' in *Yearbook of English Studies* 22 (1992), 38–62. On the general relationship of minstrel performance and romance form see two articles by A. C. Baugh, 'The Middle English Romance: Some Questions of Creation, Presentation and Preservation', *Speculum* 42 (1967), 1–31 and 'Improvisation in the Middle English Romance', *Proceedings of the American Philosophical Society* 103 (1959), 418–54.

[29] For the phrase from *King Horn* (which only appears in Cambridge, University Library, MS Gg.4.27), see *Horn*, ed. Allen, textual note to 'after [line] 1560' (p. 256). See also *King Horn*, ed. Hall, 'C', lines 1525–8.

axiomatic that this idea can never be fully captured by *any* materiality. Thus, Horn often 'recounts his own life as if it were a romance',
presenting himself to others, not by means of his name or some self-
description, but in the form of a 'tale' which has the same function for
its auditors as *King Horn* (on the whole), but which actually bears no
significant narrative relationship to the larger romance:[30]

> Horn sat upon chaere
> And bad hem alle ihere:
> 'King', he sede, 'þu leste
> A tale mid þe beste.
> I ne seie hit for no blame
> Horn is mi name.
> Ibore of gode kenne,
> Þe kinges of Suddenne.
> Þu me to kniȝte houe;
> And kniȝthood haue proue.
> To þe, king, men seide
> Þat i þe bitraide;
> Þu makedest me fleme
> And þi lond to reme;
> Þu wendest þat i wroȝte
> Þat y neure ne þoȝte:
> Bi Rymenhild to forligge.
> Bi Driȝte i þat wiþsegge!'

[Horn sat on a chair and bid them all listen to him. 'King', he said, 'listen here
to one of the best stories. I do not say it in reproach of you: Horn is my name;
born of good family, that of the king of Suddene; you made me knight, and I
have proved my knighthood. King, men said to you that I betrayed you; you
made me flee and leave your land; you thought that I did what I had never
thought of, to lie by Rymenhild, and that I deny, by God.']

(1289–306)

In this case, the mere denial of certain misconceptions seems enough
to capture the excellence of spirit generally called 'Horn'. Romances
even press this point by explicitly comparing such summaries to
the whole of which they are a part. For example, at the conclusion

---

[30] Susan Crane, *Insular Romance: Politics, Faith and Culture in Anglo-Norman
and Middle English Literature* (Berkeley: University of California Press, 1986), 38–9.
For trenchant accounts of *King Horn* and *Havelok the Dane* in relation to 'the tensions
of insular feudalism' see this volume pp. 13–52 (the phrase I quote here can be found
on p. 35).

of *Havelok the Dane*, the most oblique summary of the events of Havelok's illustrious life (itself amounting to no more than a litany of the wrongs done to Havelok and Goldboru) is held to be equivalent to 'all' that has been narrated in the 'story' [gest] which precedes it:

> Nu haue ye herd þe gest all þoru
> Of Hauelok and of Goldeborw;
> Hw he weren born and hw fedde,
> And hwou he woren with wronge ledde
> In here youþe, with trecherie,
> With tresoun, and with felounye,
> And hwou þe swikes haueden tith
> Reuen hem þat was here rith,
> And hwou he weren wreken wel.

[Now you have heard the story of Havelok and Goldboru all through: how they were born and brought up, and how they were betrayed in their youth by treachery, by treason and crime; and how the villains had thought to rob them of what was rightfully theirs, and how they were avenged.]

(2985–93)

There is, however, no better example of a romance knowing that any version of the excellence of its hero and heroine will do than the conclusion of *Floris and Blancheflour*, where a summary of the events that might be taken to *dis*prove that excellence, still manages to prove it. The pertinent facts in the case are that, in rescuing Blancheflour from the Emir, Floris has committed a 'trespass' against him for which he has been sentenced to death:

> Now þey bydden al y-wys
> Þat þe Admyral graunted þis,
> To forʒeue þat trespas
> ʒif Florys told how it was.
> Now euery word he haþ him tolde,
> How þat maide was for him solde,
> And how he was of spayn a kynges sone,
> For grete loue þeder y-come,
> For to fonde, with sum gynne,
> Þat feire maide for to wynne,
> And how þe porter was his man by-come,
> For his gold and for his warysoun,
> And how he was in þe Florys borne.

[Now they all asked that the Emir should agree to forgive the wrong if Floris told how it had happened. And so he told them every word: how that young

woman was sold for him, and how he was the king of Spain's son, how he had
come there out of great love, in order to attempt to win that young woman
with some skill, and how the porter had become his man, for his gold and
reward, and how he was carried in the flowers.]

(1040–52)

It could be said that the 'great love' Floris and Blancheflour have
demonstrated is what moves the Emir and all his men in this case;
on the other hand, it was in order to prevent exactly such a result
that the Emir imprisoned Blancheflour in the first place. Although
all Floris actually does is admit the guilt of which he is accused, the
Emir has no choice but to be impressed because the events of this
narrative—however told and to whom—precisely because they never
fully capture the excellence that is 'Floris' (as well as 'Blancheflour'),
always capture that excellence, no matter what form these events
take.

Since the whole of romance form is never more than an approximation of the idea it exists to capture, it is also the case that a
romance may be changed in shape without necessarily being altered
in form: that is, since any version of a given romance will do—since
any material object we call *Horn* knows that 'Horn' is an excellence
but not *all* the particular ways that this is true—the form of a
romance is, to a surprisingly large extent, independent of the words
that comprise it. This means that the variation that is the condition
of every text produced prior to printing is *part* of romance form,
rather than a disruption to it. In fact, where it had been axiomatic
that any change to an earlier Middle English form was an altera-
tion, romance form exists *by virtue* of such change: it is, in fact, only
the persistence of a given thought through material variation which
can prove that it is always ethereal to some extent. Although this
formal fact cannot be visible in the case of *Havelok the Dane*, which
survives in only a single manuscript (Laud misc. 108), the three
surviving versions of *King Horn* (Cambridge, University Library,
MS Gg.4.27; again, Laud misc. 108, and London, British Library,
MS Harley 2253) and the four surviving versions of *Floris and
Blancheflour* (British Library, MS Egerton 2862 (The 'Trentham
MS') and MS Cotton Vitellius D.III; Edinburgh, National Library
of Scotland MS Adv. 19.2.1 (The 'Auchinleck MS'), and, again,
Gg.4.27) are sufficiently divergent from one another that it has often
seemed wisest to print each of these romances as a set of parallel

texts.[31] It has been said of *King Horn*, in fact, that 'nearly every line of
the texts preserved in the three manuscripts . . . contains divergent
readings'.[32] Thus, the line from *Horn* that I took as an epitome of
romance form generally ('Þer nas no kniʒt hym ilik') is only present in
one of these texts (Gg.4.27). This line is therefore also an epitome
of romance form in so far as *Horn* is unchanged by such exclusion:
like every other line of this romance, in fact, what this line knows best
is that 'Horn' always exceeds a text's grasp (*no* particular set of
words can capture this idea). This means of course that the distinctions we make between the manuscripts of one romance (which we
call *Havelok*) and of another (which we call *Horn*) is arbitrary, that
inasmuch as every text of a romance is only an approximation of an
ungraspable excellence, every romance text is the *same* romance.
This is not to say that the differences in plot, detail, and cognomen
that we normally use to distinguish *Horn*, *Havelok*, and *Floris and
Blancheflour* are irrelevant, but that no difference between these texts
is sufficient to completely distinguish one from the other.

It is even tempting to say that the characteristics of romance form
ensure that there is really only one romance. It is therefore also
tempting to say that the amorphousness that is so frustrating to those
who have tried to describe romance is exactly what romance form is.
Either claim would seem to neglect too much that is interesting and
worth describing about the variant texts themselves (all those particularities that each version of *Horn* have in common, for example)
even as both claims beg the question of why something so formless
should seem so generally worth characterizing. On the other hand,
to insist upon the vagueness which constitutes this form is to notice
the degree to which any material instance of romance effectively
de-materializes—that, just like the bodies it often describes, part of
what makes a romance a romance is the extent to which its matter
tends to vanish beneath the blinding glare of the idea it conveys—
as if it were not some shape designed by an idea but an idea itself.

---

[31] On these manuscripts see *Havelok*, ed. Smithers, xi–xiv; *King Horn*, ed. Allen,
2–17; and *King Horn, Floriz and Blauncheflur*, ed. Lumby, xlii–xliii. Lumby prints the
versions of both *Floris and Blancheflour* and *Horn* in parallel; Hall prints *King Horn*
in parallel. On the 'Trentham' and 'Auchinleck' manuscripts see also Guddat-Figge,
Catalogue, 121–6 and 182–4.

[32] *Horn*, ed. Allen, 33. Because Allen posits an 'original' text behind manuscripts
that are 'heavily corrupted' she must emend nearly every line of her text, often 'conjec-
turally' (on this topic see her introduction, pp. 1, 33–5 and 91–9).

The process can be seen to have begun in the oldest manuscripts of romance we have, where the texts they copy are only sometimes presented as narratives or stories, 'þe *gest* of Kyng Horn' say (as this text is called in the incipit in Harley 2253), and more often they are identified by nothing but the excellence they posit, as 'Horn' say (as *King Horn* is described in Gg.4.27) or 'Florence and Blancheflour' (as *Floris and Blancheflour* is named in Egerton 2862).[33] This effect is itself still evident in our commitment to naming romances eponymously, as if they were the essence of some non-existent person rather than a mode of representation.[34]

The most important manifestation of this process can be found in the way the textual objects that we now call romances use the term 'romance', *but never of themselves*, as if a condition for using this very term is the recognition that 'romance' never can be any material text (or set of them) but must always be somewhere *else*. Thus, the text we call *Havelok* and use to define a certain type of romance must describe itself as a 'tale' (13) or a 'spelle' (338) or a 'gest' (2985) to itself, but when it uses the term 'romance' for the first time in the English record, it refers to the kind of text that is 'read' at Havelok's crowning:[35]

> Hwan he was king, þer mouthe men se
> Þe moste ioie þat mouhte be—
> Buttinge with sharpe speres,
> Skirming with taleuaces þat men beres,
> Wrastling with laddes, putting of ston,
> Harping and piping ful god won,
> Leyk of mine, of hasard ok,
> Romanz-reding on þe bok.

---

[33] For these titles in their respective manuscripts see Guddat-Figge, *Catalogue*, 99, 183 and 197.

[34] On the modern penchant for eponomy in naming romances see the extensive list of surviving texts in *MWME* 1: 13–16. There are exceptions of course (e.g. *The Seege of Troye, The Siege of Jerusalem*), although they are rare enough to count as exceptions to a rule. Texts named after pairs of persons (e.g. *Floris and Blancheflour, Ywain and Gawain*) may simply be understood as an expansion of the basic form.

[35] *MED*, s.v. 'romaunce n.', 1e. According to the system by which the *MED* quotations are dated there are instances of 'romance' in texts which the dictionary thinks of as composed earlier than *Havelock* (*Richard Coer de Lyon*, for example). In all the instances of such 'earlier' use in this entry, however, these romances survive in copies made later than the version of *Havelok* in Laud misc. 108.

[When he was king, men might see there the greatest joy that ever could be: thrusting with sharp spears, fencing with large shields, wrestling of young men and casting of stones, a great deal of harping and piping, backgammon and dice games, romance-reading in books.]

(2321–8)

As a form embedded in a 'book' the one attribute this use of 'romance' insists upon is romance form's materiality, but it also makes clear that the material of this romance is *not* any book in which the form we call *Havelok* takes solid shape. What *Havelok* recognizes by means of this precise gesture, in other words, is that a 'romance' is most material when it remains an idea, that, just as the spirit of every romance hero finally seems more substantial than the bodies or events on which that spirit is marked, what the word 'romance' means is not some thing, but some idea *with the status of a thing.* *Havelok*'s use of the term 'romance' is therefore a crucial moment in the history of English literary form, not because that history suddenly acquires a new classification or term, but because English literature suddenly sheds the trappings of materiality and, like Havelok himself, suddenly acquires the capacity to shine. This use of the word 'romance' marks the first time English literature *knows* that it exists more vividly when it is not engrossed in the particularities of matter. It is the first time, in other words, that English literature not only exists as no more than an idea, but, in that singularity, exists as an idea more vivid than any solid thing.

THE SOUL IS THE PRISON OF THE BODY

These consequences may seem to violate the Hegelian principles which I set out in my introduction and which have formed the basis of formal descriptions throughout this book, in particular, the Hegelian tenet that Charles Taylor has called the 'principle of necessary embodiment', the belief that 'thinking always and necessarily expresses itself in a medium', that there is no thought which does not unfold in some mind or the things that mind has shaped.[36] Although Marx in highest dudgeon tended to assume that Hegel believed in pure ideality I have also assumed throughout these chapters that,

---

[36] Charles Taylor, *Hegel* (Cambridge: Cambridge University Press, 1975), 83.

as Hegel put the view in his *Philosophy of History*, 'Spirit' ('Geist') is
not really the opposite of matter but that which exists by matter's
means, never purely ethereal but 'a circle of progressive embodiments'
('ein Kreislauf von Stufen').[37] Romance form can therefore also be
defined as an attempt to confute this principle, to use matter to know
rather than to embody an idea, thereby creating a 'spirit' that somehow floats beyond materiality. But, as I would now like to suggest,
romance form can also be understood as an attempt to *maintain*
the principle of necessary embodiment against all odds, to execute a
curious logical reversal whereby the very presumption that thought
always lodges in matter somehow becomes the opportunity to claim
that immateriality can itself be a thing, the insistence that pure spirit
simply *is* matter. From this perspective, romance form is not so much
the shape a set of textual objects assumes, but a perceptual *error* those
shapes encourage; it is a curious back-formation of an over-zealous
metaphysics, but it is a formation we are always prepared to see
precisely because it is latent in our philosophy.

The strange effect I have called romance form is therefore so
likely to occur that it occurs often, as can be illustrated generally in
relation to that immateriality which is even more usually thought to
resist embodiment, what we usually call 'the soul' or *anima*. In fact,
in Middle English romance 'soul' can be the name given to the defining
excellence I have been calling spirit, as in *Havelok*, for example,
where it describes a surplus value so great that it cannot be measured
in 'silver' or 'gold':

> Ricth he louede of alle þinge—
> To wronge micht him noman bringe
> Ne for siluer ne for gold,
> So was he his soule hold.

[He loved justice above all other things—no one could make him do wrong,
neither for silver nor for gold, he was so concerned with the good of his soul.]
(71–4)

As Aelred of Rievaulx (*c*.1110–67) defined the 'soul', it was always
surplus to any material measure because it resisted embodiment as
the very condition of its existence:

---

[37] Georg W. F. Hegel, *The Philosophy of History*, trans J. Sibree (Amherst, NY:
Prometheus Books, 1991), 79; Georg Wilhelm Friedrich Hegel, *Vorlesungen über die
Philosophie der Geschichte* (Stuttgart: Philipp Reclam, 1961), 137.

The soul is not a body nor the likeness of a body: it is not earth, air, fire or water, nor is it anything that is made up from these four, or from three of them, and certainly not from two. It is not the shape or form of a body, which by its nature can be seen with the eyes, heard by the ears, felt by touch, sensed by smell or perceived by taste.[38]

It is inherent to such a definition of what is essentially a *not*-thing that it is best described in terms of all the material attributes it lacks ('not circumscribed by local boundaries, which has neither length, breadth, nor height' [nec localibus terminis circumscribi, quod et longitudine careat et latitudine et altitudine]).[39] But, like the empty space within a solid outline, it is also inherent to an immateriality so defined that its outline will seem to give it a shape, that a 'soul' with no width, breadth, or height will seem to be a *'substance'* [substantia . . . carens longitudine, latitudine, altitudine].[40] As Bartholomaeus Anglicus put it in the *De proprietatibus rerum* (*c.*1245), such a 'soul' is a 'bodiless substance' [substantia incorporea], and it therefore is, for all intents and purposes, a 'thing' [res].[41] Where the 'soul' has fallen so firmly into earthliness, the term 'spirit' has sometimes entered as a way of naming an even purer immateriality; as it is defined in the Cistercian treatise concerned with this distinction, the *De spiritu et anima*, 'spirit' is that which is more immaterial than the 'soul': 'The two powers of the one essence are distinguished by saying that one is superior and is "spirit", while the other is inferior and is "soul". In this division the soul and what is proper to animals remain below; the spirit, however, and whatever is spiritual, soar to heights.'[42] But, for

[38] Aelred of Rievaulx, *Dialogue on the Soul*, trans. C. H. Talbot, Cistercian Fathers Series 22 (Kalamazoo, Mich.: Cistercian Publications, 1981), 39. 'Non est anima corpus, non corporis similitudo, non terra, non aer, non aqua, non ignis, non aliquid quod ex his quattuor, uel his tribus, uel certe duobus compositum sit. Non est aliqua species uel forma corporea, quam in sui natura uel oculis cernere, uel audire auribus, uel tactu attrectare, uel olfactu percipere, uel gustu possumus discernere', *De anima*, 683–754 in *Aelredi Rievallensis Opera omnia I: Opera ascetica*, Corpus Christianorum, Continuatio Medievalis, vol. 1, ed. A. Hoste and C. H. Talbot (Turnholt: Brepols, 1971), 687.
[39] Aelred of Rievaulx, *Dialogue on the Soul*, 35; *De anima*, ed. Hoste and Talbot, 685.
[40] Aelred of Rievaulx, *Dialogue on the Soul*, 49; *De anima*, ed. Hoste and Talbot, 694.
[41] Bartholomaeus Anglicus, *De proprietatibus rerum* (Basel: Ruppel, *c.*1468), fo. 8ᵛ (III.3 and III.2).
[42] 'Treatise on the Spirit and the Soul', trans. Erasmo Leiva and Sr Benedicta Ward, 181–288 in *Three Treatises on Man: A Cistercian Anthropology*, ed. Bernard McGinn (Kalamazoo, Mich.: Cistercian Publications, 1977), 235. 'Cum ad

exactly the same reason that the soul is so vulnerable to materialization, the 'spirit' is too. In fact, by the time it distinguishes the 'spirit' from the 'soul' in this way, the *De spiritu et anima* has already defined the 'spirit' as if it were a thing, that which is 'not a body' but which is therefore 'analogous to the body' [nec ipse spiritus corpus est, sed corpori similis].[43]

As can be seen from these few examples, metaphysics succumbs to the principle of necessary embodiment by inadvertence, as if a kind of materialism was the inevitable result of trying to detect ideals in a world from which they are, by definition, absent. This materialism is therefore a precise mirror image of the effect we normally call ideology: rather than ideas we hold without knowing we hold them, 'soul' and 'spirit' are the kind of objects we make without knowing we have made them. This also means that such objects can be broken apart and resolved back into the thoughts they ought to be by little more than scorn; and, therefore, shadowing the steady production of such inadvertent things, there has always been an equally corrosive procedure of *un*making or critique. The most precise and influential of these critiques was *On the Genealogy of Morals* (1887), for Nietzsche defined the 'soul' as the object that human beings make when they are forbidden to make anything else; it was the 'entire inner world' constructed by a 'moral sense' strict enough to deny us the real pleasures of the material world:

All instincts that do not discharge themselves outwardly turn inward—this is what I call the internalisation of man: thus it was that man first developed what was later called his 'soul'. The entire inner world, originally as thin as if it were stretched between two membranes, expanded and extended itself, acquired depth, breadth, and height, in the same measure as outward discharge was inhibited.[44]

The 'inner world' Nietzsche describes has exactly the 'depth, breadth, and height' that the Middle Ages expressly denied to the soul for it is

---

distinctionem ponitur gemina vis eiusdem essentiae, una superior per spiritum, alia inferior per animam designatur. In hac utique divisione anima et quod animale est, in imo remanet; spiritus autem et quod spirituale est, ad summa evolat', *De spiritu et anima* in *Patrologia Latina*, ed. J.-P. Migne (Paris, 1844–64), vol. 40, cols. 779–832 (col. 804).

[43] 'Treatise on the Spirit and the Soul', 193; *De spiritu et anima*, col. 785.
[44] Friedrich Nietzsche, *On the Genealogy of Morals*, 437–599 in *Basic Writings of Nietzsche*, trans. Walter Kaufmann (New York: Random House, 1966), 520.

also Nietzsche's point that such denial was still a means of production. As Judith Butler has observed, such a critique emphasizes the
extent to which the immateriality of the 'soul' is a 'fabrication', if not
noticed or valued as a made thing then, nonetheless, an 'artistic
accomplishment'.[45] And, as Butler has shown best in our own period,
this often means that the body is no more than the by-product of such
a 'soul', a 'surface' on which the immaterial soul can seem to exist as
'signification' or 'inscription'.[46] This means that the 'soul' which is
so often said to reside 'within' the body is actually no more than a
regime of 'punishment, supervision, and constraint' which shapes the
body in the soul's name, that, as Foucault showed us, the procedures
and technologies which we understand as 'philosophical reflection'
are no more than rules that conscript action ('the soul is the prison
of the body').[47] Although the Middle Ages could not, on the whole,
effect such an unflinching reversal of basic presumptions, it is a mark
of the legerdemain required to maintain the soul's immateriality that
Foucault's insight was very precisely anticipated 800 years earlier. As
Aelred of Rievaulx put it, 'there has been no lack of very learned men
who felt that the soul was in no way contained in the body, but rather
that the soul contained the body' [Non defuerunt uiri doctissimi, qui
sentirent animam nullo modo corpore contineri, cum potius corpus
ipsa contineat].[48]

It was Marx of course whose critiques were most firmly focused
on unpacking such metaphysical conceits, but for him the larger perceptual sin was not the secreting of made things in the guise of ideals,
but the tendency to absorb the whole world of things to this charade.
Marx attributed this error to what he called 'speculative philosophy',
but what he disliked most about this philosophy was not its speculation or idealism, but what it had to say about solid objects when they
came into view. As he observed in *The Holy Family*, the speculative
philosopher will only 'relinqui[sh] . . . abstraction . . . in a speculative, mystical fashion' so that 'he rises above his abstraction only

[45] Judith Butler, *The Psychic Life of Power: Theories in Subjection* (Stanford, Calif.:
Stanford University Press, 1997), 74.
[46] Judith Butler, *Gender Trouble: Feminism and the Subversion of Identity*
(London: Routledge, Chapman & Hall, 1990), 135.
[47] Michel Foucault, *Discipline and Punish: The Birth of the Prison*, trans. Alan
Sheridan (Harmondsworth: Penguin Books, 1977), 29–30.
[48] Aelred of Rievaulx, *Dialogue on the Soul*, 35–6; *De anima*, ed. Hoste and Talbot,
685.

in appearance'.[49] In his most acid caricature of this process, Marx describes how 'real' fruit thereby appears in such thinking, not as a pear or an apple or an almond, but as a 'Unity', a 'Substance', as 'Fruit':

> The different profane fruits are different manifestations of the life of the one 'Fruit'; they are crystallizations of 'Fruit' itself. In the apple 'Fruit' gives itself an apple-like existence, in the pear a pear-like existence. We must therefore no longer say as from the standpoint of Substance: a pear is 'Fruit', an apple is 'Fruit', an almond is 'Fruit', but 'Fruit' presents itself as a pear, 'Fruit' presents itself as an apple, 'Fruit' presents itself as an almond; and the differences which distinguish apples, pears, and almonds from one another are the self-differentiations of 'Fruit' making the particular fruits subordinate members of the life-process of 'Fruit'. Thus 'Fruit' is no longer a contentless, undifferentiated unity; it is oneness as allness, a 'totalness' of fruits which constitute an 'organic ramified series'. In every member of that series 'Fruit' gives itself a more developed, more explicit existence, until it is finally the 'summary' of all fruits and at the same time living unity which contains all those fruits dissolved in itself just as much as it produces them from within itself. (136–7)

The process by which material fruit is transformed in such speculation could be likened to generalization (ideas thought to govern every material apple are used to characterize a whole category), but Marx's point is that the very simplicity of the procedure is exactly what makes it so dangerous and powerful. The very truth of the speculative philosopher's idea may so enthral him that he will no longer be able to see the pear or apple or almond he might pick up and eat. In such cases, abstraction or speculation really amount to 'creation', and rather than knowing the world he pretends to describe the speculative philosopher fills it up with projections from his fevered brain, 'representing universally known qualities of the apple, the pear, etc. which exist in reality, as definitions discovered by him' (137–8). By 'giving the names of real things to what abstract reason alone can create', such speculation knows the 'category' as a kind of 'self-existing subject incarnating itself in real situations', thereby turning no particular object topsy-turvy (as occurs in commodity formation), but, rather, the whole world, which now consists of nothing *but* ideas (138).

---

[49] Karl Marx, *The Holy Family*, 129–55 in *Selected Writings*, ed. David McLellan (Oxford: Oxford University Press, 1977), 136. Subsequent quotations from Marx in this paragraph and the next are taken from *The Holy Family* and cited by page number in the text.

Such a disproportionate attention to ideas not only makes general-izations and abstractions seem more solid than the things from which they are derived, it causes things to evanesce as if they were somehow *less* solid than ideas. Because it views the world through the softening gauze of abstraction, in other words, even when speculative philosophy discerns 'real natural fruits' it endows them with 'a preternatural significance' that 'transform[s] them into so many abstractions'; where there was 'Fruit' on the one hand and 'real profane fruits' on the other, there are now only 'semblances of apples, semblances of pears, semblances of almonds, and semblances of raisins', fruit that is only real in that 'speculative quality which gives each of them a definite place in the life-process of "Absolute Fruit"'' (137). Thus, Marx concludes, the attempt to isolate a pure ideality not only represents the 'speculative . . . as real' it represents 'the real as speculative' (138). By ridding the world of all the material to which an idea might actually refer such a mode of apprehension frees itself 'from all dis-turbing complications, [and] from all ambiguous disguises', but only at the cost of making a given idea more vivid 'to the eye in its naked beauty' than any material object could be (138).

Although Marx himself would not have been able to make the analogy, it is useful to imagine such a brightly shining idea as if it were the 'virtual object' produced by that mode of projection we now call *holography* (Fig. 8). In this process, a photographic film, usu-ally called a 'hologram', reassembles (or diffracts) light emitted from some intense source (say, a laser) in such a way that that light seems to have been reflected from some two- or three-dimensional object; this object then appears as such a solid-seeming 'image . . . in space' that, despite its unnatural luminescence, it seems to be a thing that is very materially there.[50] The intense light which passes through the hologram can therefore be likened to the speculative mind intent upon a particular idea; the photographic film can be likened to those 'universally known qualities' extracted from real objects in order to fashion that idea; and the virtual image can be likened to the ideality which consequently shines much more brightly than any real thing ('Absolute Fruit'). The analogy is particularly useful because it shows that virtual things are always a function of perspective: just as the speculative thought will seem solid only to the philosopher willing to accord ideas such importance, the virtual object will only be visible

[50] For the phrases I quote here see *OED*, s.v. 'hologram'.

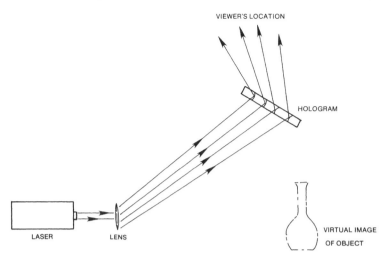

FIG. 8 Schematic of the procedure for generating a virtual object by means of a hologram.

to the viewer who places him or herself along the sight lines toward which the holograph is directed (again, see Fig. 8). The analogy is particularly strong because holography can be understood to possess just the kind of arrogance that Marx abhorred in speculation: because it believes the virtuality it projects to be essentially equivalent to the thing it really only represents, holography describes itself as that kind of 'writing' ('-graphy') which is more 'whole' or 'complete' ('holo-') than any other.[51]

Romance form, it should by now be clear, is holography by another name; the object any romance text makes is also 'complete' or 'whole' because it is 'virtual', a shining idea whose very immateriality, when seen from the right perspective, can seem to be as solid as any thing. This means, however, that the romance *text* is not equivalent to a virtual object, but to the hologram, the photographic film which contains neither a photograph nor any other simulacrum of the given shape, but rather that set of 'interference patterns' which bend a given beam of light, or reflect it, so as to create the sensory impression that an object sits where there is really empty space.[52] A given romance

---

[51] See *OED*, s.vv. 'holography', 'holo-' and '-graphy'.
[52] Joseph E. Kasper and Steven A. Feller, *Complete Book of Holograms: How They Work and How to Make Them* (New York: John Wiley, 1987), 1–4.

text is not shaped by the thought that a given reader will see *as* that romance, in other words, but, like the hologram, it contains *information about* that form sufficient to project that thought. The inevitable result is that, just as 'Fruit' substitutes itself for the apple one can touch in speculative philosophy, and just as the virtual object rather than the photographic film will come to seem like the 'hologram' (for this has become the custom in the use of this term), the idea conveyed by the romance will seem to *be* that romance and the materialities of the romance text will simply fade from view.[53] Indeed, just as the brightly shining virtual object inevitably distracts any viewer's gaze from the solid hologram that projects it, the idea emanating from any romance text will seem *more* solid than that text, an immateriality that appears to be solid because it shines so brightly, an idea that acquires all the characteristics of a thing but only because it is compounded of nothing *but* light and air.

THE GROUNDING OF A THING IN AIR

Given the place he has assumed in the history of the virtual object we now call 'literature' it is not surprising that Chaucer was aware of the intricacies of such a physics, nor that he could make this understanding particularly clear when he described his Doctor of Physic as a man 'grounded in astronomye' (I.414).[54] The richness of this observation is lost, however, if we understand 'grounded' to mean no more than 'well instructed' (as the *Riverside Chaucer* suggests); its wit is to recognize that studious attention to the touchable things of the world can result in a kind of speculation that not only transforms things into thoughts, but, as a result, tends to confine its perceptions to the world

---

[53] As the *OED* defines 'hologram' in the first instance it is 'A pattern produced when light (or other radiation) reflected, diffracted, or transmitted by an object placed in a coherent beam is allowed to interfere with an undiffracted background or reference beam related in phase to the first (or identical with it)'. It goes on to note that a 'hologram' is also 'a photographic plate or film containing such a pattern'. See *OED*, s.v. 'hologram'.

[54] Chaucer is quoted here and throughout from Geoffrey Chaucer, *The Riverside Chaucer*, ed. Larry D. Benson, 3rd edn. (Boston: Houghton Mifflin, 1987). Subsequent citations will be by line number in the text (accompanying roman numerals indicate fragment number in the case of *The Canterbury Tales*, and book in the case of *Troilus and Criseyde*).

of thinking ('Wel knew he the olde Esculapius, | And Deyscorides, and eek Rufus, | Olde Ypocras, Haly, and Galyen . . .' I.429–31). Chaucer is therefore also in a position to notice (just as Marx would later) that the Doctor not only makes thoughts into things, but he purveys the airy result as if it were an object useful in material life ('wel koude he fortunen the ascendent | of his ymages for his pacient', I.417–18). In fact, the Doctor and his labour are already deeply embedded in a system of exchange that trades in little but metaphysical subtleties ('For gold in phisik is a cordial, | Therefore he lovede gold in special', I.443–4). If we are surprised to find Chaucer so alert, so early, to the delusions and powers of capitalism, it is only because we do not tend to see Chaucer himself as someone who traffics in air. And yet, even if Chaucer's own subtleties were not yet coinable in gold—if we still must think of him as writing for preferment rather than pay—Chaucer knew what such coining would look like because the virtual objects the Doctor of Physic purveyed were exactly like what, in Chaucer's day, the literary thing had already become.

As we shall see, Chaucer had a different name for this thing once he had burnished it to perfection, but, by the end of the fourteenth century, this object was not only widely available in what I have called romance form, but that form had become so well elaborated, even sophisticated, that it lent itself to broader adaptations and transformations. The key change can be noted in *Sir Gawain and the Green Knight* (c.1380–1400), a romance which still produces the virtual object necessary for the form (a 'romance' that is not this text, but is itself a 'book'), but which is perceptive enough about such procedures to know that, in every material instance, it must be a hologram, information about an idea rather than the idea itself ('as' the romance is told in the solidity of some 'book' but is not that 'book' itself):

> Þe kyng comfortez þe kny3t, and alle the court als
> La3en loude þerat, and luflyly acorden
> Þat lordes and ladis þat longed to þe Table,
> Vche burne of þe broþerhede, a bauderyk schulde haue,
> A bende abelef hym aboute of a bry3t grene,
> And þat, for sake of þat segge, in swete to were.
> For þat watz acorded þe renoun of þe Rounde Table,
> And he hounoured þat hit hade euermore after,
> As hit is breued in þe best boke of romaunce.

[The king comforts the knight, and all the court laughs aloud about it, and the lords and ladies that belonged to the Table graciously agree that each man of the fellowship should have a baldric, wrapped cross-wise around him, in bright green, to wear as a livery, for the sake of that man. For that was thought to redound to the renown of the Round Table, and he who had it would be honoured ever after, as it is told in the very best book of romance.][55]

Such perspicacity about the nature of romance form, within that form, made it possible for English writing in this period to employ its holographic capacities incidentally, as a small component of a much larger (and differently complex) form. Thus, the psychological allegory in John Gower's *Confessio Amantis* (*c*.1390–3) is elaborated, at one point, by the claim that 'Amans' is an exemplary spirit who has been 'fed' (or formed) by the immaterialities projected from the solid objects he 'reads' ('often it happens that I am sustained by reading the romance of Ydoine and Amadas' (fulofte time it falleth so, | min ere . . . Is fedd of redinge of romance | Of Ydoine and of Amadas)).[56] The most important result of understanding the powers of romance form so clearly, however, is that other forms can become holograms, projecting rather than being shaped by their defining idea, even where that idea is not the spirit of some romance. It is as the first step in just such an elaboration that Chaucer's first original production, *The Book of the Duchess* (1369), begins with the reading of yet another 'romance' that is a solid thing or 'book', held in the narrator's hands (but therefore in no hands that exist or ever existed):

> So whan I saw I might not slepe
> Til now late this other night,
> Upon my bed I sat upright
> And bad oon reche me a book,

[55] *Sir Gawain and the Green Knight*, ed. J. R. R. Tolkien and E. V. Gordon, 2nd edn., rev. Norman Davis (Oxford: Clarendon Press, 1967), lines 2513–21. The translation here is my own.
[56] John Gower, *Confessio Amantis* in *The English Works of John Gower*, ed. G. C. Macaulay, 2 vols., EETS, ES 81–2 (1900–1), book 6, lines 876–79 (2: 191). On the form of the *Confessio Amantis* generally see James Simpson, *Sciences and the Self in Medieval Poetry: Alan of Lille's* Anticlaudianus *and John Gower's* Confessio Amantis (Cambridge: Cambridge University Press, 1995), 134–271. On the exempla in the *Confessio* which might themselves be termed romances (and the 'vital role they play in holding the work together') see Jeremy Dimmick, ' "Redinge of Romance" in Gower's *Confessio Amantis*', 125–37 in *Tradition and Transformation in Medieval Romance*, ed. Rosalind Field (Woodbridge: D. S. Brewer, 1999) (I quote from p. 128).
The romance Amans reads could be in English, but 'Ydoine and Amadas' was probably meant to evoke a French text since *Amadas et Idoine* does not survive in any English form. For the French text see *Amadas et Ydoine: roman du XIIIe siècle*, ed. John R. Reinhard (Paris: H. Champion, 1926).

A romance, and he it me tok
To rede and drive the night away.
(*The Book of the Duchess*, 44–9)

This evocation is also sophisticated enough to identify what is then read as a virtual object, or 'wonder thing' (61); even more importantly, it is a use of 'romance' which equates this form with holography as such, since the story the narrator tells at this point does not posit a certain immaterial excellence (and is not a 'romance' in any of the more traditional senses).[57] *The Book of the Duchess* therefore employs romance to observe that any writing whose solidity seems to reside in the idea or 'wonder thing' is equivalent to a romance, and it exploits that equivalence to present itself as just such a 'wonder thing', not a 'romance' but 'this book' (96), as the narrator emphatically puts it. Since this term will appear in every version of *The Book of the Duchess* that is copied or printed, such self-reference cannot designate any version of this *Book* but must, rather, refer to *all* of them. This means that, for the first time, not only does English writing know about virtual objects, but such an object actually knows itself.[58] Where it had been a defining aspect of romance form that its virtuality was a bar to such self-naming—where the 'book' a romance referred to could only be some *other* romance, where romance holography could only proceed on the condition that all knowledge of its procedures was born in those procedures alone—English can now create virtual objects that *proclaim* their immateriality. As one might expect, this is taken to be an advantage rather than a giving away of some game, an opportunity for virtual objects to present themselves not as frail or insubstantial, but wondrous.

Although *The Book of the Duchess* occupies an important place in Chaucer's career, and therefore in the history of English literature,

---

[57] Although it clearly derives from Ovid's *Metamorphoses* and resembles versions told in the *Ovide moralisé* (early 14th c.) and Machaut's *Le dit de la fonteinne amoureuse* (c.1360) Chaucer's story of 'Ceyx' and 'Alcyone' seems to have no specific source. See James Wimsatt, 'The Sources of Chaucer's "Seys and Alcyone"', *MÆ* 36 (1967), 231–41; and Strohm, 'Origin and Meaning of Middle English *Romaunce*', 14–16.

[58] Chaucer has already used the phrase 'this book' in this way in the *Romant of the Rose* (37). It is a mark of Chaucer's unusual way with this phrase that neither this nor the use I have just described in the *Book of the Duchess* appear in the relevant *MED* entry. In fact, both uses fall between the *MED*'s sense that a 'book' is either a 'material object' (1a) or a 'written composition' (2a). See *MED*, s.v. 'bok. n1'. For all of Chaucer's uses of this term see Larry D. Benson, *A Glossarial Concordance to the Riverside Chaucer*, 2 vols. (New York: Garland Press, 1993), s.v. 'bok n1'.

it is probably best understood, not as a particularly momentous adaptation of romance form, but as a particularly careful measure through use of the value romance form had acquired by 1369—an instance of just how much could be done with romance once it was clear exactly what sort of material it was—an indication of how its airy substance came to be the grounds for literary making, and, in this way, the grounds for English literature subsequently. It has long been recognized of course that Chaucer's writing was heavily indebted to romance, and, in particular, to the habits of diction sometimes traceable to the books of romance Chaucer did hold in his hands.[59] What has been less clear is that these more particular borrowings were only a symptom of Chaucer's larger debt to the kind of holography romances were capable of—that what Chaucer (like his contemporaries) learned from particular romance texts was how to *de*-materialize things, how to make the solidity of any writing a kind of hologram whose materiality could create immaterialities luminescent enough to seem even more solid than things themselves. If it has long been known that Chaucer acknowledged his debts to romance form in the diction and style he employs in *The Tale of Sir Thopas* (1392–5), in other words, it has never been recognized that this *Tale* also acknowledges the power of romance to produce spirits as if they too were material:

> Men speken of romances of prys,
> Of Horn child and of Ypotys,
>   Of Beves and sir Gy,
> Of sir Lybeaux and Pleyndamour—
> But sir Thopas, he bereth the flour
>   Of roial chivalry!

> (VII. 897–902)

---

[59] On this debt generally see D. S. Brewer, 'The Relationship of Chaucer to the English and European Traditions', 1–38 in *Chaucer and Chaucerians*, ed. D. S. Brewer, (London: Thomas Nelson & Sons, 1966); Kean, *Chaucer and the Making of English Poetry*, 1: 1–23; and John Burrow, *Ricardian Poetry* (London: Routledge & Kegan Paul, 1971), 11–28. On Chaucer's debt to the Auchinleck manuscript in particular see Laura Hibbard Loomis, 'Chaucer and the Auchinleck MS: *Thopas* and *Guy of Warwick*', 131–49 in *Adventures in the Middle Ages* (New York: Burt Franklin, 1962). (This essay first appeared in *Essays and Studies in Honor of Carleton Brown*, ed. P. W. Long (New York: New York University Press 1940), 111–28.) See also Laura Hibbard Loomis, *Sir Thopas*, 486–559 in *Sources and Analogues of Chaucer's Canterbury Tales*, ed. W. F. Bryan and Germaine Dempster (Chicago: University of Chicago Press, 1941).

Just as important here as Chaucer's mention of extant romances such as *Bevis of Hamtoun* (*c*.1300) and *Guy of Warwick* (*c*.1300) is the way that these romances are known, not as writing one might read in a 'book' (or tell as a 'tale' or 'gest'), but as the spirits, 'Beves' and 'sir Gy', which cannot be embodied in any text. In fact, *prys*, the Middle English term Chaucer here uses to name such spirits, is one of the more precise specifications such immaterial projections have ever received: when describing 'human traits' this word denoted a kind of surplus, 'high quality, excellence, high rank, nobility, [or] gentility', but, more generally, the term meant 'monetary or exchange value' (it is, in fact, the word that gives us Modern English *price*).[60] Such perspicuity in *Thopas* not only allows it to be a conventional romance, despite the burlesque of its tone—that materiality which projects the 'prys' it then names 'Thopas'—it ensures that it is a romance unusual in being elaborated *by means of* other romances, that the 'prys' of 'Beves' and 'sir Gy' (as projected by all the material versions of *Bevis of Hamtoun* and *Guy of Warwick*) will be the substance out of which the 'prys' of Thopas is made. In this sense, *The Tale of Sir Thopas* also marks the moment when the spirit of romance has finally become its own raw material, the substance of which still more romances may be made.

Even less clear than the depth of such acknowledgements has been their breadth, for what *Sir Thopas* also indicates in the few lines I have just quoted is just how *general* the importance of romance had become for shaping English literary ambition by the end of the fourteenth century. As important as all the care with which Chaucer evokes so many past romance names in *Thopas* is the way that that evocation resembles the pantheon of non-English models for literary making that Chaucer had described at the end of *Troilus and Criseyde* (1382–6):

> Go, litel bok, go, litel myn tragedye,
> Ther God thi makere yet, er that he dye,
> So sende myght to make in som comedye!
> But litel book, no makyng thow n'envie,

---

[60] See *MED*, s.v. 'pris n1'. (I quote definitions from 6b and 1a in this entry), and *OED*, s.v. 'price n.'. *Prys* is used in the Gg.4.27 version of *Horn* to describe Horn's virtues ('& þu art kniȝt of muchel pris, | & of grete strengþe | & fair o bodie lengþe' (*King Horn*, ed. Hall, 'C', lines 897–900)), and in *Havelok* to describe Goldboru's virtues ('Þe kinges douther bigan þriue | And wex þe fayrest wman on liue, | Of alle þewes was she wis | Þat gode weren and of pris' (280–3)).

> But subgit be to alle poesye;
> And kis the steppes where as thow seest pace
> Virgile, Ovide, Omer, Lucan, and Stace.

> (V.1786–92)

Here, just as the names 'Beves' or 'Gy' evoke an exemplary spirit projected by a variety of material instances, the names 'Virgile, Ovide, Omer, Lucan, and Stace' evoke the illustrious legacy of what Anne Middleton has called 'the mighty dead', spirits confined to no material particular, but each one necessarily projected by an abundance of such materials (all the copies of the *Aeneid*, say).[61] Just as such a stanza helps *Sir Thopas* project a certain *prys*, this stanza helps *Troilus* proffer itself as such an immaterial object, a 'book' in the sense that *The Book of the Duchess* is (a 'wonder thing' which exists in no particular text but in some ethereal space), a spirit as mighty as 'Virgile, Ovide, Omer, Lucan, and Stace'. Chaucer describes such spirituality with the term *poesie* in this earlier instance, and he thereby connects it to an emergent vocabulary in English for designating the results of such de-materialization (other terms include *poete, poetical, poetrie*).[62] What *Thopas* also knows when it looks back to this rich formal self-description is that holography was not a procedure discovered by English writers—that writing of a certain *prys* had long been available before English romance, not only in writers such as Virgil, Ovid, Homer, Lucan, and Statius,[63] but in more immediate medieval

---

[61] Anne Middleton, 'Chaucer's "New Men" and the Good of Literature in the *Canterbury Tales*', 15–56 in *Literature and Society*, ed. Edward Said, Selected Papers from the English Institute, NS 3 (Baltimore: Johns Hopkins University Press, 1980), 36. The phrase comes in the context of a detailed reading of this stanza in relation to Chaucer's aspirations (pp. 34–9).

[62] *Poesie* first appears in the English record in *Piers Plowman*, although this priority is only as secure as the dates provided by the *MED* for its citations (in this case, '*c.*1385' for *Troilus* and '*c.*1378' for the B-text of *Piers Plowman*). Chaucer uses the word *poetrie* for the first time in the English record in *The House of Fame*, 858, 1001, and 1478, in the last instance in relation to a similar pantheon of the mighty dead. *Poet* appears surprisingly early in the record, *c.*1325, in the *Cursor Mundi* (line 8351), although it does not appear again until *c.*1376 in the A-text of *Piers Plowman* (XI.130). *Poetical* appears first in *The House of Fame*, 1095. See *MED* s.vv. 'poesie n.', 'poete n.', 'poetical adj.', and 'poetrie n.'

[63] The stanza of *Troilus* I quote has a very close precedent in the evocation of Virgil in the *Thebaid*: 'Vive, precor; nec tu divinam Aeneida tempta, | sed longe sequere et vestigia semper adora' [O live, I pray!, nor rival the divine *Aeneid*, but follow afar and ever venerate its footsteps'], *The Thebaid* in *Statius*, ed. and trans. J. H. Mozley, 2 vols., rev. edn. (London: W. Heinemann, 1955–7), 12.816–17.

predecessors such as Jean de Meun, Dante, and Boccaccio.[64] What the *Tale of Sir Thopas* also knows about romance form, then, is that its grounding function was as tutelary as innovative—that even as it provided an English fund of such airy things, it was a form that prepared and trained English writers to exploit and extend much older instances of this procedure.

Chaucer's extraordinarily knowledgeable forms may therefore teach us how the spirit of English romance became the spirit of English literature, even as they show us the cost of such de-materialization. This last calculation is particularly difficult to make because Chaucer's own ambitions were so great: however similar to any minstrel Chaucer may have known he was in function, he wanted to be a thing no less wondrous than 'Virgile' or 'Omer', not Chaucer but 'Chaucer', a man with his own high *prys* whose name would become synonymous with surplus value in English literature. Chaucer's perspicuity in this case is also distorted by his success in such a transumption, for however carefully he exposes the procedures by which immaterial things are made, the very brightness of his own projection as well as that of all his imitators has allowed centuries of admirers of the pantheon of resulting 'poesye' to ignore both its grounds and the materialities behind such gossamer attainments. This forgetfulness is momentously apparent in that passage in Eliot's 'Tradition and the Individual Talent' which has something like the last stanza of *Troilus* as its model, and which describes the immaterialities of 'art' in ways that would make any holographer proud:

The poet . . . must be quite aware of the obvious fact that art never improves, but that the material of art is never quite the same. He must be aware that the mind of Europe—the mind of his own country—a mind which he learns in time to be much more important than his own private mind—is a mind which changes, and that this change is a development which abandons nothing *en route*, which does not superannuate either Shakespeare, or Homer, or the rock drawing of the Magdalenian draughtsmen.[65]

[64] On this form of acknowledgement in other medieval writers and its influence on Chaucer see David Wallace, 'Chaucer's Continental Inheritance: The Early Poems and *Troilus and Criseyde*', 19–37 in *The Cambridge Chaucer Companion*, ed. Piero Boitani and Jill Mann (Cambridge: Cambridge University Press, 1986), 29 and 36 n. 33, and, also by Wallace, *Chaucer and the Early Writings of Boccaccio* (Woodbridge: D. S. Brewer, 1985), 46–53.

[65] T. S. Eliot, 'Tradition and the Individual Talent', 42–53 in *The Sacred Wood* (London: Methuen, 1920), 46.

By deleting the possibility that 'art' consists of material instances—
or, rather, by insisting that the 'material of art' consists of a 'mind' as
big as 'Europe'—Eliot stares straight at the virtual object Chaucer
hoped to create and refuses to notice that it is not there. In fact, what
Eliot refuses to know, as the person who stands at an angle perfect for
viewing the airy projection, is what a writer such as Chaucer had to
know in order to produce it: the virtual object of 'art' or 'poesye' is an
illusion which can only be taken seriously at the expense of all the
things that actually exist.

Such comparisons do not make clear why a writer such as Chaucer
should aspire to such pretension when he was aware of the insub-
stantiality of what he sought—especially when he stood at a juncture
where earlier kinds of English literature provided substantial models.
Why, in short, would English writing have turned from the richness
of things to building this house of cards, particularly at the moment
when it was so acutely aware of the chimerical nature of the results?
For an answer we may look again to the parallel of capitalism, where
decreasing attention to the particularity of things and their making
seems to yield more and more (and more and more) value. What we
get when we exchange a 'geste' for the immaterialities of 'romance',
a 'tale' for the 'wondrous thing' of a 'book', an 'individual talent' or
'private mind' for 'art' or 'alle poesye', is air and light in the place of
objects, and, since it is a condition of the substitution that the original
material cannot be seen, the movement from something to nothing
seems like an increase in subtlety. To prefer literature of this kind is to
prefer shimmering apparitions to solid things, to equate immateriality with richness, to embrace the view that thoughts are likely to be
more complex and valuable to the extent that they can separate
themselves from matter, but it is not to *know* one prefers this. It is to
believe that the nothing one embraces is, in fact, all there is.

Where this view of literature is in the ascendant, writings that
refuse to participate in this system will themselves seem to be worth-
less or meaningless. This book has been written to demonstrate that
early Middle English is the most important body of writing to suffer
from such a categorical exclusion, and that such writing therefore
offers the most obvious place to put the Archimedean lever if we are
finally to shift our own settlements and begin to learn all that we have
forgotten about the possibilities of literary making. It must also be
true, however, that many written objects made after 1400 will benefit
from the understanding that careful attention to early Middle English

must foster. This is no place to try to list the kinds of things that might be reclaimed for literature in this way, but I hope the foregoing has also made clear how such things will be recognized: as every early Middle English text has survived to prove, the written form that lasts through time *because* of its eccentricity, or strangeness, or spectacular incomprehensibility almost certainly *is* literature—where, of course, we are happy to define the literary as that which deflates metaphysical pretension rather than that which fosters it.

Works Cited

Aase, Jan-Geir Johansen, ' "The Worcester Fragments": (Worcester Cathedral MS 174, ff. 63ʳ–66ᵛ): An Edition, with Diplomatic Transcription, Notes, and Glossary' (University of Sheffield, Ph.D. Thesis, 1984).

Aelred of Rievaulx, *De anima*, 683–754 in *Aelredi Rievallensis Opera Omnia I: Opera Ascetica*, Corpus Christianorum, Continuatio Medievalis, vol. 1, ed. A. Hoste and C. H. Talbot (Turnholt: Brepols, 1971).

—— *Dialogue on the Soul*, trans. C. H. Talbot, Cistercian Fathers Series 22 (Kalamazoo, Mich.: Cistercian Publications, 1981).

Allen, Hope Emily, 'The Origin of the *Ancrene Riwle*', *PMLA* 33 (1918), 474–546.

Allen, Rosamund, 'The Implied Audience of Laȝamon's *Brut*', 121–39 in *The Text and Tradition of Laȝamon's 'Brut'*, ed. Françoise Le Saux (Cambridge: D. S. Brewer, 1994).

Altfranzösisches Wörterbuch, ed. Adolf Tobler and Erhard Lommatzsch, 10 vols. (Stuttgart: Steiner, 1915–).

Althusser, Louis, 'Marx's Relation to Hegel', 161–86 in *Politics and History: Montesquieu, Rousseau, Hegel and Marx*, trans. Ben Brewster (London: NLB, 1972).

—— 'The Object of *Capital*', 71–198 in Louis Althusser and Étienne Balibar, *Reading Capital*, trans. Ben Brewster (London: Verso, 1979).

Amadas et Ydoine: roman du XIIIe siècle, ed. John R. Reinhard (Paris: H. Champion, 1926).

Anchoritic Spirituality: Ancrene Wisse and Associated Works, trans. Anne Savage and Nicholas Watson (New York: Paulist Press, 1991).

Ancrene Wisse: Guide for Anchoresses, trans. Hugh White (Harmondsworth: Penguin, 1993).

Ancrene Wisse: Parts Six and Seven, ed. Geoffrey Shepherd (Exeter: Short Run Press, 1985; 1st published 1959).

Andreas Capellanus on Love, ed. and trans. P. G. Walsh (London: Duckworth, 1982).

The Anglo-Saxon Chronicle, trans. G. N. Garmonsway, 2nd edn. (London: J. M. Dent, 1972; 1st published 1953).

An Anglo-Saxon Dictionary, ed. Joseph Bosworth and T. Northcote Toller (Oxford: Oxford University Press, 1972; 1st published 1878).

Aquinas, Thomas, *On Being and Essence*, trans. Armand Maurer, 2nd rev. edn. (Toronto: Pontifical Institute of Mediaeval Studies, 1968).

—— *Sermo seu tractatus de ente et essentia*, ed. Ludwig Baur, Opuscula et Textus, Series Scholastica, I (Münster: Aschendorff, 1933).

—— *Summa theologiae*, vol. 11, ed. and trans. Timothy Suttor (London: Eyre & Spottiswoode, 1970).

Arendt, Hannah, 'The Concept of History', 41–90 in *Between Past and Future: Eight Exercises in Political Thought* (New York: Viking, 1961).

—— 'Tradition and the Modern Age', 17–40 in *Between Past and Future*.

Aristoteles Latinus, VII.1: Physica, ed. Fernand Bossier and Jozef Brams (Leiden: Brill, 1990).

Aristotle, *The Complete Works of Aristotle*, ed. Jonathan Barnes, 2 vols., rev. edn. (Princeton: Princeton University Press, 1984).

—— *Nichomachean Ethics*, 2: 1729–1867 in *Complete Works*, ed. Barnes.

—— 'On the Soul', 1: 641–92 in *Complete Works*, ed. Barnes.

—— *Physics*, 1: 315–446 in *Complete Works*, ed. Barnes.

—— *Poetics*, 2: 2316–40 in *Complete Works*, ed. Barnes.

—— *Problems*, 2: 1319–527 in *Complete Works*, ed. Barnes.

Aristotle's De anima in the Version of William of Moerbeke, trans. Kenelm Foster and Silvester Humphries (London: Routledge, 1951).

The Art of Art History: A Critical Anthology, ed. Donald Preziosi (Oxford: Oxford University Press, 1998).

Augustine, *Confessions*, trans. Henry Chadwick (Oxford: Oxford University Press, 1991).

—— *Confessions*, trans. William Watts, 2 vols. (Cambridge, Mass.: Harvard University Press, 1995; 1st published 1912).

—— *De dialectica*, ed. Jan Pinborg, trans B. Darrell Jackson (Dördrecht, Holland: D. Reidel, 1975).

—— *De doctrina Christiana*, ed. and trans. R. P. H. Green (Oxford: Clarendon Press, 1995).

—— 'De magistro', ed. K.-D. Daur, 155–203 in *Contra academicos; De beata vita; De ordine; De magistro; De libero arbitrio*, Corpus Christianorum, Series Latina 29 (Turnholt: Brepols, 1970).

—— 'The Teacher', 113–186 in *The Greatness of the Soul; The Teacher*, trans. Joseph M. Colleran (London: Longmans, Green, 1950).

Averrois Cordubensis commentarium magnum in Aristotelis de anima libros, ed. F. Stuart Crawford (Cambridge, Mass.: The Medieval Academy of America, 1953).

Baldick, Chris, *The Social Mission of English Criticism, 1848–1932* (Oxford: Clarendon Press, 1983).

Barker, Francis, *The Tremulous Private Body: Essays on Subjection*, 2nd edn. (Ann Arbor: University of Michigan Press, 1995).

Barratt, Alexandra, 'Flying in the Face of Tradition: A New View of the *Owl and the Nightingale*', *University of Toronto Quarterly* 56 (1987), 471–85.

Bartholomaeus Anglicus, *De proprietatibus rerum* (Basel: Ruppel, *c.*1468).
—— *On the Properties of Things*, 2 vols., ed. M. C. Seymour (Oxford: Clarendon Press, 1975).
'The Battle of Lewes', 72–121 in *The Political Songs of England*, ed. Thomas Wright, Camden Society Publications 6 (London, 1839).
Baugh, A. C., 'Improvisation in the Middle English Romance', *Proceedings of the American Philosophical Society* 103 (1959), 418–54.
—— 'The Middle English Romance: Some Questions of Creation, Presentation and Preservation', *Speculum* 42 (1967), 1–31.
Baxandall, Michael, *Patterns of Intention: On the Historical Explanation of Pictures* (New Haven: Yale University Press, 1985).
Beckwith, Sarah, 'Passionate Regulation: Enclosure, Ascesis, and the Feminist Imaginary', *South Atlantic Quarterly* 93 (1994), 803–24.
Bede, *Ecclesiastical History of the English People*, ed. and trans. Bertram Colgrave and R. A. B. Mynors (Oxford: Clarendon Press, 1969).
Beer, Gillian, *The Romance* (London: Methuen, 1970).
Bennett, J. A. W., *Middle English Literature* (Oxford: Clarendon Press, 1986).
Benson, Larry D., *A Glossarial Concordance to the Riverside Chaucer*, 2 vols. (New York: Garland Press, 1993).
Bernard, *Tractatus de moribus et officio episcoporum*, cols. 809–54, *Patrologia Latina*, 182, ed. Migne.
Bertrand, Simone, 'A Study of the Bayeux Tapestry', 31–8 in *The Study of the Bayeux Tapestry*, ed. Gameson (originally published as 'Étude sur la Tapisserie de Bayeux', *Annales de Normandie* 10 (1960), 197–206).
Bloch, R. Howard, *Etymologies and Genealogies: A Literary Anthropology of the French Middle Ages* (Chicago: University of Chicago Press, 1983).
—— *Medieval Misogyny and the Invention of Western Romantic Love* (Chicago: University of Chicago Press, 1991).
Bodel, Jehan, *La Chanson des Saisnes*, ed. Annette Brasseur, 2 vols., Textes Littéraires Français 369 (Geneva: Librairie Droz, 1989).
Boethius, *Philosophiae consolationis liber quinque*, ed. Karl Büchner (Heidelberg: Carl Winter, 1977).
—— *The Consolation of Philosophy*, trans. V. E. Watts (Harmondsworth: Penguin, 1969).
Bourdieu, Pierre, *The Logic of Practice*, trans. Richard Nice (Cambridge: Polity Press, 1990).
Bracton: De legibus et consuetudinibus Angliae, ed. George E. Woodbine, trans. with revisions and notes, Samuel E. Thorne, 4 vols. (Cambridge, Mass.: Harvard University Press, 1968–77).
Brehe, S. K., 'Reassembling the *First Worcester Fragment*', *Speculum* 65 (1990), 521–36.
Brewer, D. S., 'The Relationship of Chaucer to the English and European Traditions', 1–38 in *Chaucer and Chaucerians*, ed. D. S. Brewer (London: Thomas Nelson & Sons, 1966).

Brilliant, Richard, 'The Bayeux Tapestry: A Stripped Narrative for their Eyes and Ears', 111–37 in *Study of the Bayeux Tapestry*, ed. Gameson.

Brown, Catherine, *Contrary Things: Exegesis, Dialectic, and the Poetics of Didacticism* (Stanford, Calif.: Stanford University Press, 1998).

Burchfield, R. W., 'The Language and Orthography of the *Ormulum* MS', *Transactions of the Philological Society* (1956), 56–87.

Burke, Kenneth, *The Philosophy of Literary Form: Studies in Symbolic Action* (Baton Rouge, La.: Louisiana State University Press, 1941).

—— *The Rhetoric of Religion: Studies in Logology* (Berkeley: University of California Press, 1970).

Burrow, John, *Medieval Writers and Their Work: Middle English Literature and its Background, 1100–1500* (Oxford: Oxford University Press, 1982).

—— *Ricardian Poetry* (London: Routledge & Kegan Paul, 1971).

Butler, Judith, *Bodies that Matter: On the Discursive Limits of Sex* (London: Routledge, 1993).

—— *Gender Trouble: Feminism and the Subversion of Identity* (London: Routledge, Chapman & Hall, 1990).

—— *The Psychic Life of Power: Theories in Subjection* (Stanford, Calif.: Stanford University Press, 1997).

The Cambridge History of English Literature, ed. A. W. Ward and A. R. Waller, vol. 1 (Cambridge: Cambridge University Press, 1908).

The Cambridge History of Later Medieval Philosophy, ed. Norman Kretzmann, Anthony Kenny, and Jan Pinborg (Cambridge: Cambridge University Press, 1982).

Cartlidge, Neil, 'The Composition and Social Context of Oxford, Jesus College, MS 29 (II) and London, British Library, MS Cotton Caligula A.IX', *MÆ* 66 (1997), 250–69.

—— 'The Date of *The Owl and the Nightingale*', *MÆ* 65 (1996), 230–47.

Casey, Edward S., *The Fate of Place: A Philosophical History* (Berkeley: University of California Press, 1997).

Chambers, R. W., 'The Lost Literature of Medieval England', *The Library*, 4th ser., 5 (1925), 293–321.

—— *On the Continuity of English Prose from Alfred to More and his School*, EETS OS 191a (London: Oxford University Press, 1932).

Chaucer, Geoffrey, *The Riverside Chaucer*, ed. Larry D. Benson, 3rd edn. (Boston: Houghton Mifflin, 1987).

Chibnall, Marjorie, 'Pliny's *Natural History* and the Middle Ages', 57–78 in *Empire and Aftermath: Silver Latin II*, ed. T. A. Dorey (London: Routledge & Kegan Paul, 1975).

Cicero, *Ad Herennium*, ed. and trans. Harry Caplan, Loeb Classical Library (Cambridge, Mass.: Harvard University Press, 1976; 1st printed 1942).

—— *Topica*, 377–459 in *De inventione, De optimo genere oratorum, Topica*, ed. and trans. H. M. Hubbell (London: William Heinemann, 1968).

Coke, Edward, *Reports*, ed. John Henry Thomas and John Farquhar Fraser, 6 vols. (London: J. Butterworth & Son, 1826).

Coleman, Janet, 'The Owl and the Nightingale and Papal Theories of Marriage', *Journal of Ecclesiastical History* 38 (1987), 517–68.

Colish, Marcia L., *The Mirror of Language: A Study in the Medieval Theory of Knowledge*. rev. edn. (Lincoln: University of Nebraska Press, 1983).

Collingwood, R. G., *The Idea of History* (Oxford: Clarendon Press, 1946).

—— *The Principles of History and Other Writings in the Philosophy of History*, ed. W. H. Dray and W. J. van der Dussen (Oxford: Clarendon Press, 1999).

A Concordance to Ancrene Wisse, MS Corpus Christi College Cambridge 402, ed. Jennifer Potts, Lorna Stevenson, and Jocelyn Wogan-Browne (Cambridge: D. S. Brewer, 1993).

Cornelius, Roberta D., *The Figurative Castle: A Study in the Mediaeval Allegory of the Edifice with Especial Reference to Religious Writings* (Bryn Mawr: [no publisher], 1930).

Crane, Susan, *Insular Romance: Politics, Faith and Culture in Anglo-Norman and Middle English Literature* (Berkeley: University of California Press, 1986).

Croce, Benedetto, *Theory and History of Historiography*, trans. Douglas Ainslie (London: George G. Harrap, 1921).

Curtius, Ernst Robert, *European Literature and the Latin Middle Ages*, trans. Willard R. Trask, Bollingen Series 36 (Princeton: Princeton University Press, 1953).

Dahood, Roger, 'Ancrene Wisse, the Katherine Group and the Wohunge Group', 1–33 in *Middle English Prose: A Critical Guide to Major Authors and Genres* (New Brunswick, NJ: Rutgers University Press, 1984).

Dance, Richard, 'The AB Language: the Recluse, the Gossip and the Language Historian', 57–82 in *A Companion to Ancrene Wisse*, ed. Yoko Wada (Cambridge: D. S. Brewer, 2003).

Davies, Brian, *The Thought of Thomas Aquinas* (Oxford: Clarendon Press, 1992).

Davies, R. R., *Conquest, Coexistence and Change, Wales, 1063–1415* (Oxford: Clarendon Press, 1987).

—— *Lordship and Society in the March of Wales, 1282–1400* (Oxford: Clarendon Press, 1978).

Davis, Colin, *Levinas: An Introduction* (Cambridge: Polity Press, 1996).

De coniuge non ducenda: Gawain on Marriage: The Textual Tradition of the De coniuge non ducenda with Critical Edition and Translation, by A. G. Rigg (Toronto: Pontifical Institute of Mediaeval Studies, 1986).

de Spinoza, Benedict, *Ethics*, ed. and trans. Edwin Curley (Harmondsworth: Penguin, 1996).

De spiritu et anima, 40, cols. 779–832 in *Patrologia Latina*, ed. Migne.

Derrida, Jacques, *Of Grammatology*, trans. Gayatri Chakravorty Spivak (Baltimore: Johns Hopkins University Press, 1976).

—— 'Restitutions of the Truth in Pointing [*pointure*]', 432–49 in *The Art of Art History*, ed. Preziosi.

—— *The Truth in Painting*, trans. G. Bennington and I. McLeod (Chicago: University of Chicago Press, 1987; 1st published 1978).

Dimmick, Jeremy, ' "Redinge of Romance" in Gower's *Confessio Amantis*', 125–37 in *Tradition and Transformation in Medieval Romance*, ed. Rosalind Field (Woodbridge: D. S. Brewer, 1999).

Dobson, E. J., *English Prononuciation: 1500–1700*, 2 vols., 2nd edn. (Oxford: Clarendon Press, 1968; 1st edn. 1957).

—— *The Origins of Ancrene Wisse* (Oxford: Clarendon Press, 1976).

Dod, Bernard G., 'Aristoteles latinus', 45–79 in *The Cambridge History of Later Medieval Philosophy*, ed. Kretzmann, Kenny, and Pinborg.

Domesday Book, ed. John Morris, vol. 31, part 1 (Lincolnshire), ed. Philip Morgan and Caroline Thorn (Chichester: Phillimore, 1986).

Donoghue, Daniel, 'Laȝamon's Ambivalence', *Speculum* 65 (1990), 537–63.

Douglas, David, *The Norman Conquest and British Historians* (Glasgow: Jackson, Son, 1946).

Duns Scotus, John, *De rerum principio*, 4: 267–717 in *Opera omnia*, 26 vols., ed. Luke Wadding (Farnborough: Gregg International, 1969; 1st published Paris: Vivés, 1891–5).

—— *God and Creatures: The Quodlibetal Questions*, trans. Felix Alluntis and Allan B. Wolter (Princeton: Princeton University Press, 1975).

—— *Questiones quodlibetales*, 25: 1–586 in *Opera omnia*, ed. Wadding.

Early Middle English Verse and Prose, ed. J. A. W. Bennett and G. V. Smithers, with a glossary by Norman Davis, 2nd edn. (Oxford: Oxford University Press, 1968).

The Early South-English Legendary, ed. Carl Horstmann, EETS os 87 (London, 1887).

Edson, Evelyn, *Mapping Time and Space: How Medieval Mapmakers Viewed Their World* (London: The British Library, 1997).

Eliot, T. S., 'Tradition and the Individual Talent', 42–53 in *The Sacred Wood* (London: Methuen, 1920).

English Historical Documents, vol. 2, ed. David C. Douglas and George W. Greenaway, gen. ed. David C. Douglas, 2nd edn. (London: Eyre Methuen, 1981; 1st edn. 1953).

English Historical Documents, vol. 3, ed. Henry Rothwell, gen. ed. David C. Douglas (London: Eyre & Spottiswoode, 1975).

The English Text of the Ancrene Riwle (edited from B. M. Cotton MS Cleopatra C.vi), ed. E. J. Dobson, EETS os 267 (1972).

The English Text of the Ancrene Riwle (edited from B. M. Cotton MS Nero A.xiv), ed. Mabel Day, EETS os 225 (1952).

The English Text of the Ancrene Riwle: Ancrene Wisse (edited from MS Corpus Christi College, Cambridge 402), ed. J. R. R. Tolkien, EETS OS 249 (London, 1962).

Essays and Studies in Honor of Carleton Brown, ed. P. W. Long (New York: New York University Press, 1940).

Fleming, Robin, *Kings and Lords in Conquest England* (Cambridge: Cambridge University Press, 1991).

Floris and Blancheflour, 71–110 in *King Horn, Floris and Blauncheflur, The Assumption of Our Lady*, ed. J. Rawson Lumby, rev. George H. McKnight, EETS OS 14 (London, 1901).

Fortescue, John, *De Laudibus Legum Angliae*, ed. and trans. S. B. Chrimes (Cambridge: Cambridge University Press, 1942).

Foucault, Michel, *Discipline and Punish: The Birth of the Prison*, trans. Alan Sheridan (Harmondsworth: Penguin Books, 1977).

Franzen, Christine, *The Tremulous Hand of Worcester: A Study of Old English in the Thirteenth Century* (Oxford: Clarendon Press, 1991).

Freeman, E. A., *The History of the Norman Conquest: Its Causes and Results*, 6 vols. (Oxford: Clarendon Press, 1867–77; 2nd edn. of vols. 1–3, 1870–5).

—— 'The Authority of the Bayeux Tapestry', 7–18 in *The Study of the Bayeux Tapestry*, ed. Gameson.

Fremantle, W. H., *The Principal Works of St Jerome*, Select Library of Nicene and Post-Nicene Fathers, vi (Oxford: James Parker, 1893).

Fulk, Robert D., 'Consonant Doubling and Open Syllable Lengthening in the *Ormulum*', *Anglia* 114 (1996), 481–513.

Galbraith, V. H., *Domesday Book: Its Place in Administrative History* (Oxford: Clarendon Press, 1974).

Gameson, Richard, 'Origin, Art, and Message of the Bayeux Tapestry', in *The Study of the Bayeux Tapestry*, ed. Gameson.

Genette, Gerard, *Mimologics*, trans. Thaïs E. Morgan (Lincoln: University of Nebraska Press, 1995).

Geoffrey of Monmouth, *The Historia regum Britannie of Geoffrey of Monmouth*, I (Bern, Burgerbibliothek, MS 568), ed. Neil Wright (Cambridge: D. S. Brewer, 1984).

—— *The History of the Kings of Britain*, trans. Lewis Thorpe (Harmondsworth: Penguin, 1966).

Georgianna, Linda, 'Coming to Terms with the Norman Conquest: Nationalism and English Literary History', *REAL: Yearbook of Research in English and American Literature* 14 (1998), 33–53.

—— *The Solitary Self: Individuality in the Ancrene Wisse* (Cambridge, Mass.: Harvard University Press, 1981).

Die Gesetze der Angelsachsen, ed. Felix Liebermann, 3 vols. (Halle: Niemeyer, 1903–16).

The Gesta Guillelmi of William of Poitiers, ed. and trans. R. H. C. Davis and Marjorie Chibnall (Oxford: Clarendon Press, 1998).

Gilchrist, Roberta, *Contemplation and Action: The Other Monasticism* (London: Leicester University Press, 1995).

Gildas, *The Ruin of Britain and Other Works*, ed. and trans. Michael Winterbottom (London: Phillimore, 1978).

Gillespy, Frances, *Laȝamon's Brut: A Comparative Study in Narrative Art*, University of California Publications in Modern Philology 3 (Berkeley, 1916).

Goldberg, Jonathan, *Writing Matter: From the Hands of the English Renaissance* (Stanford, Calif.: Stanford University Press, 1990).

Görlach, Manfred, 'Chaucer's English: What Remains to Be Done', *Arbeiten aus Anglistik und Amerikanistik* 3 (1978), 61–79.

—— *The Textual Tradition of the South English Legendary*, Leeds Studies in English Texts and Monographs, NS 6 (University of Leeds: School of English, 1974).

Gower, John, *Confessio Amantis*, 1:1–2:480 in *The English Works of John Gower*, ed. G. C. Macaulay, 2 vols., EETS ES 81–2 (1900–1).

Grammatici Latini, ed. Heinrich Keil, 7 vols. (Leipzig: B. G. Teubner, 1857–80).

Gransden, Antonia, *Historical Writing in England c.550 to c.1307* (London: Routledge & Kegan Paul, 1974).

Grape, Wolfgang, *The Bayeux Tapestry* (Munich: Prestel, 1994).

Greenblatt, Stephen, 'What is the History of Literature?', *Critical Inquiry* 23 (1997), 460–81.

Greg, W. W., 'What is Bibliography?', *Transactions of the Bibliographical Society* 12 (1914), 39–53.

Guddat-Figge, Gisela, *Catalogue of Manuscripts Containing Middle English Romances*, Texte und Untersuchungen zur Englischen Philologie, vol. 4 (Munich: Wilhelm Fink, 1976).

Guillory, John, *Cultural Capital: The Problem of Literary Canon Formation* (Chicago: University of Chicago Press, 1993).

Hahn, Thomas, 'Early Middle English', 61–91 in *The Cambridge History of Medieval English Literature*, ed. David Wallace (Cambridge: Cambridge University Press, 1999).

Hargreaves, A. D., *An Introduction to the Principles of Land Law*, 4th edn. (London: Sweet & Maxwell, 1963).

Harris, C. R. S., *Duns Scotus*, 2 vols. (Oxford: Clarendon Press, 1927).

Harvey, P. D. A., 'Local and Regional Cartography in Medieval Europe', 464–501 in *History of Cartography*, ed. Harley and Woodward, vol. 1.

Havelok the Dane, ed. Kenneth Sisam, 2nd edn. (Oxford: Clarendon Press, 1915).

Havelok, ed. G. V. Smithers (Oxford: Clarendon Press, 1987).

Hegel, Georg Wilhelm Friedrich, *Philosophy of Right*, trans. T. M. Knox (Oxford: Clarendon Press, 1952).

—— *Phänomenologie des Geistes*, ed. Wolfgang Bonsiepen and Reinhard Heede, vol. 9 in *Gesammelte Werke* (Hamburg: Felix Meiner, 1980).

—— *Phenomenology of Spirit*, trans. A. V. Miller (Oxford: Oxford University Press, 1977).

—— *The Philosophy of History*, trans J. Sibree (Amherst, NY: Prometheus Books, 1991).

—— *Vorlesungen über die Philosophie der Geschichte* (Stuttgart: Philipp Reclam, 1961).

Heidegger, Martin 'The Origin of the Work of Art', 139–212 in *Basic Writings*, ed. David Farrell Krell, rev. edn. (London: Routledge, 1993; 1st published 1978).

Helgerson, Richard, *Forms of Nationhood: The Elizabethan Writing of England* (Chicago: University of Chicago Press, 1992).

Henry, Archdeacon of Huntingdon, *Historia Anglorum* [*The History of the English People*], ed. and trans. Diana Greenway (Oxford: Clarendon Press, 1996).

Hieatt, Constance, 'The Subject of the Mock-Debate Between the Owl and the Nightingale', *Studia Neophilologica* 40 (1968), 155–60.

Hill, Betty, 'The History of Jesus College, Oxford MS 29', *MÆ* 32 (1955), 203–13.

Hill, Christopher, 'The Norman Yoke', 46–111 in *Puritanism and Revolution: Studies in Interpretation of the English Revolution of the Seventeenth Century* (London: Martin Secker & Warburg, 1958).

Hilton, R. H., *A Medieval Society: The West Midlands at the End of the Thirteenth Century* (New York: Wiley, 1966).

Hinckley, Henry Barret, 'Science and Folk-Lore in *The Owl and the Nightingale*', *PMLA* 47 (1932), 303–14.

The History of Cartography, ed. J. B. Harley and David Woodward, vol. 1 (Chicago: University of Chicago Press, 1987).

A History of Herefordshire, 4 vols. in *The Victoria History of the Counties of England*, ed. William Page (London: Eyre & Spottiswoode, 1908; repr. 1975).

Hogg, A. H. A., and King, D. J. C., 'Early Castles in Wales and the Marches', *Archaeologia Cambrensis* 112 (1963), 77–124.

Holdsworth, W. S., *A History of English Law*, 17 vols. (London: Methuen, 1922–72).

Holm, Sigurd, *Corrections and Additions in the Ormulum Manuscript* (Uppsala: Almqvist & Wiksells, 1922).

Holsinger, Bruce W., *Music, Body, and Desire in Medieval Culture: Hildegard of Bingen to Chaucer* (Stanford, Calif.: Stanford University Press, 2001).

—— 'Vernacular Legality: The English Jurisdictions of *The Owl and the Nightingale*', 154–184 in *The Letter of the Law: Legal Practice and Literary Production in Medieval England*, ed. Emily Steiner and Candace Barrington (Ithaca, NY: Cornell University Press, 2002).

Holt, J. C., '1086', 41–64 in *Domesday Studies*, ed. J. C. Holt (Woodbridge: Boydell & Brewer, 1987).

—— 'The Origins of the Constitutional Tradition in England', 1–22 in his *Magna Carta and Medieval Government* (London: Hambledon Press, 1985).

Hudson, John, 'Anglo-Norman Land Law and the Origins of Property', 198–222 in *Law and Government in Medieval England and Normandy*, ed. Garnett and Hudson.

—— *Land, Law, and Lordship in Anglo-Norman England* (Oxford: Clarendon Press, 1994).

Hume, Kathryn, 'The Formal Nature of Middle English Romance', *Philological Quarterly* 53 (1974), 158–80.

—— *The Owl and the Nightingale: the Poem and its Critics* (Toronto: University of Toronto Press, 1975).

Inquisitio Comitatus Cantabridgiensis, ed. N. E. S. A. Hamilton (London: Royal Society of Literature Publications, 1876).

Isidore of Seville, *Etymologiarum sive originum libri XX*, 2 vols., ed. W. M. Lindsay (Oxford: Clarendon Press, 1911).

—— *Etymologies: Book II, Rhetoric*, ed. and trans. Peter K. Marshall (Paris: Les Belles Lettres, 1983).

—— *Étymologies: Livre XII (Des animaux)*, ed. and trans. Jacques André (Paris: Les Belles Lettres, 1986).

Jameson, Fredric, *Marxism and Form: Twentieth-Century Dialectical Theories of Literature* (Princeton: Princeton University Press, 1971).

John of Salisbury, *Metalogicon*, ed. Clemens C. I. Webb (Oxford: Clarendon Press, 1929).

Johnson, Barbara, *The Critical Difference: Essays in the Contemporary Rhetoric of Reading* (Baltimore: Johns Hopkins University Press, 1980).

Jolivet, Jean, 'Quelques cas de "platonisme grammatical" du viiᵉ au xiiᵉ siècle', 93–9 in *Mélanges offerts à René Crozet*, vol. 1 (of 2) ed. Pierre Gallais and Yves-Jean Riou (Poitiers: Société d'Études Médiévales, 1966).

Juvenal and Persius, ed. G. G. Ramsay (London: Harvard University Press, 1918; repr., 1990).

Kane, George, *Middle English Literature: A Critical Study of the Romances, the Religious Lyrics, Piers Plowman* (London: Methuen, 1951; repr. 1970).

Kasper, Joseph E., and Feller, Steven A., *The Complete Book of Holograms: How They Work and How to Make Them* (New York: John Wiley, 1987).

The Katherine-Group edited from MS Bodley 34, ed. S. T. R. O. d'Ardenne, Bibliothèque de la Faculté de Philosophie et Lettres de l'Université de Liège, Fascicule 215 (Paris: Les Belles Lettres, 1977).

Kean, P. M., *Chaucer and the Making of English Poetry*, 2 vols. (London: Routledge & Kegan Paul, 1972).

Ker, N. R., *Catalogue of Manuscripts Containing Anglo-Saxon* (Oxford: Clarendon Press, 1990; 1st published, 1957).

—— 'Unpublished Parts of the *Ormulum* printed from MS. Lambeth 783', *MÆ* 9 (1940), 1–22.

Ker, W. P., *Epic and Romance: Essays on Medieval Literature*, 2nd edn. (London: Macmillan & Co., 1908; 1st edn. 1896).

King Horn: A Middle English Romance, ed. Joseph Hall (Oxford: Clarendon Press, 1901).

King Horn: An Edition Based on Cambridge University Library MS Gg.4.27 (2), ed. Rosamund Allen (London: Garland Publishing, 1984).

Knight, Stephen, 'The Social Function of the Middle English Romances', 99–122 in *Medieval Literature: Criticism, Ideology and History*, ed. David Aers (Brighton: Harvester, 1986).

Knowles, David, *The Monastic Order in England* (Cambridge: Cambridge University Press, 1949; 1st published 1940).

Laȝamon, *Brut, or Hystoria Brutonum*, ed. and trans. W. R. J. Barron and S. C. Weinberg (Harlow: Longman, 1995).

Lapidge, Michael, *The Cult of St Swithun*, Winchester Studies 4.ii (Oxford: Clarendon Press, 2003).

Law and Government in Medieval England and Normandy: Essays in Honour of Sir James Holt, ed. George Garnett and John Hudson (Cambridge: Cambridge University Press, 1994).

Law, Vivien, *Grammar and Grammarians in the Early Middle Ages* (London: Longman, 1997).

The Laws of the Kings of England from Edmund to Henry I, ed. and trans. A. J. Robertson (Cambridge: Cambridge University Press, 1925).

Le Saux, Françoise H. M., *Laȝamon's Brut: The Poem and its Sources* (Woodbridge: D. S. Brewer, 1989).

Leavis, F. R., 'Literature and Society', *Scrutiny* 12 (1943), 2–11.

Leges Henrici Primi, ed. and trans. L. J. Downer (Oxford: Clarendon Press, 1972).

Legouis, Émile and Cazamian, Louis, *A History of English Literature*, trans. Helen Douglas Irvine, 2 vols. (London: J. M. Dent, 1926).

Lerer, Seth, 'Old English and its Afterlife', 7–34 in *The Cambridge History of Medieval English Literature*, ed. David Wallace (Cambridge: Cambridge University Press, 1999).

Levinas, Emmanuel, *Totalité et Infini: Essai sur l'extériorité* ([Paris]: Martinus Nijhoff, 1971).

—— *Totality and Infinity: An Essay on Exteriority*, trans. Alphonso Lingis (Pittsburgh: Duquesne University Press, 1969).

Lévi-Strauss, Claude, *The Savage Mind* (*La Pensée Sauvage*) (London: Weidenfeld & Nicolson, 1966).

Lewis, Charlton T. and Short, Charles, *A Latin Dictionary* (Oxford: Clarendon Press, 1879).

Lewis, Suzanne, *The Art of Matthew Paris in the Chronica Majora* (Aldershot: Scolar Press, 1987).

—— *The Rhetoric of Power in the Bayeux Tapestry* (Cambridge: Cambridge University Press, 1999).

Liebermann, Felix, *Über die Leges Anglorum saeculo XIII Londoniis collectae* (Halle: Niemeyer, 1894).

Loomis, Laura Hibbard, 'Chaucer and the Auchinleck MS: *Thopas* and *Guy of Warwick*', 131–49 in *Adventures in the Middle Ages* (New York: Burt Franklin, 1962).

—— *Sir Thopas*, 486–559 in *Sources and Analogues of Chaucer's Canterbury Tales*, ed. W. F. Bryan and Germaine Dempster (Chicago: University of Chicago Press, 1941).

Loyn, H. R., *The Vikings in Britain* (London: B. T. Batsford, 1977).

Maitland, Frederic W., *Domesday Book and Beyond* (Cambridge: Cambridge University Press, 1987; 1st published 1897).

Map, Walter, *De nugis curialium* (*Courtiers' Trifles*), ed. and trans. M. R. James, rev. C. N. L. Brooke and R. A. B. Mynors (Oxford: Clarendon Press, 1983).

Marie de France, 'Laüstic', 97–101 in *Lais*, ed. Alfred Ewert, intro. Glyn S. Burgess (London: Duckworth, 1995; 1st published 1944).

Marx, Karl, *The Holy Family*, 131–55 in *Selected Writings*, ed. McLellan.

—— *A Critique of Political Economy*, 388–92 in *Selected Writings*, ed. McLellan.

—— *Capital: A Critique of Political Economy*, vol. 1, trans. Samuel Moore and Edward Aveling, ed. Frederick Engels (London: Lawrence & Wishart, 1954).

—— *Selected Writings*, ed. David McLellan (Oxford: Oxford University Press, 1977).

—— *The Eighteenth Brumaire of Louis Bonaparte*, 300–25 in *Selected Writings*, ed. McLellan.

—— *The Holy Family*, 129–55 in *Selected Writings*, ed. McLellan.

Matthes, Heinrich C., *Die Einheitlichkeit des Orrmulum: Studien zur Textkritik, zu den Quellen und zur sprachlichen Form von Orrmins Evangelienbuch* (Heidelberg: Carl Winter, 1933).

Matthew of Vendôme, *Ars versificatoria*, 106–93 in *Les arts poétique du XIIe et du XIIIe siècle*, ed. Edmond Faral (Paris: Champion, 1924).

Mayr-Harting, H., 'Functions of a Twelfth-Century Recluse', *History* 60 (1975), 337–52.

Mehl, Dieter, *The Middle English Romances of the Thirteenth and Fourteenth Centuries* (London: Routledge & Kegan Paul, 1968).

Merleau-Ponty, M., *Phénoménologie de la perception* (Paris: Librairie Gallimard, 1942).

Merleau-Ponty, M., *Phenomenology of Perception*, trans. Colin Smith (London: Routledge, 1962).

The Metalogicon of John of Salisbury, trans. Daniel D. McGarry (Berkeley: University of California Press, 1955).

Middleton, Anne, 'Chaucer's "New Men" and the Good of Literature in the *Canterbury Tales*', 15–56 in *Literature and Society*, ed. Edward Said, Selected Papers from the English Institute, NS 3 (Baltimore: Johns Hopkins University Press, 1980).

—— 'William Langland's "Kynde Name": Authorial Signature and Social Identity in Late Fourteenth-Century England', 15–82 in *Literary Practice and Social Change in Britain, 1380–1530*, ed. Lee Patterson (Berkeley: University of California Press, 1990).

Millett, Bella, 'The Origins of *Ancrene Wisse*: New Answers, New Questions', *MÆ* 61 (1992), 206–28.

Milroy, James, 'Middle English Dialectology', 156–206 in *The Cambridge History of the English Language*, vol. 2, ed. Norman Blake (Cambridge: Cambridge University Press, 1994).

Minio-Paluello, L., 'Iacobus Veneticus Grecus: Canonist and Translator of Aristotle', *Traditio* 8 (1952), 265–304.

Moffat, Douglas, 'The Recovery of Worcester Cathedral MS F. 174', *Notes and Queries* NS 32 (1985), 300–2.

Morrison, Stephen, 'New Sources for the *Ormulum*', *Neophilologus* 68 (1984), 444–50.

Morrison, Stephen, 'Orm's English Sources', *Archiv für das Studium der Neueren Sprachen (und Literaturen)* 221 (1984), 54–64.

—— 'Sources for the *Ormulum*: A Re-examination', *Neuphilologische Mitteilungen* 84 (1983), 419–36.

Mulhern, Francis, *The Moment of 'Scrutiny'* (London: Verso, 1981; 1st published 1979).

Müller, Herman, 'Der Musiktraktat in dem Werke des Bartholomaeus Anglicus *De proprietatibus rerum*', 241–55 in *Riemann-Festschrift: Gesammelte Studien* (Leipzig: Max Hesses, 1909).

Murphy, James J., 'Rhetoric and Dialectic in *The Owl and the Nightingale*', 198–230 in James J. Murphy, *Medieval Eloquence: Studies in the Theory and Practice of Medieval Rhetoric* (Berkeley: University of California Press, 1978).

Mustanoja, T. F., *A Middle English Syntax: Part 1 (Parts of Speech)*, Mémoires de la Société de Helsinki 23 (Helsinki, 1960).

Neckam, Alexander, *De naturis rerum libri duo*, 2 vols., ed. Thomas Wright, Rolls Series 34 (London, 1863).

Nietzsche, Friedrich, *On the Genealogy of Morals*, 437–599 in *Basic Writings of Nietzsche*, trans. Walter Kaufmann (New York: Random House, 1966).

The Norman Conquest of England: Sources and Documents, ed. R. Allen Brown (Woodbridge: Boydell Press, 1984).

Oakden, J. P., *Alliterative Poetry in Middle English*, 2 vols. (Manchester: Manchester University Press, 1930–5).

An Old English Miscellany, ed. Richard Morris, EETS os 49 (1872).

The Ormulum, ed. Robert Holt, notes and glossary by R. M. White, 2 vols. (Oxford: Clarendon Press, 1878).

Otter, Monika, '1066: The Moment of Transition in Two Narratives of the Norman Conquest', *Speculum* 74 (1999), 565–86.

Ovid, *Ars Amatoria*, 12–175 in *The Art of Love and Other Poems*, ed. J. H. Mozley, rev. G. P. Goold (London: William Heinemann, 1979).

—— *Metamorphoses*, 2 vols., trans. F. J. Miller (London: Heinemann, 1966–8).

The Owl and the Nightingale, ed. Eric Gerald Stanley (Manchester: Manchester University Press, 1960; rev. 1972).

The Owl and the Nightingale: Text and Translation, ed. Neil Cartlidge (Exeter: University of Exeter Press, 2001).

Oxford Dictionary of Saints, ed. David Hugh Farmer, 4th edn. (Oxford: Oxford University Press, 1997; 1st published 1978).

Oxford Latin Dictionary (Oxford: Clarendon Press, 1968–82).

Pächt, Otto, *The Rise of Pictorial Narrative in Twelfth Century England* (Oxford: Clarendon Press, 1962).

[Paris, Matthew] Mathæi Parisiensis, *Chronica majora*, ed. Henry Richards Luard, 7 vols., Rolls Series 57 (London, 1872–3).

Parkes, M. B., 'On the Presumed Date and Possible Origin of the Manuscript of the "Ormulum": Oxford, Bodleian Library, MS Junius 1', 115–27 in *Five Hundred Years of Words and Sounds: A Festschrift for Eric Dobson*, ed. E. G. Stanley and Douglas Gray (Cambridge: D. S. Brewer, 1983).

Partner, Nancy, *Serious Entertainments: The Writing of History in Twelfth-Century England* (Chicago: University of Chicago Press, 1977).

Patrologiae cursus completus, series latina, ed. J.-P., Migne, 221 vols. (Paris, 1844–64).

Patterson, Lee, 'Literary History', 250–62 in *Critical Terms for Literary Study*, ed. Frank Lentricchia and Thomas McLaughlin (Chicago: University of Chicago Press, 1990).

Pearsall, Derek, *Old English and Middle English Poetry* (London: Routledge & Kegan Paul, 1977).

—— Review of *The Origins of Ancrene Wisse*, by E. J. Dobson, *Review of English Studies* 28 (1977), 316–18.

—— 'The Development of Middle English Romance', *Mediaeval Studies* 27 (1965), 91–116.

Peterson, Douglas L., '*The Owl and the Nightingale* and Christian Dialectic', *Journal of English and Germanic Philology* 55 (1956), 13–26.

Petrus Cantor, *Verbum abbreviatum*, cols. 21–554 in *Patrologia Latina*, 205, ed. Migne.

Plato, *The Collected Dialogues*, ed. Edith Hamilton and Huntington Cairns, Bollingen Series 71 (Princeton: Princeton University Press, 1961).

—— *Cratylus*, 421–74 in *The Collected Dialogues*, ed. Hamilton and Cairns.

—— *Timaeus*, 1151–1211 in *The Collected Dialogues*, ed. Hamilton and Cairns.

Pliny, *Natural History*, 10 vols., ed. and trans. H. Rackham (London: William Heinemann, 1940–67).

Pocock, J. G. A., *The Ancient Constitution and the Feudal Law: A Study of English Historical Thought in the Seventeenth Century*, 2nd edn. (Cambridge: Cambridge University Press, 1987; 1st published 1957).

Pollock, Frederick, and Maitland, Frederic William, *The History of English Law*, 2nd edn., 2 vols. (Cambridge: Cambridge University Press, 1968; 1st published 1898).

Poole, Austin Lane, *From Domesday Book to Magna Carta: 1087–1216*, 2nd edn. (Oxford: Clarendon Press, 1955; 1st edn. 1951).

Proctor, R., *An Index to the Early Printed Books in the British Museum*, 2 vols. (London: Kegan Paul, 1898).

Quintilian, *Institutio oratoria*, ed. and trans. Donald A. Russell, 5 vols., Loeb Classical Library (Cambridge, Mass.: Harvard University Press, 2001).

Reynolds, Susan, *Fiefs and Vassals: The Medieval Evidence Reinterpreted* (Oxford: Oxford University Press, 1994).

Richards, I. A., *Practical Criticism: A Study of Literary Judgment* (London: Kegan Paul, Trench, Trubner, 1929).

Richardson, H. G. and Sayles, G. O., *Law and Legislation from Æthelberht to Magna Carta* (Edinburgh: Edinburgh University Press, 1966).

Robertson, Elizabeth, *Early English Devotional Prose and the Female Audience* (Knoxville: University of Tennessee Press, 1990).

—— ' "This Living Hand": Thirteenth-Century Female Literacy, Materialist Immanence, and the Reader of the *Ancrene Wisse*', *Speculum* 78 (2003), 1–36.

Robinson, Ian, *Chaucer and the English Tradition* (Cambridge: Cambridge University Press, 1972).

Rotuli Hundredorum, ed. W. Illingworth and J. Caley, 2 vols. (London: Record Commission, 1812–18).

Round, J. H., 'Mr Freeman and the Battle of Hastings', 258–305 in his *Feudal England* (London: George Allen & Unwin, 1964; 1st published, 1895).

Salter, Elizabeth, 'Nicholas Love's "Myrrour of the Blessed Lyf of Jesu Christ" ', *Analecta Cartusiana* 10 (1974).

Scarry, Elaine, *The Body in Pain: The Making and Unmaking of the World* (Oxford: Oxford University Press, 1985).

—— 'The Well-Rounded Sphere: Cognition and Metaphysical Structure in Boethius's *Consolation of Philosophy*', 143–80 in *Resisting Representation* (Oxford: Oxford University Press, 1994).

Schapiro, Meyer, 'The Still Life as a Personal Object—A Note on Heidegger and van Gogh', 427–31 in *The Art of Art History*, ed. Preziosi.

Schleusener, Jay, '*The Owl and the Nightingale*: A Matter of Judgment', *Modern Philology* 70 (1972–3), 185–9.

Select Charters, ed. William Stubbs, 9th edn., rev. H. W. C. Davis (Oxford: Clarendon Press, 1913; 1st published 1870).

Seymour, M. C. and colleagues, *Bartholomaeus Anglicus and his Encyclopedia* (Aldershot: Variorum, 1992).

Sharpe Richard, 'The Prefaces of *Quadripartitus*', 148–72 in *Law and Government in Medieval England and Normandy*, ed. Garnett and Hudson.

Shepherd, G. T., 'Early Middle English', 81–117 in *The Middle Ages*, ed. W. F. Bolton (London: Sphere, 1970).

'The Shires and Hundreds of England', 145–6 in *An Old English Miscellany*, ed. Richard Morris, EETS os 49 (1872).

Simpson, A. W. B., *An Introduction to the History of the Land Law* (Oxford: Oxford University Press, 1961).

Simpson, James, *Sciences and the Self in Medieval Poetry: Alan of Lille's* Anticlaudianus *and John Gower's* Confessio Amantis (Cambridge: Cambridge University Press, 1995).

Sir Gawain and the Green Knight, ed. J. R. R. Tolkien and E. V. Gordon, 2nd edn., rev. Norman Davis (Oxford: Clarendon Press, 1967).

Smith, Thomas, *Literary and Linguistic Works*, part III (*De recta emendata linguae Anglicae scriptione dialogus*), ed. Bror Danielsson, Stockholm Studies in English 56 (Stockholm, 1983).

Solopova, Elizabeth, 'The Metre of the *Ormulum*', 423–39 in *Studies in English Language and Literature: 'Doubt Wisely', Papers in Honour of E. G. Stanley*, ed. M. J. Toswell and E. M. Tyler (London: Routledge, 1996).

Solterer, Helen, *The Master and Minerva: Disputing Women in French Medieval Culture* (Berkeley: University of California Press, 1995).

Southern, R. W., 'Aspects of the European Tradition of Historical Writing (4): The Sense of the Past', *Transactions of the Royal Historical Society*, 5th series, vol. 23 (London: Royal Historical Society, 1973), 241–63.

—— *The Making of the Middle Ages* (London: Random Century, 1967).

Spearing, A. C., *Medieval to Renaissance in English Poetry* (Cambridge: Cambridge University Press, 1985).

The Spirit of Medieval English Popular Romance, ed. Ad Putter and Jane Gilbert (Harlow: Longman, 2000).

Stanford, S. C., *The Archaeology of the Welsh Marches* (London: William Collins, 1980).

Stanley, E. G., 'Laȝamon's Antiquarian Sentiments', *MÆ* 38 (1969), 23–37.

Stenton, F. M., *Anglo-Saxon England*, 3rd edn. (Oxford: Clarendon Press, 1971; 1st published 1943).

Stevick, Robert D., 'Plus Juncture and the Spelling of the *Ormulum*', *Journal of English and Germanic Philology* 64 (1965), 84–9.

Stothard, Charles, 'Some Observations on the Bayeux Tapestry', 1–6 in *The Study of the Bayeux Tapestry*, ed. Gameson.

Strohm, Paul, 'Middle English Narrative Genres', *Genre* 13 (1980), 379–88.

—— 'The Origin and Meaning of Middle English *Romaunce*', *Genre* 10 (1977), 1–28.

—— '*Passioun, Lyf, Miracle, Legende*: Some Generic Terms in Middle English Hagiographical Narrative', *Chaucer Review* 10 (1975), 62–75 and 154–71.

The Study of the Bayeux Tapestry, ed. Richard Gameson (Woodbridge: Boydell Press, 1997).

Swanton, Michael, *English Literature Before Chaucer* (London: Longman, 1987).

Tatlock, J. S. P., *The Legendary History of Britain* (Berkeley: University of California Press, 1950).

Taylor, Andrew, 'Fragmentation, Corruption and Minstrel Narration: The Question of Middle English Romances' in *Yearbook of English Studies* 22 (1992), 38–62.

Taylor, Charles, *Hegel* (Cambridge: Cambridge University Press, 1975).

—— *Sources of the Self: The Making of Modern Identity* (Cambridge: Cambridge University Press, 1989).

The Thebaid in *Statius*, ed. and trans. J. H. Mozley, 2 vols., rev. edn. (London: W. Heinemann, 1955–7).

Thompson, Sally, *Women Religious: The Founding of English Nunneries after the Norman Conquest* (Oxford: Clarendon Press, 1991).

The Thrush and the Nightingale, 237–48 in *Middle English Debate Poetry: A Critical Anthology*, ed. John W. Conlee (East Lansing, Mich.: Colleagues Press, 1991).

Tolkien, J. R. R., '*Ancrene Wisse* and *Hali Meiðhad*', *Essays and Studies* 14 (1929), 104–26.

'Treatise on the Spirit and the Soul', trans. Erasmo Leiva and Sr Benedicta Ward, 181–288 in *Three Treatises on Man: A Cistercian Anthropology*, ed. Bernard McGinn (Kalamazoo, Mich.: Cistercian Publications, 1977).

Turville-Petre, J. E., 'Studies on the *Ormulum* MS', *Journal of English and Germanic Philology* 46 (1947), 1–27.

Turville-Petre, Thorlac, *England the Nation: Language, Literature, and National Identity, 1290–1340* (Oxford: Clarendon Press, 1996).

Two of the Saxon Chronicles Parallel (with supplementary extracts from the others), ed. John Earle, rev. Charles Plummer, 2 vols. (Oxford: Oxford University Press, 1892–9).

Ullmann, Walter, 'On the Influence of Geoffrey of Monmouth in English History', 257–76 in *Speculum Historiale: Geschichte im Spiegel von Geschichtsschreibung und Geschichtsdeutung*, ed. Clemens Bauer, Laetitia Boehm, Max Müller (Munich: Karl Alber, 1965).

Utley, Francis Lee, 'Dialogues, Debates, and Catechisms', 3: 669–745 in *MWME*.

Van Caenegem, R. C., *The Birth of the English Common Law*, 2nd edn. (Cambridge: Cambridge University Press, 1973; 2nd edn. 1988).

Vaughn, Richard, *Matthew Paris* (Cambridge: Cambridge University Press, 1958).

Visser, G. J., *Laȝamon: An Attempt at Vindication* (Assen: Van Gorcum, 1935).

Wace's 'Roman de Brut', A History of the British: Text and Translation, ed. and trans. Judith Weiss (Exeter: University of Exeter Press, 1999).

Wallace, David, 'Chaucer's Continental Inheritance: The Early Poems and *Troilus and Criseyde*', 19–37 in *The Cambridge Chaucer Companion*, ed. Piero Boitani and Jill Mann (Cambridge: Cambridge University Press, 1986).

—— *Chaucer and the Early Writings of Boccaccio* (Woodbridge: D. S. Brewer, 1985).

Warren, Ann K., *Anchorites and their Patrons in Medieval England* (Berkeley: University of California Press, 1985).

Weimann, Robert, 'The Concept of Tradition Reconsidered', *Yearbook of Comparative and General Literature* 23 (1974), 29–41.

White, Hayden, 'Interpretation in History, 51–80 in his *Tropics of Discourse*.

—— 'Historicism, 'History, and the Figurative Imagination', 101–120 in his *Tropics of Discourse*.

—— *Metahistory: The Historical Imagination in Nineteenth-Century Europe* (Baltimore: Johns Hopkins University Press, 1973).

—— 'The Fictions of Factual Representation', 121–34 in his *Tropics of Discourse*.

—— 'The Historical Text as Literary Artifact', 81–100 in his *Tropics of Discourse*.

—— 'The Value of Narrativity in the Representation of Reality', 1–25 in his *The Content of the Form: Narrative Discourse and Historical Representation* (Baltimore: Johns Hopkins University Press, 1987).

—— *Tropics of Discourse: Essays in Culture and Criticism* (Baltimore: Johns Hopkins University Press, 1978).

Williams, Raymond, 'Literature and Sociology', 13–30 in *Problems in Materialism and Culture* (London: Verso, 1980).

Williams, Raymond, *Marxism and Literature* (Oxford: Oxford University Press, 1977).

Wilson, R. M., *Early Middle English Literature* (London: Methuen, 1939).

—— *The Lost Literature of Medieval England* (London, Methuen, 1970; 1st published 1952).

Wimsatt, James, 'The Sources of Chaucer's "Seys and Alcyone"', *MÆ* 36 (1967), 231–41.

Wittgenstein, Ludwig, *Philosophical Investigations*, trans. G. E. M. Anscombe (Oxford: Oxford University Press, 1963).

Wogan-Browne, Jocelyn, 'Chaste Bodies: Frames and Experiences', 24–42 in *Framing Medieval Bodies*, ed. Sarah Kay and Miri Rubin (Manchester: Manchester University Press, 1994).

Wolter, Allan B., *The Philosophical Theology of John Duns Scotus*, ed. Marilyn McCord Adams (Ithaca, NY: Cornell University Press, 1990).

Woman Defamed and Woman Defended, ed. Alcuin Blamires (Oxford: Oxford University Press, 1992).

Woodward, David, 'Medieval Mappaemundi', 286–370 in *History of Cartography*, ed. Harley and Woodward, vol. 1.

Woolf, Rosemary, 'The Theme of Christ the Lover-Knight in Medieval English Literature', *Review of English Studies*, NS 13 (1962), 1–16.

Wormald, Patrick, ' "*Quadripartitus*" ', 111–47 in *Law and Government in Medieval England and Normandy*, ed. Garnett and Hudson.

Index